DESIGN & HISTORIC PRESERVATION

The Challenge of Compatibility

Held at GOUCHER COLLEGE Baltimore, Maryland MARCH 14–16, 2002

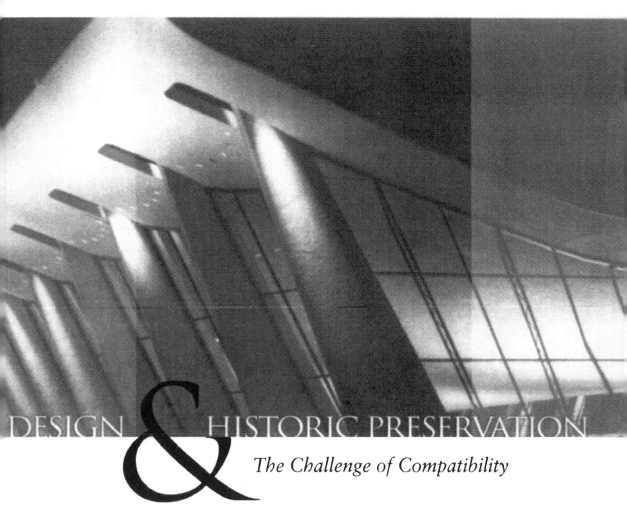

DESIGN & HISTORIC PRESERVATION

The Challenge of Compatibility

Newark: University of Delaware Press DELAWARE

edited by DAVID AMES & RICHARD WAGNER

New paperback printing 2014 by University of Delaware Press
Co-published with Rowman & Littlefield
4501 Forbes Boulevard, Suite 200, Lanham, Maryland 20706
www.rowman.com

16 Carlisle Street, London W1D 3BT, United Kingdom

978-1-61149-234-7 (paperback: alk. paper)

Originally published by Associated University Presses
2010 Eastpark Boulevard
Cranbury, NJ 08512

Library of Congress Cataloging-in-Publication Data
Design & historic preservation : the challenge of compatibility : held at Goucher
College, Baltimore, Maryland, March 14–16, 2002 / edited by David Ames &
Richard Wagner.
        p. cm.
    Includes bibliographic references and index.
    ISBN 978-0-87413-831-3 (alk. paper)
    1.   Architecture—Aesthetics—Congresses. 2. Architectures and
       history—Congresses. 3. Historic preservation—Congresses. I.
       Ames, David L. II. Wagner, Richard D. III. Goucher College. IV.
       Title: Design and historic preservation.
  NA2500.D47   2009
  720.28'8—dc22

    2008033527

CONTENTS

INTRODUCTION

▦ INTRODUCTION

DAVID L. AMES, PH.D.
Professor of Urban Affairs, Public Policy, and Geography
Director, Center for Historic Architecture and Design
University of Delaware

"The major problem with the preservation system we have created is
the separation of the world into verbal and non-verbal components.
Most regulations, guidelines, and standards are verbal, but the objects
of their application are visual."

— E. Blaine Cliver

This book collects the papers from the "Third National Forum on
Preservation Practice: A Critical Look at Design in Historic Preservation"
held at Goucher College, March 2002. The forums are a series of
ongoing critical discussions about issues central to the practice of historic
preservation in the United States since the passage of the National Historic
Preservation Act of 1966. The third forum was sponsored by the preservation
programs at Boston University, George Washington University, Goucher
College, University of Delaware, University of Kentucky, University of
Oregon, and University of Southern California, and by the Historic Resources
Committee of the American Institute of Architects in partnership with the
National Park Service.

Much of the basis for professional practice in historic preservation in
the United States is derived from nominating and listing buildings, structures,
objects, and districts in the National Register of Historic Places. To be
considered for the National Register, historic properties are first identified and
surveyed. Their historical or architectural significance is then evaluated against
National Register criteria, and, if found eligible, they are listed. In addition to

meeting the criteria, a property typically must be at least fifty years old and possess physical integrity; those physical characteristics are enough to convey its historic appearance and significance.

Although the National Historic Preservation Act of 1966 created a national preservation policy largely as a reaction to the loss of thousands of irreplaceable historic properties, a listing in the National Register was initially primarily honorific; it did not protect historic properties from incompatible alterations or even demolition. To spur the rehabilitation of historic properties and the conservation of their neighborhoods, Congress passed the first beneficial tax treatments for the rehabilitation of properties listed in the National Register as part of the Tax Reform Act of 1976. These benefits, which have been altered a number of times in the past quarter-century, allowed developers certain favorable depreciation methods and tax credits to offset the cost of rehabilitating historic structures used for income-producing purposes, such as offices, retail space, and multi-unit residential rental property. To qualify, a property must be eligible for, or listed in, the National Register individually or as part of a National Register District. The rehabilitation work must conform to the Secretary of the Interior's Standards for Rehabilitation.

Created in 1977, the Standards for Rehabilitation are the Secretary's "best advice" on how to protect the physical integrity of properties undergoing rehabilitation and adaptive reuse. William J. Murtagh, the first Keeper of the National Register, captured the essence of the Standards when he wrote that in rehabilitating an historic property, "every effort should be made to effect changes without radically altering or destroying existing historic characteristics . . . [and] . . . alterations should be minimally visible from the public right-of-way if they are visible at all."[2]

In the 1990s, based on more than a decade of experience with tens of thousands of historic properties, Standards for Preservation, Restoration, and Reconstruction were added to those for rehabilitation. Collectively known as the Secretary of the Interior's Standards for the Treatment of Historic Properties, they have been widely influential in the United States beyond their application for judging the appropriateness of changes to National Register properties. Most states and territories require that the Standards for Rehabilitation or other appropriate treatments be followed to obtain state tax credits or when using state money to alter an historic building. In addition, thousands of local government historic preservation ordinances incorporate the treatments. Thus, in the United States today, much of what constitutes best historic preservation practice, and binds the field of historic preservation itself, has evolved from our experience with the National Register and the Secretary of the Interior's Standards for the Treatment of Historic Properties.

Design and Compatibility in Historic Preservation: A Critical Topic

At first blush the notion of "design in preservation" may seem a contradiction in terms since most people associate design with creating something new, while preservation is usually associated with maintaining things that are old. However, design plays a central and critical role in preservation. A building, district, or landscape is often characterized by describing the arrangement of parts in patterns related to the principals of design. That is, we discuss the exterior appearance of a building in terms of its scale, proportions, and massing, as well as texture and color of the materials. Seen this way, the term "design" is a noun. Design can also be thought of as a verb. For example, the design of a new building in an historic district or addition to an existing building is often portrayed as a problem-solving activity or process. Thus, design is both a noun and a verb. It can refer either to the end product or to the process.[3] Considering the design of historic properties as a noun is central to the National Register evaluation process. When one moves beyond this to rehabilitating or restoring a building, design becomes a verb, or a problem-solving process.

Much of the evaluation of historic properties is about looking at design as historic objects—as nouns. One of the criteria for inclusion in the National Register is known as "Criterion C: Design/Construction." It asks if the property being considered "embod[ies] the distinctive characteristics of a type, period, or method of construction, represent[s] the work of a master, or possess[es] high artistic value."[4] Design, defined as "the combination of elements that creates the form, plan, space, structure, and style of a property," is also one of the aspects of integrity a property must exhibit to be eligible for the National Register.[5]

The Context for Design in Historic Preservation: The Secretary of the Interior's Standards for the Treatment of Historic Properties

The Secretary of the Interior's Standards for the Treatment of Historic Properties form a continuum of intervention into existing fabric, from *preserving* as much fabric as possible to *reconstructing* a property that no longer exists.[6] Between these two lies *restoration*, meaning to return a property to a particular point in time, and *rehabilitation*, which often includes alterations and sometimes additions to meet requirements of continuing or new uses.

The purpose of the Secretary of the Interior's Standards is to help promote responsible preservation practices while protecting historic resources from physical modifications that would dilute or destroy their physical integrity and with that, their historical or architectural significance. The physical features of a property that made it historically significant, that constitute its integrity and must remain intact, include such aspects of its design as form, plan, structure, and architectural style, and the materials and the workmanship with which it was built, among other features that make up its historic character.

The four related approaches to treatment—preservation, rehabilitation, restoration, and reconstruction—share common assumptions about the nature of an historic property and a philosophy of preservation. An historic property is seen as the accumulation of physical changes over time, possessing features that illustrate important aspects of its present and past. These changes are seen as historically significant and should be preserved. Future change is also seen as necessary to preserving the property in the years ahead by allowing it to be adapted to new and contemporary uses. This tension between preserving the past and changing for the future is at the core of the Secretary of the Interior's Standards for the Treatment of Historic Properties.

As defined by the Secretary of the Interior, the four treatments are as follows:[7]

1. *Preservation* is the treatment in which measures are applied to sustain the existing form, integrity, and materials of an historic property. This treatment is used when the distinctive materials, features, and spaces of a property are essentially intact and illustrate its historic significance without needing extensive repair or replacement.

2. *Rehabilitation,* sometimes called adaptive use, is the treatment called for when deteriorated and missing features must be repaired or replaced and alterations or additions are required to adapt the property to a new compatible use. The standard requires that any repairs, alterations, and additions must be done in a manner that preserves those portions or features that are historically significant and communicate its historical, cultural, or architectural value.

3. *Restoration* is the treatment in which the form, features, and character of a property are depicted accurately as it appeared at a particular period of time, often during its original period. Restoration is accomplished by removing features from other periods in the history of the property and reconstructing missing features from the restoration period. A treatment frequently applied to house museums, restoration is the most popularly understood form of preservation.

4. *Reconstruction* is the treatment in which the form, features, and detailing of a non-surviving site, landscape, building, structure, or object are recreated from new materials for the purpose of replicating its appearance at a specific period of time and its historic location.

One can also think of the four treatments as a series of increasingly exact constraints of the process for solving design problems involving historic buildings, districts, and landscapes. For example, how does one maintain and preserve the physical characteristics of a building, bring it up to code, and insert new mechanical systems, making it functionally a modern building, without changing its overall character?

While the term "treatment" implies that the historic property is a passive object being acted upon, treatment is, in fact, a series of actions and reactions between the building and design solutions. As Bryan Lawson observes, "Good design is a response to a whole series of issues. . . . A piece of good design is rather like a hologram; the whole picture is in each fragment. It is often not possible [to determine] which bit of the problem is solved by which bit of the solution."[8] Thus the problem-solving design process in the treatment of historic properties is rather like solving a simultaneous equation.

Since design and historic preservation is a vast topic, the Third National Forum on Preservation Practice sought to focus the discussion by calling for papers in four areas: compatible design, design standards and guidelines, design and cultural landscapes, and design and the recent past.

Compatible design is usually defined as "capable of existing together in harmony." When applied to historic preservation projects, it typically refers to the design of additions to historic buildings, modifying historic interiors, and constructing new buildings in historic districts or landscapes.

However, creating a compatible design is only one way in which architects relate new to old. Norman Tyler suggests two others are often used, matching the new to the old, and contrasting the new and the old.[9] In matching, new buildings or additions seek to replicate the adjacent historic properties as much as possible, making it difficult, if not impossible, to tell them apart. This approach often appeals to owners of historic properties and civic organizations. On the other hand, advocates of a contrasting approach argue that the design of new additions or buildings should be of contemporary design and clearly articulate new from old. Architects often favor the contrasting approach because they feel it gives them freedom to interpret the environment in today's architectural idioms in much the same way as the original architects did in their day.

The Secretary of the Interior's Standards prefer compatibility, where new work is "differentiated from the old and [to] be compatible with the historic materials, features, size, scale, and proportion, and massing to protect the integrity of the [historic] property and its environment."[10] The standards reject the matching approach, arguing that the integrity and significance of an historic property would be undermined if new work were not visually distinguished from the original. They also reject the contrasting approach because too much distinction between the new and old would also compromise the integrity and significance of the historic property.

Some of the questions that the papers on compatible design attempt to answer are: How much does a successful project hinge on the approach taken and how much on the skill of the designer? Must new design be subservient to existing fabric to be compatible? What enrichment does a contrasting new design bring to a district that compatibility does not? To what degree do the specific attributes and character of an historic district or property affect the nature of new design? How can design avoid the pitfalls of "themes," which is sometimes the result of compatibility?

To protect their historic architectural and landscape resources, communities often adopt *design standards and guidelines*. Although local historic districts have existed since the 1930s, it was not until the creation of the National Register in 1966 that the definition of an "historic district" was standardized. The register states that "the identity of a district results from the interrelationship of its resources, which can convey a visual sense of the overall historic environment or can be an arrangement of historically or functionally related properties."[11]

Historic districts and their properties are usually protected through local historic preservation ordinances, which are part of the local zoning code. Most preservation ordinances include standards for historic designation, provision for architectural review by a board, and guidelines or standards for rehabilitating and adding to historic buildings and landscapes as well as constructing new buildings in historic areas. Almost all local guidelines and standards incorporate or reference the Secretary of the Interior's Standards for Rehabilitation.

Among the questions raised in the papers on design guidelines and standards are: Do guidelines stifle or encourage creative design? How flexible should guidelines and their interpretation be? What are the virtues of highly specific guidelines? Of general guidelines? How specific should guidelines be to a community or district? How can guidelines avoid fostering inaccurate, historicizing treatments? What are the most effective ways to address the use of historical versus substitute materials?

Design and cultural landscapes emerged as a pivotal issue in preservation in the early 1980s. Arnold R. Alamen and Robert Z. Melnick credit the National Park Service for bringing this resource to the attention of preservationists, asserting, "More than any other American organization or agency, [the National Park Service] provided the most significant direction to the nascent cultural landscape preservation movement."[12]

By their very nature, landscapes change rapidly. Plant materials seed, grow, and die or are harvested. Woodlands are replaced with farms, and farms by subdivisions. Prairies are strip-mined and valleys dammed, transforming landscapes from natural settings to cultural landscapes.

The questions facing design and cultural landscapes are not unlike those facing the design and preservation of the built environment. However, they are often less understood and appreciated than those related to buildings and historic districts. How can design strategies best preserve the singular features of an historic landscape? Can a comprehensive rehabilitation program be applied to an historic landscape without the loss of that landscape's salient features, or should the program entail changes that are incremental and varied? What are effective strategies for adaptive use of landscapes? Can historic landscapes be changed from accommodating passive to active functions, or vice versa, without undue compromise? What constitutes appropriate/acceptable infrastructure added to an historic landscape?

Design and the recent past usually refers to historic resources created after World War II. Since a property typically must be at least fifty years old to be eligible for the National Register, we are only beginning to consider them as historic. Because of this, the post-World War II built environment of suburban communities, shopping centers, motels, and diners is especially susceptible to unsympathetic alterations.

The recent past raises new design and preservation problems ranging from the conservation of the materials of which they are constructed to how rapidly many are being demolished and replaced. Some of the questions about the recent past considered at the Forum were: How can the tendency to historicize buildings of the recent past be countered? How can they be altered to meet the challenge of incorporating new functions or systems without compromising essential historic features? What unique problems exist when designing an addition to buildings of the recent past? How should the recent past provide a source of inspiration for design in an historic context?

The Papers

Design professionals, architects, landscape architects, engineers, and historic preservationists are all represented in the papers presented at the Third National Forum on Preservation Practice. The fourteen papers presented were grouped in four sessions. In the first session, entitled "Melding Contemporary and Historic Design," architect Michael Mills tackles the concept of design in historic preservation, which he defines as a verb; design is "to plan or to fashion skillfully and artistically." Mills uses case studies to discuss how design is associated with each of the four treatments, showing that successful preservation projects require myriad design decisions.

In their paper, architect Eleanor Esser Gorski and historian Dijana Cuvalo use case studies in Chicago to show the way in which developers have interpreted design guidelines to maximize profits, often producing caricatures of historic buildings. They examine how developers' views of design conflict with citizens' preference for historically accurate replicas, while preservationists advocate compatible design.

Historic preservationist Kate Lemos uses the SoHo district in New York City to examine how design philosophies compete in the interpretation of design guidelines, producing mixed results. She claims that many design guidelines use a kit-of-parts approach that results in mediocre architecture. Lemos suggests that the level of design for new buildings and additions could be improved if guidelines were based less on architectural details found in a district and more on its underlying historic themes and design motifs.

The second session, "Design Standards in Changing Environments," opens with a paper by James Hare, a preservationist, who examines the review process of the oldest preservation ordinance in the United States, that of Charleston, South Carolina. He looks at how it has changed over time, particularly after the tripling in size of the city's historic district. In her paper, Lauren Weiss Bricker, a professor of architecture, looks at how bungalow neighborhoods are being preserved with design guidelines. She offers ways of counteracting what she considers to be the stultifying effects of guidelines on the architectural richness of these early twentieth-century residential districts.

Using the Broadway district in downtown Los Angeles as their case study, the architect and historian team of Cathleen Malmstrom and Bridget Mailey describes how design standards can be drafted to balance traditions of new immigrant populations with the preservation of historic American commercial buildings. In particular, they examine the effect that the newly arrived *mercado* market tradition has had on the exteriors of late nineteenth- and early twentieth-century commercial buildings in this revitalized area.

In the last paper in the session, Ned Crankshaw, Krista Schneider, and Julie Reisenweber report on their use of a "multi-scale" approach to design guidelines to help preserve a rural agricultural area in central Kentucky. The approach seeks to allow new development as well as to protect traditional uses.

The third session, "Modernism and Postmodernism in Preservation Design," opens with architect Pamela Whitney Hawkes' examination of the compatibility of the spare functionality of modernist design with the preservationist's need to retain as much historic fabric as possible. She believes that this is the key question in melding contemporary and historic design.

Peyton Hall, an architect, asserts in his paper that the rehabilitation of historic buildings deserves the best of contemporary design. He argues that the Secretary of the Interior's Standards for Rehabilitation are too conservative and frequently result in mediocre design. As an alternative, he suggests using the contrasting approach to enrich both the present and the past

Architectural historian Alison Hoagland looks at the role of post-modernism in preservation. She suggests that postmodernism and preservation have "an oddly symbiotic relationship" because postmodernism's emphasis on context and its use of historical design references provides preservationists with buildings that blend the new and old in compatible ways.

The last session, "Engineering and Preservation Design," opens with Michael C. Henry's paper on the reuse of monumental-span structures. An engineer and architect, Henry examines the rehabilitation and adaptive reuse of Atlantic City Convention Hall, the largest clear-span structure in the world when it was completed in 1929. He describes technical issues related to the project as well as the thought process behind using a contrasting approach for new construction within the historic large-span space.

Charles Peterson, best known as the creator of the Historic American Building Survey, describes his reluctant role in the 1930s during the early development of the Jefferson National Expansion Park. Eventually completed with Eero Saarinen's monumental arch, the park caused the destruction of one of the best collection of cast-iron commercial fronts in the United States.

In the last paper, H. Henry Ward looks at two important buildings of the recent past, Reagan National and Dulles International airports. He takes the reader through a detailed description of their recent rehabilitations and enlargements, including using contrasting, matching, and compatible approaches to design.

Session One: Melding Contemporary and Historic Design

Michael J. Mills addresses the question of what constitutes design in historic preservation in his paper, "Design in Preservation Projects." He rejects the notion that since guidelines and standards for historic buildings and districts dictate design, there is no design in preservation. Defining design as "to plan or to fashion skillfully and artistically," Mills emphasizes the design challenges in projects that illustrate all four of the Secretary of the Interior's Standards for the Treatment of Historic Properties. He reminds us that at its core, design in preservation is creative problem solving, arguing that, in many ways, the challenges faced in preservation design are greater than those in new construction.

Focusing on issues of compatibility and design guidelines, Eleanor Gorski and Dijana Cuvalo evaluate their experiences in Chicago applying design standards to the new infill construction in historic districts in "Quality Infill Design: How Do We Move Beyond the Bad and Bland?" After defining "quality infill" in the abstract as design that strikes a balance between being compatible with the historic district without replicating existing historic buildings, they show how in reality the process of design—which usually includes preservationists, architects, citizens, planners, and developers—often creates imbalance. They note that achieving quality infill design is made more complicated within the context of a heated real estate market such as Chicago that has traditionally been heavily influenced by political maneuvering.

The difficulty of designing quality infill buildings in this environment is rooted in the question of what constitutes compatibility, with the public favoring historicizing designs, developers wishing to maximize the return on their investment by building the largest possible structure, and preservationists hewing to the notion of compatibility. To further complicate the issues, as neighborhoods become historic districts and design guidelines are established, community groups have become vested in controlling what happens, often reflecting the public's desire for replication, not compatibility, in new construction.

Kate Lemos, in her paper, "Defining Context: Promoting a Greater Level of Innovation in New Design within Historic Districts" writes of her experience in New York City's SoHo district. She argues for design standards based on historic trends and depth of context, instead of ones based solely on the architectural characteristics of buildings and traditional emphasis on cohesiveness and homogeneity. Lemos believes that it is important to protect historic buildings from inappropriate change. She asks whether the point has been reached in robust urban districts where we limit our ability, through the guidelines used, to create "innovative new design that is a product of its own cultural moment?" As an alternative, she argues that guidelines should be based on a deeper understanding of a district's layers of history and its deeper architectural fabric, not just traditional principles of design.

Session Two: Design Standards in Changing Environments

James Hare examines the evolution of Charleston, South Carolina's preservation ordinance, the oldest in the United States, in his paper, "Exaggerated Reverence for the Past: The Challenges of Design Review in the Charleston Historic District." He argues that the history of design review in Charleston falls into two periods divided by 1966. In the same year that the National Historic Preservation Act was passed by Congress, the city tripled the size of the original Old and Historic Charleston District. Hare analyzes how design review changed from the earlier period when the Board of Architectural Review operated relatively informally under the four-decade-long chairmanship of architect Albert Simons, to a formal process with an active board.

After outlining the Simons era, Hare concentrates on the post-1966 period. He examines the validity of claims by the architectural community that the board subordinated innovative, contemporary architecture to imitative, traditional design, contrasting this with the claims of residents and neighborhood organizations that the board encourages architects to design modern-looking buildings. In developing his thesis, Hare surveyed over two hundred local architects, asking them to identify new buildings in the historic district they considered "successful" and "unsuccessful" designs. Based on the survey, he selected two projects: one that the architects considered successful and one that they thought unsuccessful. He then looked at how they were reviewed by the board to illustrate the differences of opinion between members of the board and the architects.

In her paper, "California's Historic Districts: Preservation in a Vacuum," Lauren Weiss Bricker looks at four towns with design guidelines. She concludes that the design review process in these communities was similar to many across the country: they discouraged creative, contemporary architecture while sanctioning mediocre design, which she concludes erodes the historic integrity of the districts they were created to protect. Ironically, she feels that the guidelines contributed to the poor design because they were biased toward buildings and did not pay enough attention to the overall design characteristics that unify and give districts their physical coherence. She also thinks that the reliance on the Secretary of the Interior's Standards for the Treatment of Historic Properties reinforces the emphasis on buildings in design reviews since they provide little guidance on urban form or landscapes.

Bricker suggests that architects designing new buildings in historic districts share some of the responsibility for poor new design in historic districts as well since they often lack understanding of the architectural history and overall character of the area. According to Bricker, the architects attempt to make new buildings compatible merely by adding decorative details derived from nearby historic buildings. To correct this problem, she argues that guidelines should reflect the climatic and other underlying considerations that influenced original architecture, rather than the details themselves. In addition, she argues that sensitive design requires understanding of *why* historically significant features have changed, as well as *how* those changes affected the character of the district as it evolved.

In "Addressing Culturally Influenced Issues in Design Guidelines" Cathleen Malmstrom, AIA, and Bridget Maley examine how the traditions of two different ethnic groups can be mediated with community-based design standards. In recent years, as the Latino merchants have moved into older downtowns, such as the Broadway area in Los Angeles, they have removed historic storefronts so they may market in the traditional *mercado* fashion of open-air displays extending out onto the public sidewalk. In addition, they often cover historic architectural detail on the upper floors with large signs. While many Americans admire this colorful tradition when they visit Central and South America, they are not comfortable when it is imported into the United States, particularly when historic buildings are involved.

To begin to address the conflict between non-indigenous-based traditions and the historic built environment, Maley and Malmstrom discuss their work in developing design guidelines that accommodate the *mercado* retail traditions for the Broadway district based on the Secretary of the Interior's Standards. Working with owners, merchants, and other principal stakeholders, their design guidelines recommend glazed infill storefronts that respect the original design of storefronts while allowing businesses to expand retail displays onto public sidewalks. The guidelines also recommended ways to meld the vivid colors of the Latino marketplace with the incredible architectural details found on many of the area's historic buildings.

In their paper, "Multi-Scale Design Guidelines for the Rural Landscape of Nelson County, Kentucky," Ned Crankshaw, Julie Riesenweber, and Krista Schneider suggest a method for developing design guidelines for rural areas. In the past, rural preservationists have traditionally emphasized preserving agricultural land but failed to address the design of new construction, whether it was a new barn in a farmstead or a new subdivision on the edge of a town. The authors suggest that design guidelines should be developed to complement rural land-preservation efforts, ones that address the locations of new development, the processes by which land division takes place, the ways in which additions to communities are designed, and the arrangement of buildings and other built elements on individual rural properties. They argue that preserving individual sites within a large rural environment is of little value when land uses are changed drastically over time, and, conversely, that conserving rural land uses without compatible design guidelines will not preserve rural landscapes.

In their case study of Nelson County, Kentucky, the authors synthesized the results of separate landscape models that measured the sensitivity of natural landscape resources to new development with two visual models that measured the landscapes most appreciated by residents. From this research they developed a "Rural Historic Sensitivity Model," consisting of contiguous agricultural holdings overlaid with the survey of historic resources to identify the areas with the greatest potential as an historic district. Using the model as the framework for extensive fieldwork, the authors identified ten potential rural historic districts. For each they developed "multi-scale" design guidelines that reinforced traditional settlement patterns and protected significant resources.

Session Three: Modernism and Postmodernism in Preservation Design

In "Is Less More?: Twentieth-Century Design Attitudes and Twenty-First-Century Preservation," Pamela Whitney Hawkes asks whether a good designer can also be a good preservationist. Is it possible, she wonders, to balance preservation with leaving space "for the imagination, for creating memories for new generations?" Although she recognizes that modernism and preservation have long been philosophically opposed, she examines the striking projects of early European modernist architects Joze Plecnik (1872–1957) and Carlo Scarpa (1906–1978) to illustrate how historic and contemporary design can be melded. She suggests that their approaches to design might apply to current preservation challenges in the United States.

Hawkes shows how Plecnik, in his work on Prague's historic Hradney Castle, and Scarpa, in his additions to the Castelvecchio in Verona, completed successful preservation projects while remaining true to modernist design principles. In doing so, they shunned direct historical references, but instead used craft and materiality, as well as dramatic selective removal of historic fabric, to create new forms with remarkable sensitivity to their surroundings.

Hawkes believes that the success of these two works rests on three underlying concepts: contrast of old and new, use of craft details, and selective removal of historic fabric. The architects did not restore missing architectural details, but designed their own by abstracting the character of the historic properties to their essence, using them to inspire a contrasting new work that heightens the appreciation of the historic features. Both also emphasized richness of materials, heightened color and texture, and highlighted subtle or bold craftsmanship. According to Hawkes, their attention to details, the way in which new and old elements were put together, and their understanding of underlying patterns gave Plecnik's and Scarpa's work authenticity, embedding them comfortably in the historic settings.

Most radically, Hawkes points out, both Plecnik and Scarpa removed elements of historic fabric to create space for new insertions of their own design. The removals, however, were not wholesale gutting, but surgical in precision, intent on striking a balance between preserving original fabric and creating new space and architecture.

Peyton Hall believes that the rehabilitation of historic buildings deserves the best in contemporary design. In his paper, "Reconsidering the Guidelines for Design of Additions to Historic Buildings," he argues that the Secretary of the Interior's Standards for Rehabilitation are too conservative in recommending that new design be subservient to the original building. This, he believes, discourages bold additions that can create a rich dialogue between old and new. The resulting designs, according to Hall, are frequently "mediocre interventions that ultimately devalue the historic resource because they do not reflect our time." Like Hawkes, he subscribes to the philosophy of modernist architect Carlo Scarpa that in restoration an architect should weave "new work into the ongoing dialogue of an evolving fabric." Considering buildings as collaborations across time, Hall wants contemporary additions to express the character of the present as much as the original design expressed the past.

In his case study, Hall examines the rehabilitation and adaptive use of Grauman's 1922 Egyptian Theatre. As the first movie palace in Hollywood, the National Register-listed theater was designed to present both live performances and films. It featured an innovative open-air forecourt that helped to create for the audience the illusion of stepping into another place and time.

Hall describes the preservation of historically significant spaces and fabric in the theater, along with the reconstruction of missing historic features, and how they contrast effectively with the design of new insertions. He takes the reader through the design process, from careful identification of areas and materials that would be preserved and restored through developing design principles for adding new contemporary elements inside the historic shell.

Looking at what postmodernism has contributed to historic preservation, Alison K. Hoagland argues in her paper, "Ironic Historicism: Postmodernism and Historic Preservation," that the two movements have had what she calls "an oddly symbiotic relationship." Postmodern architects, in their use of historical elements and allusions, have exploited the appreciation of the past fostered by the historic preservation movement. This, along with postmodernism's affinity for contextualism, has resulted in new buildings that contribute to a richer definition of compatibility in additions to historic buildings and new construction in historic districts.

Tracing postmodernism back to the 1930s as a movement advocating pluralism and eclecticism, art and poetry, improvisation and spontaneity, and regionalism and contextualism, Hoagland suggests that its use of historicism in architecture was partly influenced by historic preservation. Both movements rejected modernism. She argues that historic preservation kept traditional architecture alive by fighting demolition and encouraging restoration and rehabilitation. Postmodernism takes a different view of the past, one that insists on a critical dialogue with the past, as can be seen in the familiar works of Charles Moore's Piazza d'Italia, New Orleans, Michael Graves' Public Service Building in Portland, Oregon, and Phillip Johnson's AT&T Building in New York City, which Hoagland cites as examples. She also sees the postmodernist's interest in context and in borrowing from surrounding existing buildings for the design of the new, as well as for its reintroduced ornament and color, as contributing to its symbiotic relationship with preservation.

Hoagland notes that at the same time the Secretary of the Interior's Standards for Rehabilitation were being developed, postmodern design was seriously challenging the dominance of the International Style in architecture. She believes that postmodernist design was especially well suited for meeting the need for compatible new designs, particularly in historic areas since it has dynamic compatibility without being subservient.

Session Four: Engineering and Preservation Design

When completed in 1929, the Atlantic City Convention Hall was the largest clear-span enclosed structure in the world. Listed in the National Register of Historic Places and as a National Landmark, the building also possessed a very innovative lighting design when it opened. It was, according to Michael Henry in his paper, "Keeping the Volume Up: Infill and Adaptive Reuse of Monumental-Span Structures," a "state-of-the-art, sophisticated machine for entertainment." In the late 1990s it was replaced by a new convention center. After considering various reuses for the historic convention hall, it was determined that its primary space, the vaulted Auditorium, could be rehabilitated as space for special events attracting between 12,000 and 15,000 people.

Observing that long-span buildings have awed the public since Roman times, Henry introduces his paper with an overview of the history of long-span buildings. He discusses the challenges in preserving these types of structures, using the rehabilitation of Union Station in St. Louis, Gare d'Orsay in Paris, Union Station in Washington, D.C., and Reading Terminal in Philadelphia as examples. Henry argues that the major design problem in the adaptive use of long-span structures is how to introduce economically necessary smaller spaces within the vast interior areas without compromising their grand scale.

After describing the architecturally significant and character-defining features of the Auditorium, Henry outlines the preservation philosophy used to guide design decisions for its adaptive use. In Henry's view, developing this philosophy was a critical first step since upgrading the facility to a modern event space required significant intervention. The philosophy was based on three of the four treatments of historic properties. Preservation standards were applied to the proscenium arch and the north and south walls; restoration standards were applied to the ceiling, indirect lighting, and the loggias; while rehabilitation standards were applied below the balcony and concourse loggia, as well as in the design of the new freestanding seating bowl.

Inserted into the Auditorium's volume, the new seating was a critical component of the design. The new freestanding seating bowl provided modern seating and met sightlines and code requirements without harming primary fabric or compromising the feeling of being in a large-volume space. Constructed of contemporary materials and painted to contrast with the historic colors, the seating bowl and concourse are subordinate to, but contrast with, the original interior of the Auditorium.

In "Before the Arch: Some Early Architects and Engineers on the St. Louis Waterfront," Charles Peterson recounts his experiences as the National Park Service's landscape architect during the late 1930s in planning St. Louis's Jefferson National Expansion Memorial on the Mississippi River. The memorial, constructed in the early 1960s to Eero Saarinen's 1948 competition-winning design, was not in the first plan. Charged with evaluating the historic significance of over 500 buildings, including one the nation's best collections of nineteenth-century cast-iron commercial fronts, Peterson recounts how the attitude of the times considered resources of only truly national significance worth saving, and led to the destruction of all but three buildings. He also suggests that the promoters of the Jefferson National Expansion Memorial were not really interested in preservation and used the 1935 Historic Sites and Buildings Act, which focused on recording historic buildings rather than preserving them, as an expedient way to have Congress authorize the memorial.

While Charles Peterson's commitment to saving buildings is well known, his role as a landscape architect and planner in St. Louis, as well as his proposal for a national architectural museum and the development of preliminary plans for the Jefferson National Expansion Memorial, are not. In his paper, he describes the succession plans before Saarinen designed his arch, paying particular attention to the architects and engineers who contributed in the early days of the park.

In the final paper of this volume, "Temples of Flight: Preservation Design at Washington National and Dulles International Airports," Henry Ward examines the process and issues in the rehabilitation and restoration of Washington, D.C.'s two airports, Reagan (formerly National) and Dulles International. Completed in 1941 and 1962 respectively, both exemplify the problems of preserving the recent past, particularly those that must be constantly adapted to remain useful. Ward also points out that both National Register properties challenge popular conceptions of what is "historic" and should be preserved.

Reagan National and Dulles presented very different preservation challenges. Built before the boom in commercial aviation, Reagan National's terminal was designed to express the novelty of flight for the general public. Located close to downtown Washington, its site offered little room for expansion. By the time Dulles was completed, the jet age made flight commonplace. Its design provided a plan that would allow both the airport and its signature terminal to expand while protecting their integrity.

When the Washington Airports Authority assumed responsibility for the two airports the mid-1980s, it undertook studies of current and future needs of both facilities. At Reagan National Airport, plans called for the rehabilitation of the historic 1941 terminal, demolition of a number of additions, and the construction of a new 35-gate terminal, along with new vehicular circulation systems and greatly expanded parking structures. At Dulles, the expansion of the terminal was to follow Saarinen's original plans for doubling its size and preserving his carefully designed approach sequences. However, the mobile lounges that took passengers directly from the terminal to planes, thus eliminating long walks and Jetways, were determined to be obsolete. Instead, new mid-field terminals were to be constructed, along with major new parking facilities.

At Reagan National Airport, an early decision was made to design the new terminal to be distinctly different from the character of the 1941 horizontal modernist building with its round, glazed curtain walls and cantilevered floors that also incorporated architectural references to colonial and neoclassical styles. The design challenges at Dulles included adding a number of large new parking decks along the entry road, including locating one in front of the terminal, without destroying Saarinen's carefully planned entry sequence, as well as how to link the new mid-field terminals to the original without intruding on its historic appearance.

Perhaps the most radical challenge to preservation at Dulles, and one not anticipated by the Secretary of the Interior's Standards for Rehabilitation, was that Saarinen designed the terminal to be completed in the future. Thus the key question was whether protecting the integrity of the terminal in rehabilitation lay in following the original historic design for its expansion, or in expanding the terminal with a compatible design by another architect. Ward describes how this dilemma was solved.

Taken together, these papers by architects, engineers, preservationists, and historians examining the role of design in preservation forcefully assert that, far from being something apart from preservation, the design process is at the core of preservation practice. It is the linchpin that moves preservation from evaluation and designation—design as a noun—to the action of preserving—design as a verb. In doing so, the act of designing is also the mechanism that integrates the multifaceted knowledge and fields of practice that must be brought to bear on the physical preservation of a property, no matter which of the four treatments is utilized. The design process then translates the abstractions of historic significance and integrity into the reality of preserved properties that give us continuity with our past while continuing to do their work in the modern world. ✪

(Endnotes)

1 E. Blaine Cliver, "Revisiting Past Rehabilitation Practices," in *Past Meets Future: Saving America's Historic Environments*, ed. Antoinette J. Lee (Washington, D.C.: The Preservation Press, 1992), 175.

2 William J. Murtagh, *Keeping Time: The History and Theory of Preservation in America* (New York: Sterling Publishing Co., 1988), 123.

3 Bryan Lawson, *How Designers Think: The Design Process Demystified* (Oxford: The Architectural Press, 1997), 3.

4 Department of the Interior, National Park Service, *National Register Bulletin: How to Apply the National Register Criteria* (Washington, D.C.,1990, rev. 1998), 17.

5 Ibid., 44.

6 Kay W. Weeks, "Historic Preservation Treatments: Toward a Common Language," CRM 19, no. 1 (1996) and http://www2.cr.nps.gov/tps/common/index/htm.

7 The primary source for this discussion is the Secretary of the Interior's Standards for the Treatment of Historic Properties as published on the National Park Service Web site at http://www2.cr.nps.gov/tps/standardguide/overview/choose_treat.htm, or simply enter "Standards for the Treatment of Historic Properties" into a browser. Discussion of the standards can be found in Norman Tyler, *Historic Preservation: An Introduction to Its History, Principles, and Practice*, 1992 and Murtaugh, *Keeping Time: The History and Theory of Preservation in America*.

8 Lawson, 59.

9 Tyler, 140.

10 Department of the Interior, *Secretary of the Interior's Standards for Rehabilitation & Illustrated Guidelines for Rehabilitating Historic Buildings* (Washington, D.C.: National Park Service, Cultural Resources Preservation Assistance Division, 1992).

11 Department of the Interior, National Register Bulletin 15. *How to Apply the National Register Criteria for Evaluation* (Washington, D.C., 1991), 5.

12 Arnold R. Alamen and Robert Z. Melnick, *Preserving Cultural Landscapes in America* (Baltimore: Johns Hopkins University Press, 2000), 7.

PART ONE
Melding Contemporary and Historic Design

DESIGN IN PRESERVATION PROJECTS

MICHAEL J. MILLS, FAIA
Partner
Farewell Mills Gatsch Architects, LLC

Many property owners, agencies, and even design professionals have difficulty using the words "design" and "historic preservation" in the same sentence. They may regard historic preservation as a discrete activity that does not involve design, or think that decisions about the treatment of the architectural fabric of an historic building are either obvious and easily made or, conversely, dictated by "preservation standards." Those architects who restore historic buildings, adapt historic buildings to new uses, or design new buildings in historic settings know that these are misconceptions. Actually, myriad design decisions are required for successful historic preservation projects, or for careful treatment of historic fabric when the goal of the project is not just preservation.

The first definition of the word "design" in the *Random House Dictionary* is "to plan the form and structure of something." In the field of architecture, this is most consistent with the design of new buildings. However, the second definition is "to plan and fashion skillfully and artistically." This is an appropriate description of the type of design that characterizes historic preservation work.

The Secretary of the Interior's Standards for the Treatment of Historic Properties establishes the framework and definitions for the levels of treatment of historic buildings. Each of the four treatment categories—Preservation, Rehabilitation, Restoration, and Reconstruction—describes varying degrees of retention of historic materials.[1] Design challenges exist in all of the categories, and some of these will be explored in the following overview.

Preservation

Preservation is defined as "the act or process of applying measures necessary to sustain the existing form, integrity, and materials of an historic property."[2] The standards for this treatment require the retention of the greatest amount of historic fabric, including the features that illustrate the building's evolution over time. How can the act of merely preserving an historic building's materials be considered design? An example is the conservation of the exterior marble at Whig and Clio halls on the Princeton University campus.

Whig and Clio Halls were designed in 1893 by A. Page Brown for rival campus debating societies (Figure 1). A century of weathering and a fire in Whig Hall had caused various problems for the marble, which included long cracks in the twenty-two-foot, monolithic columns; multiple and severe cracking in the bases and plinths; cracking and exfoliation of projecting elements like the Ionic capitals; and severe sugaring, gypsum deposits, and iron staining of the marble. Another team retained by Princeton in 1992 concluded that both the substructure of the portico and columns should be replaced entirely. It was their opinion that the structural cracks in the columns were caused by "differential settlement of the foundation on which the stones bear," and that the systems of cracks in the bases and plinth stones were due to the marble's inability to span the bearing points. Their recommendations included replacing the columns with new ones formed by three drums (because it is no longer possible to quarry twenty-two-foot blocks of Vermont Danby marble) and replacing the bases and plinths with marble sectioned in four parts around a concrete core, so that the marble would not be load bearing.

Hoping to find an approach that preserved as much original fabric as possible

FIGURE 1. *Whig and Clio Halls, Princeton, New Jersey. Photograph: Taylor Photo.*

while ensuring the portico's structural integrity, the University retained our firm to provide a second opinion. We assembled the team of Robert Silman, the eminent structural engineer; Ivan Myjer, a stone expert; and Dr. George Wheeler, a conservator from the Metropolitan Museum of Art. To allay our concerns about diagonal cracks in the columns, we also retained G.B. Geotechnics to perform two types of non-destructive tests: impulse radar and ultrasonic pulse velocity. These tests provided qualitative and quantitative information about the marble itself, the nature and depth of the cracks, as well as positions of internal anchors.

From probes that were made into the portico platform and from checking alignments with a transit, we found no evidence of differential settlement of the marble structure. We concluded that the damage to the marble plinths and bases and the top of the foundations was due to a variety of factors, including water leaching through the portico floor, freeze/thaw damage from ice and de-icing chemicals, poor bedding of the original stones, and inadequate repairs that accelerated the damage.

After our detailed survey, we made the following recommendations: 1) retain the monolithic columns, as they have historic value and can no longer be replicated, 2) replace the marble bases and plinths with new stone units to match the original design, 3) correct design problems with the portico floor, 4) rebuild the tops of the rubble masonry foundations with concrete, 5) undertake cleaning, repointing, and repairs to the marble with in-kind materials and proper conservation techniques, and 6) complete limited structural pinning repairs to the stone columns and entablature. The biggest challenge was clearly to keep the columns in place while replacing their bases and plinths.

A design was then developed for two alternative shoring schemes that could accomplish this task. The first was for building shoring towers between the columns with drilled holes and temporary pinned supports for the columns, and the second was for performing the same operation, but with the use of friction clamps in place of drilled pins. After design and bidding these options, the contractor Lorenzon Brothers was added to the team with their engineer J. B. Callaghan, both of Philadelphia. Another refinement was added to the design at their suggestion, which was to build only two shoring towers at either end of the portico, install two W36 bridge steel members between them, and take the load off the columns and portico and onto the steel with a system of hydraulic jacks.[3] Friction clamps, which would "squeeze" the columns, would be hung from W36s by high-tensile strength steel rods adjusted by screw jacks. Oak blocks were designed to marry into the concave flutes of the columns and would rely on the static coefficient of friction to overcome gravity. Slip

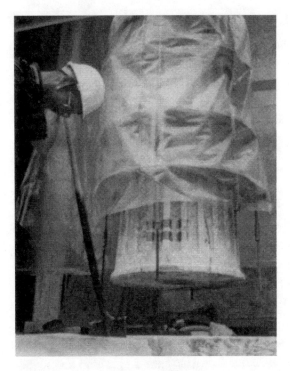

FIGURE 2. *Suspended column at Whig Hall. Photograph: Farewell Mills Gatsch Architects, LLC.*

test trials were undertaken to ensure that the compression rings would perform effectively. If the tests had failed, we would have used the drilled hole-and-pin method as originally designed to suspend the columns above their foundations.

The execution of the design resulted in an impressive orchestration of construction equipment, which included three cranes to install the shoring towers. After slip tests confirmed that the compression rings would in fact perform effectively, the hardware was installed. To ensure worker safety, a redundant set of compression rings was added to each column and a steel plate beneath. It had initially been thought that only two 28,000-pound columns at a time would be suspended. However, the load capacity of the shoring allowed the outer four columns of the pediment plus the pediment itself (310,000 pounds) to be supported at the same time, which expedited construction. Foundation repairs were made, a new marble porch deck over a waterproofed slab was installed, and the new marble bases and plinths, which were fabricated in Germany to our design, were slid into place using traditional lead shims. The middle two columns were then shored and the process repeated for both buildings (Figure 2).

The design of the shoring system also facilitated other work, such as the Dutchman repair and carving program. Many of the projecting Ionic volutes that were in danger of failure were pinned, repaired with sections of new marble, and recarved to match existing profiles. The work also included an extensive cleaning program, complete repointing, and chemical consolidation of some of the marble. We believe that our design for the shoring and repair of the column foundations was unprecedented in the United States, and will serve as an option to owners of other historic buildings that have damage to substructure beneath columns. The innovative design solutions that were explored and utilized in this project preserved the marble columns and restored them to their century-old duty of supporting the entablature, pediment, and portico roof.

Restoration

Restoration is defined as "the process of accurately depicting the form, features, and character of a property as it appeared at a particular period of time by means of removal of features from other periods in its history and reconstruction of features from the restoration period."[4] While this definition may seem straightforward, the design decisions in restoration are often quite complex. In restoration, material authenticity is often sacrificed, and certain materials may be removed or missing features rebuilt to depict a single period. No restoration is entirely pure because the work is done at a different time in history, and frequently includes modern mechanical and electrical systems as well as structural reinforcements. The restoration of the 1761 Brearley House in Lawrence Township, New Jersey, is a case in point.

This important pre-Revolutionary house, owned by a signer of the U.S. Constitution, had been vacant for many years and was in very poor condition. It was part of a tract of land purchased by the Township for a park in 1985. Without a plan for the building's preservation, the Township needed help in securing and protecting it. Our firm was retained in 1987 to design a project to stabilize and "mothball" the house. The project was featured in a National Park Service Preservation Brief on that topic.[5] The protective measures included installing temporary roofing and drainage for rainwater protection, wrapping the chimneys with plywood for structural stabilization, providing plywood covers with louvers over the windows for ventilation and security, adding a ventilation fan on a thermostat to prevent damage from condensation, installing temporary fire detection and security systems, and building a perimeter security fence. During the ensuing ten years while the protection was in place, the house was studied through the completion of historic research, a comprehensive historic structure report, and extensive archaeology. A vibrant, eighteenth-century paint scheme on the interior of the house was discovered through paint analysis.

Thus, when the decision was made to restore the property, a considerable amount of information existed on which to base the renovation. The period of significance for the design was determined to be from 1761 to the late nineteenth century, when the last Brearley descendants were living in the house. This decision not only preserved the extensive original woodwork, but also some modest later alterations made by the family, such as the porch roofs

FIGURE 3. *Brearley House, Lawrence Township, New Jersey.*
Photograph: Farewell Mills Gatsch Architects, LLC.

and some additional mantels and miscellaneous millwork. The exterior chimneys, roof, doors, windows, porches, and shutters were restored based on historic evidence (Figure 3). In order to preserve the integrity of the interior architectural fabric, new HVAC, electrical, plumbing, fire protection, and security systems were designed in a way to minimize intrusion. Major equipment and piping were installed behind historic finishes in locations that the public will never see. The new HVAC system equipment and ductwork was located in the basement to service the first floor and in the attic to service the second. The first-floor structure was reinforced in the basement and other surgical openings were made to allow repairs behind original finishes. The only evidence of the twentieth century is the floor and wall registers (an improvement over the radiators that existed before the renovation) and the electrical devices including lighting, detectors, switches, and exit signs necessitated by the fact that the Brearley House is a public building.

Reconstruction

The Brearley House project also illustrates the design decisions needed as part of a reconstruction, in this case the reconstruction of the previously removed kitchen wing. The term "reconstruction" as defined by the Secretary of the Interior's Standards means "the act or process of depicting, by means of new construction, the form, features, and detailing of a non-surviving site, landscape, building, structure, or object for the purpose of replicating its appearance at a specific period of time and in its historic location."[6] A reconstruction has the least authenticity of historic materials, since it depicts a single period in history using new materials, and is often based solely on archaeology and other documentary evidence.

Based upon our research of an historic inventory from 1845 that mentioned a kitchen wing and the lack of a cooking fireplace in the main part of the house, it was certain that a kitchen wing had once existed. On-site archaeology and the evidence of the kitchen's attachment to the gable end of the house confirmed the overall size and shape of the prior structure. Several architectural precedents were also discovered in the New Jersey HABS inventory from neighboring Burlington County. This evidence and the client's need for modern facilities to support the intended use led to the decision to proceed with the reconstruction and to create a design for a new wing.

Archaeology showed that the original kitchen contained two rooms separated by a large walk-in fireplace. Many local precedents existed that could yield detailed information on the design of the fireplace, windows, doors, moldings, and other architectural features. However, the client did not need or want the reconstruction of an eighteenth-century kitchen. Rather, the need was for facilities that would support the new use. The addition was, therefore, designed to provide a small kitchen, a storage room, public toilets, and barrier-free accessibility to the first floor of the house. The addition was built on the excavated foundations of the previous structure, which were protected by new bond beams of concrete that were installed on top of the rubblestone. While the interpretation called for rebuilding the outward form and mass of the wing, it was decided by the New Jersey Historic Preservation Office that not enough evidence existed to reconstruct the materials and details of the structure. The approved design solution was to outline the form of the kitchen wing using modern, but compatible, building materials that would not be mistaken for historic fabric (Figure 3). These materials include the fiberglass shingle roof; the featureless, clapboard walls; and the standard divided light windows that are not as detailed as the original windows in the main house.

Rehabilitation

The broadest category in the Secretary of the Interior's Standards is "rehabilitation," which is defined as "the act or process of making possible a compatible use for a property through repair, alterations, and additions while preserving those portions or features which convey its historical, cultural, or architectural values."[7] Projects in this category range from building renovation for similar uses and restoration of landmark public buildings that do not involve a change of use, to adaptation of historic structures for uses other than the original. As in a preservation approach, a large amount of material fabric is retained in a rehabilitation, as more than one period in the history of the building may be represented. However, there may be less material authenticity due to the fact that alterations and additions for the new use are required in this treatment category. Often, the highest compliment paid to a rehabilitation project is: "It looks wonderful, but I can't tell what you did." And often, these projects involve very extensive renovations to HVAC, electrical, fire protection, telecommunications, and security systems. It takes a skillful designer to incorporate new systems in a way that allows the original design and materials of historic spaces to be preserved and restored.

The Graduate College at Princeton University is listed on the National Register of Historic Places based on its architectural significance as one of the finest examples of collegiate Gothic architecture in the United States. Designed by Ralph Adams Cram in 1912, it embodies the educational ideals at the beginning of the last century espoused by Dean Andrew Fleming West, the first dean of the college. The project began as a fire code upgrade of the dormitory areas, but over time became a comprehensive rehabilitation project. The scope included a new sprinkler system, a new heating system linked to Princeton's energy management system, upgrade of toilet rooms, new fire detection and alarm systems, the connection of every room to the Princeton computer Net system, and the restoration of the finishes, which included the heart pine floors, paneled fireplaces and window seats, oak doors and trim, plaster walls, and leaded glass windows. The Graduate College encompasses over 150,000 square feet of dormitory space arranged around two courtyards, as well as public spaces like Procter Hall and Van Dyke Library. At the southeast corner of the complex is the 170-foot tall Cleveland Memorial Tower, the tallest Gothic tower on the Princeton campus.

The major design decisions were driven by the need to retain the historical integrity of the rooms, while unobtrusively integrating state-of-the-art life safety, communication, and environmental systems. One of the most important of these decisions was to keep as much of the terra cotta and plaster as possible. The plaster contained a significant amount of asbestos and cutting it would have created a health hazard. Also, cuts for utilities in the terra cotta partitions, which were tested by mock-ups, undermined the partitions' structural integrity. The biggest design problem, therefore, was how to run new utilities vertically through the building with a minimum impact on the existing spaces and partitions, and further, how to distribute the utilities horizontally through the room suites.

The design response was to remove the wood floors down to the concrete slabs to provide the space for mechanical, electrical, and telecommunications distribution within the suites. Piping and duct banks were routed through the few original chases, the backs of student closets, and existing dropped ceilings above bathrooms and stair landings. A new subfloor system was designed to provide sufficient space for the utilities while matching the elevation of the old floors (Figure 4). New heart pine floors were installed to match the existing floors. New hot water convectors replaced the steam radiators and were

FIGURE 4. *Princeton University Graduate College, Princeton, New Jersey. Photograph: Otto Baitz.*

accommodated within existing bench seats below the leaded glass windows.

In a rehabilitation project like this one, the major systems were competing for a limited amount of space in a building not originally designed for them, which created a very complex, three-dimensional puzzle. The design approach was also complicated by the romantic nature of the building, as room layouts did not align floor to floor. To enable this complex project to be designed and executed without conflicts between architectural, mechanical, electrical, fire safety, and telecommunications systems, we relied heavily upon our computer-aided design system. The resultant database permitted the intricate coordination of systems that was needed to control the quality of this rehabilitation. There were over 450 full-size drawings in the final design set. The academic environment of the Graduate College was both preserved and modernized by the careful design of its new systems (Figure 4).

Adaptive Use

The adaptive use of historic buildings that can no longer be utilized for their original purposes also requires design creativity. Adaptive use is a subset of the rehabilitation category in the Secretary of the Interior's Standards, which includes any activity that preserves the physical fabric and the evidence of evolution of a building or site, while accommodating new uses. This can be seen in many of the buildings in the historic center of Rome, where layer upon layer of historic fabric is preserved even as new layers are added to allow continued use. Historic buildings cannot all become museums, and one of the best ways to preserve a building is to ensure its continued use by adaptation.

Examples of design in adaptive use projects are very diverse and range from the conservative, where the use is fitted seamlessly into the building, to radical, where the historic fabric is juxtaposed against a new intervention. I would place the renovation of the Essex Club in Newark, New Jersey, in the first category. This gentleman's club in the Georgian Revival style was converted to the new headquarters of the New Jersey Historical Society, one

FIGURE 5. *New Jersey Historical Society, formerly the Essex Club, Newark, New Jersey. Photograph: Farewell Mills Gatsch Architects, LLC.*

of New Jersey's oldest cultural institutions (Figure 5). The basic rehabilitation program included repairs to the roof and main façade; code improvements such as a new fire stair, sprinklers, and elevator; and a new HVAC system, which was zoned to provide appropriate climate control to the collections. However, the major generator of the design was the program of use, which took advantage of the fine, Georgian Revival interior spaces. The first-floor tap room became a multi-purpose meeting room; the walnut-paneled, second-floor club room was converted to a gallery for permanent exhibits; and the large dining room became the main gallery for changing exhibits. Former kitchen and support space for the club was utilized as additional storage space for the collection. On the upper floors, a library and reading room with expansive views of the downtown and Military Park across the street was created in space that formerly housed a corporate suite. Next to the reading room, the former squash courts and their spectators' galleries were redesigned to house the library archives.

At the other end of the spectrum is our design for the conversion of an historic, wire rope factory in the Roebling Industrial Complex in Trenton into high-tech offices for the New Jersey Housing and Mortgage Finance Agency. In this case, the envelope of the building had previously been restored, and it was treated as the container for a new design intervention that engaged the existing, industrial fabric with modern forms and functional offices.

The project had a number of significant economic and social goals. Primarily, it represented the agency's commitment to keeping its workforce in the city of Trenton. The organization of the plan on an urban model gives coherence to the agency for its employees and visitors, and expresses the mandate of the agency, which is to support the construction needs of the state housing industry through economic development. Located in the wire fabrication building, a broad, top-lit, multi-bay structure, the offices were organized around four major urban squares linked by a network of interconnected corridors (Figure 6). The centers (or squares) are distinct departmental addresses, which include administration, executive, finance, and single-family housing. Each center is designed to be different in character and materials, and related to the specific activities of that department. The finance department, for example, is

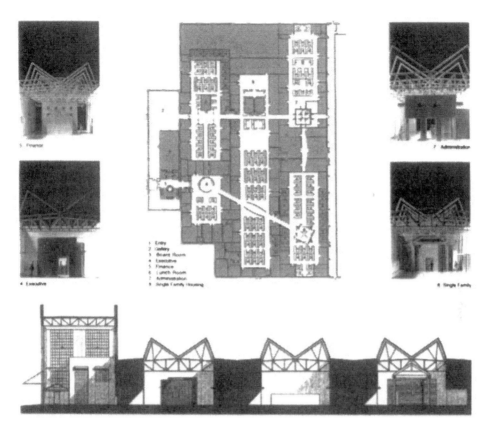

FIGURE 6. *New Jersey Housing and Mortgage Finance Agency, formerly Roebling Industrial Complex.*
Photograph: Farewell Mills Gatsch Architects, LLC.

configured as a branch bank on an urban square. Single-family housing is
expressed by a wood pavilion with a gabled roof, which is domestic in
character. The executive department, near the entry, is a gear-like structure
reflecting the dynamism of both the original Roebling plant and the new state
agency (Figure 6). The entry through the high-bay testing building is the
location of the reception area, a gallery, and meeting spaces that are used by
HMFA, other state agencies, and the greater community. The project has won
numerous awards including an international joint award from *Business Week*
and *Architectural Record.*

Additions

Designing additions to historic buildings is perhaps the most challenging
activity within the field of preservation. The Secretary of the Interior's Standards
indicate that an attached exterior addition is usually an acceptable alternative,
but only after it has been determined that the new use cannot be successfully
met by existing interior spaces. If additions are made, the standards state that

they should be designed and constructed "so that the character-defining features are not obscured, damaged, or destroyed."[8] "Design for the new work ... should always be clearly differentiated from the historic building,"[9] so that the addition does not appear to be part of the historic resource. It is a challenge for the designer to strike a balance between extending historic fabric seamlessly and differentiating the addition so that no one will mistake it for the historic building. The refinement of new materials through appropriate detailing is also of considerable significance, as such detail or ornament must simultaneously respond to the historic context while fulfilling contemporary requirements and sensibilities.

An example of our effort to do this in an important public building is our design for the Legislative Staff Building, which is an addition to the New Jersey State House. The renovation of the New Jersey State House complex has been a defining project for our firm since 1975, when we began the historical studies of the building that led to the work. The State House complex includes two major buildings: the State House and the State House Annex, and two branches of government: the Legislative and the Executive. Our planning for the project was extensive, from historic research on the complex to archaeology, master planning, site planning, a space needs analysis, code studies, and systems analysis. The design work on the historic portions of the building included preservation of historic spaces like the 1893 Assembly Chamber; restoration of the exterior envelope; restoration of the interior monumental spaces such as the Senate Chamber; reconstruction of historic spaces lost by insensitive renovations, such as the former Supreme Court Chamber and the State Library; and conservation of artwork such as the Senate murals and a ceiling mural fragment from a mid-nineteenth-century version of the State House that was found and reinstalled.

The Legislative Staff Building is an example of collaborative work in the design of preservation and new construction projects at our firm. The need for an addition was clear from the moment we entered the State House. The fine, existing spaces in the historic portions of the building had been compromised in large part by overcrowding. In a real sense, the design of an addition made it possible for the work to proceed in restoring and rehabilitating the State House.

The addition was conceived as an extension of the brownstone base of the State House, which becomes two full stories because of the change of grade next to the Delaware River. This granite-faced building recalls the battered bases of quayside, Beaux Arts architecture in France and the arcaded basements of English neoclassical architecture. Somerset House, Sir William Chamber's government building along the Thames, is one such precedent.

FIGURES 7 AND 8. *(Left) New Jersey State House, Trenton, New Jersey. Photograph: Otto Baitz; (Right) Crescent Dormitories, The Lawrenceville School, Lawrence, New Jersey. Photograph: Otto Baitz*

Another architectural metaphor that was considered in the design was the Acropolis. The Legislative Staff Building addition forms a stylobate or platform on which sits the historic, classical elements of the State House. A new, monumental entrance was created on axis with the front doors on West Street, which serves to orient one to the new connections within the complex (Figure 7).

New Buildings In Historic Settings

The final design challenge that I will briefly mention is the design of new buildings in historic settings. The design issues of compatibility versus differentiation are similar to the treatment of additions to historic buildings. Design responses vary, from the slavish replication of form and details of the original buildings, to the confrontation of the historic setting by a building that does not acknowledge that it has a context. Rare is the successful design at the extreme ends of the scale. Another approach is suggested by our work at The Lawrenceville School.

Founded in 1810 as the Maidenhead Academy, The Lawrenceville School was "refounded" in 1883, changing its name and constructing a new campus. With landscaping created by Frederick Law Olmsted and buildings designed by Peabody and Stearns, the campus of this prominent, independent secondary school exists today as a National Historic Landmark. Designed around a house system with resident masters living family-style within the dormitories, the original houses are arranged on a landscaped circle and, for that reason, are known as the Circle Houses. At Lawrenceville we were charged with the preparation of a master plan for expansion based on the trustees' decision to proceed with co-education. We recommended an extension of the campus using an existing crescent of oak trees as the organizing element. We then designed four dormitories for girls, which became known as the Crescent Houses.

In this project, we sought to reinterpret the Queen Anne style used by Peabody and Stearns to create buildings that modulate the heaviness of masonry surfaces with skeletal wood elements such as entry pavilions and bay windows. Each of the buildings provides single and double rooms for thirty-five girls and apartments for two resident masters and their families in a rear wing. While influenced by the massing, materials, and roof pitches of the earlier buildings on the circle, the new dorms exhibit a more abstract style that is not at all Queen Anne or Victorian. The Crescent Houses are articulated with brick, painted metal, and shafts of glass in a contemporary way that complements the scale of the Peabody and Stearns buildings, but does not compete with them. These buildings also stand on their own as quietly confident works of architecture (Figure 8).

Conclusion

It is my contention that historic preservation is by its nature a design activity, not a separate process that somehow results in appropriate treatment of historic fabric. The treatment of historic buildings shows as much about the intentions of the designer, the owner, and the contractor as does new construction. Discovering what the issues are in any project and deciding how to address those issues are matters of judgment and creativity. Therefore, "to plan and fashion skillfully and artistically," as design is defined, is most certainly what architects do in historic preservation. ⊛

(Endnotes)

1 Department of the Interior, National Park Service, *The Secretary of the Interior's Standards for the Treatment of Historic Properties with Guidelines for Preserving, Rehabilitating, Restoring & Reconstructing Historic Buildings*, by Kay D. Weeks and Anne E. Grimmer. Washington, D.C., 1995.

2 Ibid., 17.

3 This was a similar shoring design to that of the earlier team, which would have enabled the portico to remain in place while the columns were completely removed.

4 Weeks and Grimmer, 117.

5 Department of the Interior, National Park Service, "Preservation Briefs 31: Mothballing Historic Buildings," by Sharon C. Park, AIA. (Washington, D.C., 1993).

6 Weeks and Grimmer, 165.

7 Ibid., 61.

8 Ibid., 112.

9 Ibid., 113.

Case Studies in "Quality" Infill Design

How Do We Move beyond the Bad and the Bland?

ELEANOR ESSER GORSKI, AIA
Supervising Architect
Commission on Chicago Landmarks

DIJANA CUVALO
Permit Review
Commission on Chicago Landmarks

T he "quality" of infill design has been a hotly debated issue since the inception of historic preservation as a field. For the purposes of this paper, we are defining "quality" infill design as that which strikes a balance between being compatible with an historic district without replicating existing historic buildings. The importance of quality infill design has been widely confirmed as essential to preserving the sense of place of an historic district, but just what constitutes "quality" infill design has separated the public from the preservation professionals from the beginning—with the public preferring historicizing designs as indistinguishable as possible from the originals and the professionals promoting contemporary yet compatible designs. This debate has achieved new urgency of late with criticism in many large and small cities that historic preservation is stifling contemporary architecture.

Background

In its review of new construction, the Commission on Chicago Landmarks has adopted the following standard: "To encourage excellence in contemporary design that does not imitate, but rather recognizes and respects, existing architectural and environmental characteristics of the property or district." The success of this standard has been varied, and in practice, the standard is difficult to mandate with developers and designers. Except for a few outstanding projects, most new construction in Chicago landmark districts has either been a watered-down version of period revival styles or an awkward contemporary attempt that doesn't give enough thought to recognizing or respecting the existing district.

Encouraging such "quality" infill design has been a controversial issue ever since the Chicago City Council granted the Commission on Chicago Landmarks the authority to review the design of new construction in 1987. Prior to that, the commission only reviewed changes to existing structures within the city's historic districts. Early district designations exhibited a high degree of integrity and few vacant lots, making infill design less of an issue. But with the designations of more districts in the late 1970s and early 1980s, the importance of having design review over new construction became critical.

Residents in more affluent areas felt that in a landmark district, an inequity would arise where existing buildings would be tightly regulated while vacant lots would have no restrictions and could build out to full allowable zoning densities. It was felt that this would penalize the existing building owners, who would be limited with their property while there would be no controls on neighboring development in the district—this would ultimately result in the overbuilding on the vacant lots and eroding the historic character of the district while reducing the value of existing structures. Examples of such historic districts in Chicago include Old Town Triangle, designated in 1977, and Astor Street, designated in 1975.

For districts in struggling and economically depressed areas, landmark designation meant that existing buildings would not be allowed to be demolished, thus saving what was left, hopefully stabilizing these areas, and bringing attention to existing vacant land ripe for development. But residents in struggling districts began to see incompatible new construction built, which through its poor design detracted from the very district and neighborhood character they had sought to protect. Examples of these districts include Kenwood, designated in 1979, and Wicker Park, designated in 1981.

The city council responded to the lobbying of these groups and in 1987 granted the commission the right to review new construction within historic districts. This not only assisted in the protection of existing districts, but also changed the view on designating new districts. Residents in areas with large amounts of vacant land now clamored to become landmark districts, seeing the benefits of design review by the commission. Residents lobbied for districts such as Calumet-Giles-Prairie, designated in 1988, and Oakland, designated in 1992, both of which contained almost 50 percent vacant land.

With this added authority, the commission immediately adopted new design guidelines to assist in this review. General criteria were established by which to review new construction based on evaluating a project within the historic character of the individual district: 1) size, shape, and scale and massing, 2) site plan, 3) general historic and architectural characteristics, and 4) materials.

Today, the commission oversees thirty-five districts containing approximately 3,800 individual buildings and typically reviews about fifty to seventy new construction projects each year. The amount of new construction reviewed continues to grow as Chicago has experienced an unprecedented urban construction boom and more districts are designated every year. As the number of projects increases, the commission continues to reevaluate its process and refine the criteria it uses for the review of new construction within its historic districts. But the overall quality of infill design has remained inconsistent, at best, through the years.

Obstacles

As is typical for most landmark commissions, in Chicago there is a design review process in place for any changes or alterations to existing structures as well as for proposed new construction. The commission staff conducts the initial design review with the applicant and submits an evaluation report and a recommendation to a subcommittee of the commission responsible for reviewing applications for building permits. All new construction is reviewed at a public meeting of this committee. Because the committee has final approval over all new construction, the composition of the committee is important, and it has typically been populated by a mix of developers, architects, bankers, and planners.

Public education and participation are also a key component in the process. In 1992 the commission adopted its current set of design guidelines for new construction, which attempted to provide a user-friendly resource for owners of properties in historic districts. These guidelines were based on the Secretary of the Interior's Standards for the Treatment of Historic Properties, as well as the review criteria adopted by the commission. Community groups, which were instrumental in designating their prospective districts, formed standing committees that informally reviewed new construction and advised the commission.

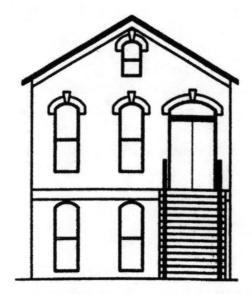

FIGURE 1. *Chicago Cottage*

By the time a design is reviewed by the commission, it is near the end of its design development process, having already been reviewed by commission staff and local community groups. But many other factors have already influenced the design of new construction beyond the commission's design criteria, such as site and zoning constraints, market demand and economics, and other city agencies. Though design review for historic districts is not directly meant to take these factors into account, it would be unrealistic and indeed counterproductive to ignore them.

Generally the private sector's approach toward the design of new construction in Chicago's landmark districts has been one marked by historicism—albeit either a watered-down or an over-aggrandized one. New construction tries to replicate historic buildings in an effort to "blend in" and be compatible. Sometimes, conversely, an alternative approach to new construction attempts to use contemporary design and materials, but often with mixed success. Some examples of recent projects best demonstrate this approach.

The Calumet-Giles-Prairie District on the city's Near South Side is noted for its historic row houses, although the district also includes a rather eclectic mix of post-Civil War cottages. The Chicago cottage is actually a "native" building type that is typical in many of the local landmark districts. A Chicago cottage is typically constructed of wood balloon-framing, one to two and one-half stories on a raised base, which is sometimes constructed out of brick (Figure 1). The building is clad with wood clapboard siding and usually has little or no ornamentation.

In this district, a developer initially proposed two very different single-family detached residences after a consultation with the commission staff encouraging innovative contemporary design. One residence was designed to appear very contemporary, yet it did not meet the review criteria listed above. The other residence more closely met the criteria, but it was overtly historicizing, replicating various design details seen throughout the district in a rather pell-mell fashion, and adding a "Burger King" crown (Figure 2). The

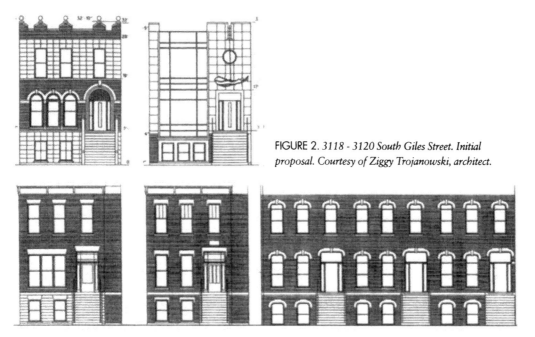

FIGURE 2. *3118 - 3120 South Giles Street. Initial proposal. Courtesy of Ziggy Trojanowski, architect.*

FIGURE 3. *3118 - 3120 South Giles Street. Final proposal. Courtesy of Ziggy Trojanowski, architect.*

commission staff and the community group, following several reiterations, worked with the developer to achieve a more compatible design (Figure 3).

Sometimes the proposed design is an over-aggrandized historicism. The Astor Street District is in an exclusive area of Chicago referred to as the Gold Coast, characterized by grand detached mansions and elegant attached town homes. An historicizing project in this district was the construction of an extensive new front on an older building that had been completely refaced in 1960s. Though the buildings in this district are often elegantly embellished, this project exceeded what would be commonly seen in terms of fenestration, detailing of materials, and architectural elements, instead adopting a "nouveau riche," generic version of history (Figure 4). This project demonstrates what constitutes too much of a good thing: too many balconies, too many French doors and divided pane windows, too many round windows, and too much rustication.

This phenomenon of over-aggrandized historicism is mostly a result of developers' perception of market tastes.

The design of new construction must also be balanced with the developer's desire to maximize profit. In some ways, density has become almost as important as the design of a building for both the neighborhoods and the landmarks commission. The demand for more and more density creates

FIGURE 4. *Astor Street. Initial proposal. Courtesy of Hutter Architects*

tangible problems in the building types that are emerging, given the massing and scale of a project and the demands on open space versus parking. Neighborhoods that consisted originally of single-family or two-unit dwellings on a lot are now zoned for more dense developments.

An example that illustrates this tension of the marketplace and the review criteria for new construction can be found in a project in the Old Town Triangle District on Chicago's Near North Side. This project illustrates how the current zoning is typically manipulated to maximize the developer's profit. The developer took advantage of the unique site situation to restore an historic cottage and add three new single-family residences on two adjacent city lots (Figure 5). Because this particular area of Old Town has through lots with street and alley access at both ends, it was possible to construct buildings on the front and rear of each lot. Zoning in the area does not allow more than one residential building on a zoning lot. The developer addressed that by constructing a common underground parking area, which connects the four buildings together as one (Figure 6). The result for zoning purposes is two buildings on two lots, which fortunately, coincides with the historic development pattern of the district of front buildings, with second buildings or coach houses at the rear of the lot.

Because of the scarcity of vacant land in this district, the land is valuable, and developers want to maximize its potential, often resulting in proposals of

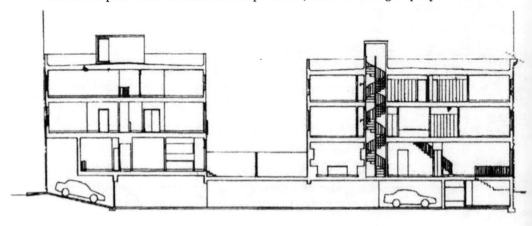

FIGURE 5. *1736 – 1738 North Sedgwick Street. Section through proposed development. Courtesy of Michael Lisec, architect.*

FIGURE 6. *1736 – 1738 North Sedgwick Street. Sedgwick Street elevation of proposed development. Courtesy of Michael Lisec, architect.*

FIGURE 7. *West Evergreen Street. Initial proposal. Courtesy of Ken Schroeder, architect.*

more density than the historic district and neighborhood can absorb. In this case, there is a high demand for parking, making it economically feasible to build a commercial-type underground parking garage for these four single-family residences. This is an extreme example of how contemporary building types have evolved to have a passing resemblance to existing historic buildings in the district.

The Old Town Triangle District was originally built as a working-class neighborhood, characterized by one-and-one-half-story frame cottages and small masonry apartment buildings. Over the years this area has seen a resurgence and has become much more affluent. As a result, the size of new single-family houses is closer to the size of the historic small masonry apartment buildings than the historic single-family houses. In response, a new building type is evolving that consists of a single-family residence "hiding" behind a multi-unit facade. This new building type has new demands such as required parking, open space in the form of balconies and rooftop decks, and a larger building footprint with little or no backyard.

The initial design for 1736-38 N. Sedgwick Street proposed only 15 feet of open space between front and rear buildings, with each building at least one story taller than adjacent historic buildings, and included rooftop decks and balconies on the façade (Figure 7). When applying the review criteria established to evaluate the proposal, the design in terms of the site plan is compatible. Though the rear-yard space is tight, it complies with zoning requirements. The commission only has review authority over what can be seen from the street and thus does not have control over the size of rear-yard open space.

In terms of massing and scale relative to the historic buildings in the district, the block where this site is found has a variety of building types and heights. Typically, a range for the building height is set based on the immediate context, and this project exceeded the range found on its block. The developer revised the design to reduce the size of the building to be no taller than the tallest building on the block. The result was that the new building would resemble the tallest masonry apartment building.

The architectural features and materials of the proposed buildings were then compared to the general historic and architectural characteristics associated with the district. The historic apartment buildings, the property type on which the proposed design is based, are typically three and one-half stories high, brick with stone trim, flat roofs, and a raised front entry. The design details are simple; usually the most prominent feature is a pressed metal cornice.

FIGURE 8. *2007 West Evergreen Street. Final proposal. Courtesy of Ken Schroeder, architect.*

The proposed design details for the Sedgwick properties borrowed from many architectural sources and were far grander and more eclectic than any found in the district. Conspicuous features included elaborate limestone window moldings, "colonial" windows, belle époque balconettes, limestone quoins, two-story projecting copper bays, all topped with elaborate copper cornices (Figure 8). This proposal was typical of what developers anticipated that the commission would require and what they perceived potential purchasers would want. But such a combination of different features and details is not typical of the district, and was thus not found to be compatible. The developer was asked to look at existing masonry apartment buildings that most closely resembled the scale of this proposal in order to get ideas on how to simplify the designs. After several iterations, the developer was able to strip down the design to something that the commission could find acceptable.

Community Groups

What role does the community play in the design review? In general, community groups in established neighborhoods are often very sophisticated. Members of these groups have seen the neighborhood grow and gentrify into the "hot" area it has now become. These groups serve an advisory role for the commission, providing insight into other neighborhood issues on a project, and can be very vocal to local officials, influencing zoning and design. The groups push issues that may not be landmark issues and are sometimes at odds with landmark guidelines. Often community groups become independent design review boards, applying their own criteria, instead of referring to local historic guidelines. But community groups are also often a developer's first point of contact in these neighborhoods, and savvy developers usually realize early on that they must please the community group in order to have a project proceed smoothly.

In Chicago, the form of government is a mayor and a city council consisting of fifty aldermen. The individual alderman in each neighborhood is also very involved in new development and design issues, for their constituents demand it of them. They often must deal with developers pushing the zoning and building code envelopes, trying to maximize profit, yet walk the tightrope between encouraging new development and preserving the sense of place that the neighborhood demands. Again, often the commission is caught as an arbiter in such cases. The commission is seen as an objective body that is preserving the "good" of the neighborhood and will balance these competing interests among all parties.

Disagreement

The final example is a project that the commission chose to give one of its annual preservation awards, a contemporary yet compatible infill design in the Wicker Park District. This district is characterized by an exceptional variety of building types, sizes, and styles dating to the late nineteenth and early twentieth centuries. Initially, this site was considered for an historicizing design that was more favored by the community, but did not meet the review criteria set by the commission. As built, the project matched the site, massing, and scale characteristics of the district, but the project was innovative in the use of architectural detailing and materials. Common elements found in the district such as three-story projecting bays, raised front entrances, decorative windows, punched window openings, and cornices were used as starting points and translated into a contemporary design vocabulary. Modern materials were used that were sympathetic to the district, yet would not show the shortcomings in craftsmanship that the historicizing-type designs often showed. Beige cast stone is the main façade material accented by a clear aluminum bay and stainless steel cornice. A perforated stainless steel bridge forms the entry sequence for the building. Colored glass block and a colorfully painted front door accent an otherwise neutral materials palette. This design complements the district, but does not draw undue attention to itself nor replicate buildings and features in the district. However, the community was not at all receptive of this design, and it remains a sticky point in the neighborhood. The community group felt that the overall design approach was not appropriate, including the architectural characteristics, the materials, and contemporary vocabulary. As is often the case, the community and the public at large (and often developers and architects responding to them) prefer more overtly historicizing design for new construction. In this case, the developer wanted to make a contemporary design statement and worked closely with their architect to achieve this goal.

Lessons Learned

Design review is a community process. The criteria set by the commission in its rules and regulations are broad in their scope, and the design guidelines are necessary to clarify the commission's policy on specific design issues. The commission is currently in the process of improving the guidelines to better respond to changing planning practices and new building types. Concurrently, the commission staff is working with other city departments that are revising city zoning and building codes to reduce conflicts in preservation practice. Community groups are generally receptive to this, because added regulations aid their review process; however, developers are wary of what they perceive as additional restrictions. And the architectural community continues to criticize and blame the commission for what it sees as an overall conservative climate for the design of new construction.

The design guidelines are the commission's primary tool for education of all parties involved in developing, designing, and reviewing the new infill design. Emphasizing appropriate contemporary design is one way to begin to shift the discussion of what is "quality" infill construction in historic districts. Annual design awards were started by the commission to also raise the awareness of the public to the importance of historic preservation and infill design in Chicago.

Design review for infill construction is a time-consuming process for everyone involved, because the review involves not only objective elements but also subjective ones. A typical new design review process might take two to three months before a building permit can be issued. This is a surprise to many developers and designers, and leads to limited review time for each project and inevitable compromises. These compromises may not always meet the "letter" of preservation theory, but are a reality of preservation practice.

The design review and approval process, the different players involved in that process, larger neighborhood issues, code requirements, and the economics and tastes of the marketplace all impact infill design in historic districts in Chicago. What constitutes good infill design has been a hotly debated issue since the inception of historic preservation as a discipline. We chose the word "quality" to express the subjectivity that often accompanies design review and criticism. Quality means many different things to many different people, all of which need to be successfully addressed in the design review process to achieve a solid, "quality" infill design. ⊗

▨ DEFINING CONTEXT

Promoting a Greater Level of Innovation in New Design within Historic Districts

KATE R. LEMOS
Associate
Beyer Blinder Belle Architects & Planners

Historic district designation in urban settings has served this country well by successfully protecting the special character of significant groups of historic buildings. Our laws are firm, constitutionally tested, and generally accepted by the communities they serve. Over the past decade, however, preservation has been criticized for resisting change and impeding creativity. Is there truth in this? Have we reached a point of backlash where our own framework for regulating urban historic districts limits our ability to elicit innovative new design that is a product of its own cultural moment?

In the sense that a narrow interpretation of the physical fabric of a district leads to a narrow idea of what might be an appropriate intervention, the answer is yes. An innovative contemporary building that could enhance its historic context but contrasts visually with it may not be found appropriate if the criteria is limited to compatibility with existing materials, fenestration patterns, cornice heights, colors, and the like. Most designation reports, significance statements, and design guidelines present interpretations of context that emphasize cohesion and focus on the "kit of parts"—the superficial formal elements common throughout the district.

Exclusive interest in visual character-defining context, perpetuated by approvals of new buildings that relate to their context by adopting its dominant stylistic features or compositional elements, fuels criticism that preservation limits design innovation. This focus fosters an impression that preservationists prefer contemporary design that relates only superficially to its historic context. Such a framework further compromises preservationists' and architects' abilities to embrace existing formal variety in the urban fabric, itself a condition of historical circumstances. As a result, the process can become intrinsically resistant to new designs that do not reference the dominant formal qualities of the district. Finally, as a matter of curatorial management, emphasis on visual coherence leaves the preservationist unable to acknowledge the necessity of visual difference as a means of distinguishing between "new" and "old."

Too much emphasis on visual coherence for its own sake creates a harmful public and critical misconception of the purpose and regulation of historic districts and creates a false sense of what is the generally accepted means of designing within them. This seems in direct opposition to the following conditions, and raises a number of philosophical questions for preservationists. First, preservationists celebrate architectural excellence and do not necessarily favor historical imitation as the only form of appropriate new design. Second, banal, historical imitations compromise the architectural quality and obfuscate the authenticity of historic districts comprised of buildings whose designs are products of their own cultural moments. Third, visual compatibility is not the only way a new design can relate to the historic character of a protected district. There are many levels of meaning embedded in the historic fabric, which allow endless possibilities for interpretation, resulting in novelty and innovation in new designs. Accordingly, should not design interventions perpetuate rather than halt the continuum of contemporary cultural production in protected districts? Would it not be appropriate that preservationists, keen to observe the historicity of form, be at the forefront of the movement to advance the proposition that contemporary architecture be distinct from that of the past—even if it compromises the alleged visual coherence of an historic district?

Context can be interpreted to reveal deeper, more abstract levels of significance in the history of the district and special characteristics of the fabric. New designs can draw from these, and arguments can be made for their appropriateness. I believe the most interesting and successful interventions are those that relate to their context on deeper and more abstract levels than by simply extending the formal and visual characteristics of the district. Such innovative design can furnish an engaging interpretation of an historic context's significant character and in so doing, enrich our understanding of the historic fabric itself. To illustrate this, I use the SoHo Cast Iron Historic District in New York City as a case study for ways in which historic fabric has been interpreted on abstract levels to produce and support the approval of highly innovative contemporary design.

Interpretations of context in any form can not dictate good design, nor make good architects out of less talented ones, and not all innovative modern design is appropriate just because it is new and different. But by pointing out abstract yet meaningful relationships between new and old, penetrating interpretations of context can broaden the assumed criteria for appropriateness, help to elicit more interesting new designs, and increase the frequency of precedent-setting approvals of new design. Preservationists can play a vital role in the process of responding sensitively and creatively to historic context by providing this kind of interpretation in the design process, and bearing it in mind in the approval process. Without compromising our laws and hard-fought battles to protect historic districts, it is time to embrace a paradigm shift from protecting to enhancing their aesthetic quality and preserving the authenticity of both the old and the new.

Defining Context and Historic District Control

Historic district designation and control in the United States shares many fundamentals of approach and implementation. William J. Murtagh, the first Keeper of the National Register of Historic Places, defined the features necessary to the establishment of an historic district in the late 1980s:

> The total design of a neighborhood—as a product of its spaces, its objects, its buildings, and their style ... must convey a sense of cohesiveness. This cohesiveness can have a very strict rhythm, such as one sees in the streetscapes of Baltimore, Philadelphia, or Beacon Hill row houses, or a disparity, such as one sees in Georgetown or Savannah. Despite the dissimilarity of design in these latter neighborhoods, the abstracts of aesthetic quality, such as building scale, height, materials, and proportions are generally compatible. It is the odd building in such a neighborhood, out of mass and scale and constructed of incompatible materials, in the wrong color, with the wrong textures, that planners call a nonconforming intrusion.[1]

The foregoing reveals a riveting fascination with visual features, and represents a philosophy shared by many neighborhood preservation groups and picked up by developers and architects as accepted guidelines for "compatibility" within an historic context. Though some preservationists see this as outdated, it has become institutionalized in design control. In the wake of urban renewal programs and the rise of modern design considered incongruent in historic settings, historic district designation has become a legitimate tool to protect historic urban fabric not only from the wrecking ball, but also from the threat of the "nonconforming intrusion."

Designation reports carefully point out the physical characteristics of the buildings that, when combined, create the patterns and rhythms that make the district distinct and cohesive. These reports typically include arguments for historical and cultural significance, but district boundaries must be justified, and the included buildings must be decisively shown to share qualities that merit designation as a collective whole. Determinations of significance must therefore make, above all, the case for the *cohesiveness* of the district, resulting in an intrinsic emphasis on similarity and homogeneity. Even in historic districts designated to protect buildings that are not stylistically cohesive but represent a common historical use or period of development, emphasis is often placed on the resulting coherence of the streetscapes.[2]

Such definitions of context rely heavily on stylistic elements and compositional features—such as window configurations, cornice heights, base articulation, materials, vertical articulation, fenestration patterns—to create a "kit of parts," the most clearly defined set of contextual cues from which most architects feel they are expected to derive their designs. Found within the language of the designation report, further emphasized in design guidelines where they exist, and reiterated in the language of landmarks commissions' approvals of proposed new design, the "kit of parts" presents a limited set of possibilities for appropriate new design.

The New York City Landmarks Preservation Commission (LPC) relies in part on the designation reports in making its decisions on appropriateness. The New York City Landmarks Law[3] contains language stating that when the LPC reviews a proposed new building in an historic district, it shall consider, "in addition to any other pertinent matters, the factors of aesthetic, historical, and architectural values and significance, architectural style, design, arrangement, texture, material, and color."[4] These factors are all defined in the designation reports. Certificates of Appropriateness, the documents explaining why a proposed intervention into an historic district or addition to an individual landmark is found appropriate, clearly cite the significant characteristics of the district or building, as described in its designation report. Therefore, in cities like New York especially, definitions of context can play an important role in the design review process.

A narrow interpretation of context is problematic in any district, but especially in those that include buildings from more than one period of development, and thus possess a variety of styles, scales, and materials. Contemporary architects designing interventions into urban contexts, and preservationists charged with managing change in protected districts, operate with modern-day interpretations of an absolute context, which in reality was built up gradually, through many different periods of growth and change. Indeed, complexity in the historic urban fabric, heightened by the cultural expressions of each successive generation of designers and builders, is our architectural inheritance. Further, the buildings we are left with are the manifestations of cultural, political, and economic trends, and material and technological innovations of each successive period of development. Interpreting an historic context as a single artifact, and emphasizing order in what was not necessarily designed as ordered urban space, undermines the unique qualities of the individual assets in the district and impairs contemporary cognition of the mechanisms of growth and change that made the area what it is today. If patterns in the existing urban fabric are interpreted to the extent that complexities are filtered out, the essence of a district becomes the product of a dozen or so formal elements, reliance on which overlooks deeper levels of meaning embedded in the urban fabric.

The SoHo Cast Iron Historic District

SoHo is one such district with a complex history and a complexity of architectural expressions. There the LPC has approved both banal, literal derivations of its typical formal features and strikingly innovative contemporary design. Its context can be characterized by its many nineteenth-century architectural expressions erected in cast iron, brick, and stone masonry, which exist as the legacy of the ascendancy of Broadway as a vital commercial corridor. Combinations of exuberantly articulated mid- to late-nineteenth-century commercial styles and simpler expressions

FIGURE 1. *The color and fabric of SoHo, Greene Street south of Spring Street. Photograph: Kate R. Lemos.*

of an urban industrial vernacular, as well as the occasional Federal period row house, form the streetscapes of the district. Each street possesses its own level of architectural cohesiveness or complexity, offering changing vistas, a multitude of colors, materials, forms, window patterns, building heights, and exterior details (Figure 1). Here, the "nonconforming intrusion" might be a positive addition and, without imitating existing formal elements, could reference an abstract but significant aspect of the district's history in a contemporary commercial expression or a modern industrial vernacular.

The district was designated in 1973, after a decade of rediscovery and adaptive use of its loft space by artists transformed it from an area on the decline to a cultural center.

The introduction of the designation report summarizes the most important factors contributing to the significance of the area, citing:

- its varied and colorful social, cultural, and economic history;
- its complete, well-documented, and geographically compact illustration of nineteenth-century commercial architectural styles;
- its demonstration of how cast iron was used in nineteenth-century commercial construction;
- its illustration in a tangible way of all sides of a great aesthetic debate— some of the more thoughtful nineteenth-century theorists hoped, through a synthesis between engineering and architecture, to develop a truly representative contemporary style.[5]

In the body of the report, a chapter describes SoHo's physical context through a description of the area's development and the architectural expressions that emerged as a result, and a section on cast iron describes the significance of this material in nineteenth-century architectural and technological history. Another chapter focuses on the regularity and repetition of forms and fenestration patterns, and the similarities in architectural elements and compositions associated with its dominant styles. In general, the text stresses regularity and uniformity, which, while true of many streetscapes in SoHo, diminishes the ideas of a diverse and varied architectural and cultural history and the history of technological innovation described in the introduction. It also undermines the actual visual complexity of the district.

A more penetrating interpretation of the context might concentrate on the cultural and technical reasons for experimenting with cast iron. The repeated forms of the cast iron façades do create a perceptible rhythm and legible patterns (Figure 2). These result in large part from the prefabrication of

FIGURES 2 AND 3. *(Left) Elaborate details in cast iron and stone, corner of Greene and Broome streets. (Right) Juxtaposition of heights, cast iron streetscape, south side of Broome Street. Photographs: Kate R. Lemos.*

entire façades, which was itself the direct result of technological and material innovation and economic restraints, leading to the replication of stone for more affordable, efficient construction. Nineteenth-century views of cast iron were contradictory: for some it provided an effective means of imitating traditional forms in stone, while others saw its possibilities for developing an architecture appropriate to the age. This dilemma has played out vividly in SoHo's cast iron buildings, which are products both of experimentation with new construction technology and of the desire to work out forms of commercial expression that were at once economical and indicative of the stature of the businesses located in the district (Figure 3). Or one might simply study the rich variety of architectural expressions, materials, and colors in the district's cast iron and masonry buildings. Context thus defined holds many levels of significance from which innovative new designs might be derived. Traditional emphasis on cohesiveness and homogeneity can not yield the same depth of possibility.

Two projects recently approved in SoHo—one by Aldo Rossi, the other by Jean Nouvel—are especially compelling as examples of the type of design and level of interpretation of context I advocate.[6] Aldo Rossi designed the Scholastic Building on a lot between Broadway and Mercer Street that contained a two-story non-contributing building. The Broadway face of Rossi's scheme references the trabeated Neo-Grec architectural expressions throughout SoHo using modern materials and bold, simple forms, combining steel, terra cotta, stone, and glass (Figure 4). Set between the delicate "Little Singer" Building to the north and the Rouse Building, a more robust, masonry structure to the south, the design creates a connecting piece with a life and identity of its own.

The Mercer Street elevation, which is more successful as a less formal reference to its context, takes cues from the industrial vernacular of the district, articulating this in a legible industrial language of repetitive steel trusses and abundant glazing, which does not actually exist anywhere in the district (Figure 5). Playing with meaning, and referencing the history of a place without replicating its existing forms should be promoted.

William Higgins praised the building in *World Architecture Review*:

> With its unique double presence, Rossi's design reflects SoHo's confluence of people, ideas, and creative enterprise, and its diverse context of history and architecture. Here Rossi reached toward his ideal of the "urban artifact": a response to the city as a field of memory and idea realized in three dimensions; in the architect's words, not just a "physical thing." But "history, geography, structure, and connection with general life."[7]

FIGURE 4. *Aldo Rossi's Scholastic Building, on Broadway in SoHo. Photograph: Kate R. Lemos.*

The LPC deferred to Rossi's esteemed level of accomplishment and ability to understand and interpret urban typologies and cultural character of historic cities. The proposal was approved with enthusiasm. Chairwoman Jennifer Raab was quoted in the *New York Times* as saying Rossi's building offered a "textbook example" of how to build new infill in an historic district. "Mr. Rossi was able to design a new façade that respected the character of Broadway but didn't inappropriately try to mimic it," she said. "And then he was more daring on the utilitarian Mercer Street façade."[8]

Jean Nouvel's proposed hotel on a vacant corner lot at Broadway and Grand Street (Figure 6) embodies

FIGURES 5 AND 6. *(Left) Aldo Rossi's Scholastic Building, sketch of Mercer Street elevation. Courtesy of Studio di Architettura, New York City. (Right) Jean Nouvel's final design for 40 Mercer, formerly Hotel Broadway, courtesy Atelier Jean Nouvel.*

the idea of modern expression in a contemporary material inherent in the historical cast-iron buildings in SoHo. With these buildings, glazing is often recessed from the frame. Depth of articulation and layering of metal and glass planes creates dramatic effects of shadow and reflection as well as patterns of solid and void. In later cast iron buildings, architects and builders experimented with greater proportions of glass to metal, pushing the envelope of technological innovation to create façades with ever-increasing attenuation of metal structural members. Similarly, Nouvel's design celebrates the frame and the elegance and depth of articulation of the historic cast iron façades, and in so doing, makes one notice all the more the significance of the historical precedents in the area. In this way a modern intervention declares its presence while provoking greater attention to its historic context.[9]

I worked on the presentation for this project's landmarks hearing, illustrating elements of the context to which the proposed building related and creating an argument for its appropriateness. Display boards presented at the hearing illustrated the depth of articulation, the layering of grids, the geometric patterns on the façades, the materials, the colors, and other salient contributors to SoHo's architectural context. This was indeed falling under the sway of the "kit of parts," pointing out ways the proposal could be considered "contextual," because that has become a necessary way to show a proposed new design is "appropriate." But the presentation highlighted abstract attributes of SoHo buildings, which were not detailed in the designation report, but evident after a detailed study and interpretation of the historic fabric.

Wanting to reach deeper and test my ideas about context, I suggested that we argue that the proposal captured the essence of SoHo's commercial façades in a bold modern statement without imitating any formal features of SoHo's cast iron and masonry buildings. Its use of modern materials did not make it a standard-issue modern metal and glass building that could be erected anywhere (the same incongruent modern intervention historic district regulation was initiated to deter). Instead, its expression and celebration of the frame, façade depth and articulation, layering of grids, and experimentation with large areas of glass and delicate metal components, combined to create a new building that was inherently "SoHo." It didn't just relate to its context, it stimulated it.

The LPC loved the design and approved it, and most commissioners stated as their reasoning exactly the same abstract contextual relationships that had impressed me. The Certificate of Appropriateness describes the success of the building in completing the streetwall and terminating the block, reflecting in its massing the variations in heights found in the district, and relating to the depth of articulation and layering of grids in the façades of SoHo. Specifically, and most gratifyingly, the commissioners found:

> ... that use of metal and glass in this building recalls the evolution of these materials in this historic district, which initially featured heavy cast iron elements to imitate stone and later used thinner elements to allow for more glass; that this contemporary design is a continuation of the innovative use of the materials that grew out of the architecture of this historic district; and that the SoHo Cast Iron Historic District was a place of innovative architecture, therefore, this innovative design and use of materials will enhance the special architectural and historic character of this historic district.[10]

This is exactly the kind of interpretation of and relationship to context that preservationists should promote in historic districts. Unfortunately, not every architect or developer has the desire or resources to look beyond the most obvious contextual approach, and the easiest and most painless path to approval is perceived as relating new design to the context in a literal, formal manner. This perception is supported by the record of past approvals of buildings that imitate formal elements and/or mutely blend in with their surroundings. Indeed, Certificates of Appropriateness consistently read like a checklist from the "kit of parts." The appropriateness of windows, proportions, materials, storefronts, cornices, height, massing, et cetera, are separately cited, treating each proposal more as a sum of "appropriate" parts than as a comprehensive design.

Conclusion

Preservationists celebrate good design, both contemporary and historical. We understand and appreciate the dynamic relationships between the new and the old, created when modern interventions successfully draw from or relate to their context in imaginative or challenging ways. We can read and find significance in the manifestations of historical changes, social trends, and technological innovations that created the historic context we work to protect. Likewise, we can find a place as a conduit for good, forward-looking, contemporary design that complements and enlivens its context.

Since context is the litmus test for appropriateness, preservationists should rigorously promote broader, more abstract interpretation. Instead of typical design guidelines, design-related publications could focus on deeper levels of significance such as the history of material and technological innovation in SoHo. Similarly, designation reports written for new districts should place less emphasis on the "kit of parts" and cohesiveness, and more on the richness and complexity of the particular historical, cultural, architectural, and urban character with the definition of the historic context setting the tone for what is considered appropriate new design. By publishing broader definitions of significance and interpretations of historic context to help elicit and inform modern interventions, and through precedent-setting approvals, preservationists can and should promote a greater level of innovation in new design within historic districts. ✹

(Endnotes)

1 William J. Murtagh, *Keeping Time: The History and Theory of Preservation in America* (New York: John Wiley & Sons, Inc., 1997), 108–9.

2 In the "NoHo Designation Report," NYC Landmarks Preservation Commission, June 29, 1999, the phrase "unifying streetscapes" is used repeatedly to describe the effect of the commercial buildings within the district. NoHo is similar to SoHo, described in detail in this paper, in terms of its architectural variety and visual complexity.

3 *The New York City Landmarks Law, New York City Charter*, secs. 3020–21, and *New York City Administrative Code*, Title 25, Chapter 3.

4 New York City Landmarks Law, secs. 25-307, subsection b

5 New York City Landmarks Preservation Commission, "SoHo-Cast Iron Historic District Designation Report," (New York, 1973).

6 Others, not designed by internationally famous architects, have been approved in other districts—I choose these because they are in SoHo.

7 "Scholastic Building, New York, New York," *World Architecture Review* 97 (2003): 36.

8 David W. Dunlap, "A New Building Fits in by Standing Out," *New York Times*, April 23, 2000, sec. XI. CMS 17, 188

9 Subsequent to completion of this paper the building was redesigned slightly and reprogrammed for residential use, which received a second Landmarks Preservation Commission approval. The building opened in 2007.

10 New York City Landmarks Preservation Commission, CofA#: 01-5693, 465 Broadway, Manhattan, May 5, 2001.

PART TWO
Design Standards in Changing Environments

◼ EXAGGERATED REVERENCE FOR THE PAST

The Challenge of Design Review in the Charleston Historic District Design

JAMES HARE
Executive Director
Cornerstones Community Partnerships

Architectural design review has become a common preservation practice in the United States. This powerful mechanism for managing change is intended to protect individual buildings as well as entire historic districts, and because design review frequently regulates the way the exteriors of new buildings look, the people that control the process have a powerful influence over the evolution of architecture in their communities.

This power troubles many architects who claim it subordinates architectural innovation to subjective standards and preferences for imitative design that relies too heavily on traditional architectural styles. In Charleston, South Carolina, which is famous for being the first city to use design review to manage change in its historic district, the charges made by architects are contradicted by claims made by residents and neighborhood organizations that its design review board—known locally as the Board of Architectural Review or BAR—encourages "architects to avoid traditionalism and embrace more modern-looking designs that jar with the city's historic buildings."[1]

As others note in this collection of essays, preservation by nature is a design activity, and design review is its most invasive procedure. For this reason, as well as for the diverse nature of the criticisms that are directed against the boards that manage the design review process, it is important that preservation professionals assess the strengths and weaknesses of the process so that it does not cause more harm than good to the architectural character of the historic buildings and districts it is intended to protect. A look at how architectural design review in Charleston came about and has evolved over the past seventy years helps provide a basis from which a perspective on the process can be developed.

Charleston's 1931 zoning ordinance has been heralded as the precedent-setting mechanism for protecting the historic fabric of American cities. The Charleston zoning ordinance earned this recognition by legally defining its historic district and establishing a design review board to manage it. This was not accomplished, however, in a straightforward fashion. In fact, in order to circumvent what might have been seen as a powerful attack on private property rights of Charlestonians, the 1931 ordinance had to take an indirect route to achieve its goal.

The authority of Charleston's BAR was limited by the wording of the ordinance to judge only primary architectural features—the general design, arrangement, texture, material, and color of new construction. Expected to judge the relationship of such factors to similar features in neighboring buildings, the board was specifically proscribed from judging detailed design, the relative size of buildings in plan, interior arrangements, or building features that were not subject to public view. In general, its actions were to prevent changes to the district that were "obviously incongruous with the district's historic aspects."[2]

It is important to note that the 1931 ordinance clearly avoided requiring conformity to any particular historic style or period of architecture, and, most crucially, it did not give the BAR power to prevent demolitions in the district. Rather, the board was only allowed to indirectly control the demolition or inappropriate alteration of buildings in the historic district by withholding approval for the new construction that would follow. And yet, despite the restrictions in the 1931 ordinance, the legislation opened the door for both the BAR, whose members were expected to have a basic understanding of architectural and historic design issues, and members of the public, who might or might not be so well versed, to have a powerful say in the way new buildings would look in the historic district.

Charlestonians had a tightly defined preservation ethic when the original historic district, officially called the Old and Historic Charleston District, was created in 1931. The ethic was based largely on a hierarchy that glorified the city's colonial heritage and sanctified its eighteenth- and early nineteenth-century buildings. Elsewhere in the city, Charlestonians were very tolerant, at least until the late 1950s, of new, non-traditional architecture as long as it did

FIGURE 1. *Albert Simons, FAIA. Photo: L. Schwartz, ca. 1960.*

not impact the official historic district. Today the numerous art deco and Art Moderne buildings that were erected outside the original historic district boundary demonstrate this.

To understand how design review in Charleston was implemented, it is also important to consider the influence of one individual, Albert Simons, who was instrumental in defining Charleston's early preservation ethic and was the only architect to serve on the BAR for the first forty-three years of its operation (Figure 1). In 1917, Simons drew the architectural illustrations for Alice Huger Smith's influential volume, *The Dwelling Houses of Charleston*, which cautioned that "new and strange" ideas in architecture "which however suitable to places that developed them ... would perhaps destroy those very differences that make [Charleston] so interesting."[3] Through this work, as well as by his own publications and research, Simons exhibited a refined connoisseurship of the city's historic architecture. This, together with architectural training at the University of Pennsylvania under Beaux Arts classicist Paul Philippe Cret, provided Simons with the requisite understanding of design as it pertained to eighteenth- and early nineteenth-century Charleston architecture. His education and sensitivity allowed him to sit comfortably in judgment of the proposals for new construction that were brought before the BAR, while his high social standing in the city enabled him to redirect the architectural aspirations of his fellow citizens with assurance.

Simons advocated operating the board as an architectural clinic capable of disposing good design advice to the building public. Although he had some early doubts about whether this method would work, it was Simons's concept of the design review process as an architectural clinic—essentially a collegial discussion between him and the architects, builders, and property owners applying to the board—that prevailed for the first thirty-five years in Charleston. In a 1954 letter from BAR chairman Frederick H. McDonald to Boston's Historic Beacon Hill Law Committee, Charleston's process was described as a "voluntary and guided method" for reaching agreements about contested design proposals. McDonald's letter confirmed that the community respected the purpose of design review and the results that were gained from it, and noted that the board, which functioned "largely as an advisory architectural clinic," had never had to resort to enforcement measures.[4]

A comparison of the Old and Historic Charleston District as it was delineated in 1931 with the district that exists today shows why the BAR operated as smoothly as reported during its first four decades. Originally, the Old and Historic Charleston District took in a very small area of the modern city and it was composed almost entirely of residential structures. Crucially, the adjacent commercial streets were not included within its boundaries. This meant new commercial construction was virtually eliminated as a matter of concern for the BAR; its energies were chiefly spent reviewing minor exterior alterations to the district's historic houses.

The BAR entered an important subsequent phase in its evolution when World War II came to an end and the economic forces bottled up by the depression and World War II were uncorked in and around Charleston. As the region entered the 1950s, the demand for new construction began to exert strong and unaccustomed pressure on the historic and architecturally significant sections of the city that had been excluded from the historic district designation in 1931.

These pressures came to a head in 1958 when a design for the new Charleston County Free Library was proposed for a location outside the historic district, but adjacent to the Old Citadel complex on Marion Square. A raucous public debate over modern architecture in Charleston broke out when the design by the local firm of Cummings and McCrady was made public. It featured curtain-wall construction that responded to the client's request for natural light, minimal walls, flexible internal arrangements, low maintenance costs, and rapid construction (Figure 2).[5]

FIGURE 2. *Charleston County Free Library, Charleston, S.C. Photograph: K. Saunders, 1998.*

FIGURES 3 AND 4. *(Left) Model of proposed addition to Carolina Yacht Club. Photograph: News & Courier, 1971. (Right) Carolina Yacht Club addition as built. Photograph: D. Noyola, 2002.*

The controversy that the "modern-style" design provoked was so intense that a bill was introduced in the State House which would have required the plans for all city and county buildings in Charleston to be approved by the BAR.[6] At a public hearing both of the city's influential preservation organizations, the Preservation Society of Charleston and the Historic Charleston Foundation, condemned the design. Twenty members of the public sided with a local rabbi who stated it was "unthinkable that public buildings in Charleston should be executed in anything but traditional designs."[7]

Ultimately budget constraints and the client's program for a large functional space won out and county council approved the design originally proposed.[8] What is important about the library debate is the community's willingness to increase the purview of the BAR beyond the established historic district and its expressed disdain for non-traditional architecture in the city, at least as far as public buildings were concerned.

In 1966, the historic district was tripled in size. By the mid-1970s, it had expanded further to include large numbers of late nineteenth- and early twentieth-century commercial buildings. Today, it encompasses the entire peninsula below U.S. Highway 17.[9] At the beginning of these expansions in 1966, the composition of the BAR increased from five to seven members. And, most importantly, the review board was finally given direct authority to deny the demolition of buildings under its jurisdiction. The board no longer had to rely on withholding approval for the design of new construction to discourage demolitions. Also by this time, however, the accepted public purpose of the design review process was as much the aesthetic regulation of new construction in the city as it was the prevention of the demolition or inappropriate alteration of the city's historic and architecturally significant buildings.

An important consequence of these changes was the abandonment of Albert Simons's concept of the BAR as architectural clinic. Growth pressures and the increased design review caseload caused by the expansion of the historic district made his informal approach to design review neither practical nor possible. By necessity, the design review process in Charleston became more bureaucratic, less personally directed, and more public with regularly scheduled hearings at which citizen participation became a key factor in board deliberations.

As this transition was occurring, one of the rare new commercial construction projects proposed for the original portion of the historic district was brought before the design review board. In December 1971, a design for a large addition to the Carolina Yacht Club was presented to the review board (Figure 3). The Yacht Club, an important Charleston social institution, was housed in an antebellum cotton warehouse close to the center of the original historic district. The way in which the proposed design was altered during the design review process indicates what the board considered at that time to be appropriate new construction for the historic district. More importantly, it demonstrates how public opinion had become a key factor in the success or failure of any new construction proposal in the area of the BAR's jurisdiction.

According to the project architects—Middleton, Wilkerson and McMillan of Charlotte, North Carolina—the proposal, which required the demolition of a circa-1910 addition to the warehouse, was "easy to look at while not violating any of the design qualities of the early cotton-classing portion being saved." The architects also stated that they had done extensive studies to determine the proper scale for the new construction.[10] Despite the demolition involved in the proposal, the BAR gave the proposal conceptual approval. Yet, as soon as the design was published in the newspaper, unfavorable public reaction forced the board to reconsider its position and to intervene much more strongly in the design decisions of the architects.

The board suggested that the firm address concerns that had been expressed to BAR members about the scale of the project and, specifically, the large areas of unbroken wall surface on the west and north sides of the building. In making this request, the BAR stated:

> There is no desire on our part to insist on a building of traditional design, as this could, no doubt, be a handicap to the most functional plan. A spirited modern design would be welcomed. This design, however, should take cognizance of its location in Old and Historic Charleston. Furthermore, because of the retention of the oldest part of the Yacht Club complex, some relation with this old building is very much desired and hoped for by the board.[11]

The architects reacted so strongly to the board's intervention, however, that their design was withdrawn by the Yacht Club and the addition eventually emerged as an understated background structure that contrasted sharply with the original proposal (Figure 4). As a result, the inventory of Charleston architecture is absent what future generations might consider to be an interesting example of late-modernist architecture. Moreover, it could have been no more incompatible with the overall architectural inventory of the city than were two of Charleston's most popular buildings when they were constructed—the 1876 George Walton Williams residence (commonly known as the Calhoun Mansion) and the 1892 Victorian Romanesque Circular Church. In a world-famous historic district possessing excellent examples of every phase of American architecture from the colonial period to the New Deal, mid-century modernism is noticeably underrepresented.

Throughout his career, Albert Simons questioned both the good and bad effects that design review might have on the architectural continuum in Charleston. In his early years, he dryly quipped to architect Hal Hentz, of the Atlanta firm of Hentz, Adler & Shutze, that he had "come to the conclusion that, in their exaggerated reverence for the past, [Charlestonians] classify architects with Indians, and believe that the only good ones are the dead ones."[12] Toward the end of his tenure on the BAR, he applauded the fact that it had been an important force in the preservation of Charleston, but he also reflected that:

> As time goes on and our links with the traditional past of Charleston become more and more tenuous, it will become increasingly difficult to require conformity to traditions no longer familiar nor readily understood ... I believe that properly designed contemporary buildings may be assimilated in Charleston provided they are sympathetically studied in relation to their surroundings and are akin to them in scale, materials, colors, texture, and to that indefinable quality ... so happily summarized as the *genius loci* of a community. We cannot go on indefinitely serving up "warmed over" colonial and expect it to be forever palatable to a constantly evolving culture. Honest architecture is never quite that easy.[13]

In the three decades since Simons helped define the direction of Charleston's design review board, local architects have become increasingly vocal in their criticism of the intervention the BAR makes in the design of new construction in the city. The latitude, however, that Charleston's review board actually gives to architects has grown so wide that an emerging alternate camp in the city claims the BAR is composed of "forces of the modernist past who bash opponents with the blunt instruments of authenticity, originality, and contemporary life at bi-weekly public meetings."[14]

In light of the forces arrayed against the BAR—one side condemning the board for a perceived preference for traditional design and the other appalled by what they say is a devotion to non-traditional architecture—the real impact the BAR has on new construction is obscured by the rhetoric swirling around it. For that reason the author conducted a survey that asked 228 local American Institute of Architects (AIA) members to determine the level of exposure they had to Charleston's design review process. The survey solicited their opinions about the effect of the process on their design work in the historic district. It also asked them to identify examples of successful and unsuccessful new construction projects in the district so that the author could prepare case studies of several buildings. In all, forty-one recent projects were noted either for their successful or unsuccessful designs, with two projects—Majestic Square and Cannon Park Place—appearing on both lists. Eighteen architects thought that Majestic Square was one of the best-designed new buildings in the city, while three considered it to be among the worst. Ten architects cited Cannon Park as one of the worst new buildings, while only one thought it one of the best. It is worth noting that both projects were conceived as important elements to the city's commercial revitalization efforts, and that both were designed by well-established local firms that had extensive experience within the historic district.

The Majestic Square project was presented to the BAR for conceptual approval in September of 1994.[15] The location selected for the multi-story mixed-use project was near the center of the city's retail shopping corridor, which had been incorporated into the historic district in 1966. The architectural context of the project location consisted of a highly cohesive assemblage of late eighteenth- and early nineteenth-century commercial buildings punctuated by the art deco architecture of the compatibly scaled 1931 Riviera Theatre. A predominantly residential neighborhood called Harleston Village stretched behind and to the west of the project site.

To win the board's favor at the Conceptual Approval Hearing, the first phase in Charleston's review process, the architect, Samuel Logan, explained how his firm, LS3P Architects, resolved two major design challenges: management of traffic in and out of the structure, and accommodation of the scale of the project—which consumed an entire city block—with its surroundings.

In commenting on the design during the public portion of the hearing that followed the architect's presentation, representatives from both the

Historic Charleston Foundation and the Preservation Society of Charleston approved of the design, which attempted to complement its surroundings through the use of a red brick exterior skin, glass awnings, and cast stone details inspired by the adjacent Riviera Theatre, with suggestions that additional thought be given to breaking up the façade and reducing the overall height. The Harleston Village Association cited traffic impact as its only concern and the city's chief preservation officer recommended conceptual approval by the review board, noting that the height, scale, and mass of the proposal were appropriate for the site.[16]

BAR members briefly questioned the architect about the ratio used to divide the façade (2 to 2 as opposed to a more typical 1 to 3 ratio). There was also a short discussion about the decision to place the main entrance on the corner of the building. The architect explained this was a common treatment for late nineteenth- and early twentieth-century mercantile buildings in Charleston. It was worth exploiting because of the high volume of pedestrian traffic in the area. That said, a second motion for approval was made and the board unanimously granted conceptual approval.

At the subsequent Preliminary Approval Hearing in January 1995, the members of the BAR focused primarily on secondary issues of the design. There was no substantive discussion about the design philosophy that the architect had outlined in previous presentations, nor were alternative designs suggested for the project. It's also interesting to note that Logan's confession during his presentation that his design "really does not tell you exactly what it is," did not initiate more heated debate. If accusations that the BAR imposes a non-traditional agenda on new construction in the city are valid, this confessed disregard for a cornerstone of modernist design philosophy probably would not have gone unchallenged.[17]

Final approval was granted to the project in February 1995 based on minor revisions to secondary architectural details—chiefly the colors of some of the proposed materials and the design of the exterior light fixtures (Figure 5). After the Majestic Square project was completed, it received one of the eight merit awards granted by the South Atlantic Regional Conference of the AIA.[18]

The relative ease with which the Majestic Square project passed through the design review process contrasts sharply with the approval procedure for Cannon Park Place. This project came before the BAR for conceptual approval in December of 1995. The proposal consisted of a medical office and mixed-use commercial facility planned for the northeastern edge of the expanded historic district. Unlike the solid commercial context that influenced the design of Majestic Square, Cannon Park Place had to be reconciled with a more diverse

FIGURES 5 AND 6. *(Left) Majestic Square, Charleston, S.C. Photograph: K. Saunders, 1998. (Right) Cannon Park Place, Charleston, S.C. Photograph: D. Noyola, 2002.*

urban context in what is considered to be one of the least attractive sections of Charleston under BAR jurisdiction. To the north, the Medical University of South Carolina complex envelops the edge of the historic district. This zone is filled with both low- and high-rise structures that lack any coherent architectural appearance and are part of a long commercial strip that runs from King Street to the Ashley River. A group of late nineteenth-century homes flank the building site on the east side. Adjacent to the project on the south is Cannon Park, which had been designed by the firm of Frederick Law Olmsted after the Civil War and subsequently obliterated when Thompson Auditorium was constructed on the site for a reunion of Confederate veterans in the 1890s. When the auditorium, which subsequently housed the Charleston Museum, burned in 1980, the space was restored to its use as a park.

Like Majestic Square, the space that Cannon Park Place was intended to occupy was considered to be important by the city, which felt the project had potential to smooth the transition between the institutional character of the Medical University and the residential neighborhood of Harleston Village (Figure 6). The architectural firm for the project was Epps-Edwards Architects, whose principal, Robert Epps, had recently received an honor award from the local chapter of the AIA.[19]

To position his project for conceptual approval by the BAR, Epps explained that his intention was to follow guidelines established in a 1980s' city planning study called the Calhoun Street Corridor Plan. He also said he intended his design, which appears to have been strongly influenced by the work of contemporary Italian architect Aldo Rossi, to bridge the "institutional hospital character" on the north side of the site with the park and residential elements on its other sides. Following his presentation, board members questioned why he chose a flat roof for the building, and they also grilled him about parking requirements and flood plain restrictions. But most of all they questioned how his firm intended to integrate the building with the adjacent park.

As with Majestic Square, spokesmen from the Preservation Society of Charleston and the Historic Charleston Foundation initiated the public portion of the hearing. They acknowledged the difficulties the site posed for the designer. For this reason, both organizations and the Harleston Village Association requested that the application be deferred for further study. City staff, however, recommended that the application be given conceptual approval, noting that architectural details would be given the attention they required during the preliminary phase of the approval process.[20]

Despite this recommendation, the board was evenly split when a motion to defer approval on the design was put forward since only six of the seven board members were present at the hearing. The board was also split when a counter motion to approve the design was offered. Thus stalemated, board rules required that the application be disapproved.

Epps and Edwards did not win final approval from the BAR until late in 1996, nine months after their application for conceptual approval. During this period the building proposal was significantly changed. The change, however, was more one of height rather than design. According to the architects, the BAR expressed an interest in seeing a taller building on the site after the conceptual hearing concluded. Although this was not the client's initial desire, he capitalized on the opportunity to build a bigger building.[21] As a result, the approval process was greatly lengthened for the revised Cannon Park Place proposal.

Ultimately, Epps and Edwards appeared before the review board seven times. Final approval was eventually granted in September of 1996. Throughout this laborious approval process, a variety of concerns continued to impede the advance of the project. The Preservation Society of Charleston objected that the "contemporary nature" of the design was inappropriate for such a prominent site.[22] The review board also imposed a number of design requirements on the architects. First, they asked for a restudy of the base windows to make them more pedestrian in scale.[23] Then they asked for a greater recess of the windows into the brick walls. This was followed by a request for a restudy of the brick-to-glass ratio on the north elevation of the building.[24] Finally, they required a restudy of the pedestrian scale of the wall on Calhoun Street, to revise the screening for rooftop HVAC, and to adjust the depth of the glazing in the window openings.[25]

With the exception of the Preservation Society's complaint, the non-traditional design of the building was not the main focus of the design review process. Rather, the debate centered on the refinement of secondary design details. But most of all, it hinged on the apparent inability of the designers to fit the building comfortably into an architectural context that defied clear articulation by the BAR, city staff, both preservation groups, and the public. In the long run, other than the minor concessions that were made to accommodate the board's revision requirements, the design initially proposed by Epps and Edwards changed little during the review process.[26]

However one feels about the design of the resulting buildings, the examples offered by Majestic Square and Cannon Park Place foil the assertion that the BAR in Charleston exerts a heavy hand in the design process, whether it be to impose traditional design values or to enforce modernist architectural doctrine. Rather, these examples accentuate the problem faced by curators of highly diverse historic districts such as that found in Charleston. The Majestic Square project benefited from a location with a well-defined architectural context that derived primarily from mid to late nineteenth-century commercial buildings of comparable size. Cannon Park Place, by contrast, suffered from a location in the historic district that had been heavily impacted by a diverse mixture of institutional, commercial, and residential structures that also varied dramatically in terms of height, scale, and mass. As a result, neither the design review board, the city's preservation planning department, the preservation organizations, nor local residents could adequately explain how the Epps-Edwards project might positively or negatively impact the historic character of that part of the Charleston Historic District. In the long run, the architects of both projects were allowed to execute final designs that were very close to their original conceptions.

The deliberations by the design review board indicate in both the Majestic Square and Cannon Park Place case studies that debates about architectural style do not dominate Charleston's design review hearings. Rather the BAR tends to focus on secondary architectural details, something that the

1931 ordinance sought to avoid. This tendency is a flaw inherent in the review process, most clearly demonstrated in the Cannon Park Place deliberations, that has more to do with human nature than it does with disregard for legal charter. It should be noted that Charleston's design board members are not alone in this regard; the primary groups that choose to participate in public discussions at BAR hearings—the influential and professionally trained staffs of Charleston's preservation organizations, who are assumed to understand the specifics of the design review ordinance, and city residents, who probably have only a general understanding of the ordinance—consistently make secondary architectural details the primary focus of their commentary. It also appears, based on the cases examined here, that both preservationists and members of the public who have not had academic training in architecture or design issues lack the ability to adequately articulate the opinions they have about primary architectural features—height, scale, and mass—and as a result make the examination and critique of secondary details the foundation for their appeals to the review board. This is the point at which requests are made to make the architectural details of new construction more like those of historic buildings. The result is that design review board deliberations are based more on details of individual taste rather than a reasoned examination of the broader issue of the compatibility of new with old architecture.

It has been suggested that the problems Charleston's design review process has in this regard might be less severe if the BAR operated with a set of well-articulated design guidelines for its historic district. Many historic communities, such as Santa Fe, New Mexico, which will be examined below, rely on specific guidelines to direct the design review process. Charleston, however, has never incorporated them into its process. Considering the training that Albert Simons had in both architecture and local architectural history, as well as the relative newness of the process and the size of the community when Charleston enacted the 1931 ordinance, it is not surprising that the early BAR was never called upon to produce a written set of design guidelines for the city's builders and architects to follow. What is puzzling is why this precedent continues to stand in Charleston given the dramatic changes that have taken place in the composition of the historic district and the city's economy, not to mention the national marketing and distribution of mass-produced, non-traditional building materials.

The managers of Charleston's design review process, however, have steadfastly resisted the promulgation of design guidelines for the historic district. This, according to one former chief preservation officer, is because guidelines "become a checklist of details for developers who just want to speed through the process."[27] While this may be valid, I also suspect that the BAR has resisted guidelines in an effort to minimize what is already perceived to be an excessively intrusive process in a city that has historically taken a strong position in the defense of private property rights.

Whether or not this is the case, the current managers of the design review process in Charleston would do well to remember that the early efforts of the BAR succeeded because the review process rested primarily in the hands of one individual, Albert Simons. Simons was the board's intellectual and architectural authority. His in-depth knowledge of Charleston's history and architecture and his influential personality let the early BAR define and manage change in the small, homogeneous historic district outlined in 1931.

In considering Charleston's position on design guidelines, it is worth examining the contrasting approach taken by another prominent historic community, Santa Fe, New Mexico. Like Charleston, Santa Fe has implemented a design review process in the form of an Historical Style Committee (HSC). As with Charleston's BAR, the function of Santa Fe's HSC is to control demolition of historic structures as well as to "review and approve or deny all applications for new construction [and] exterior alteration" in the historic district based on two official architectural styles, Old Santa Fe Style and Recent Santa Fe Style. Design guidelines for both styles are extensively defined in the body of the Santa Fe Ordinance.[28]

The use of design guidelines in Santa Fe, however, has not been without its critics. Santa Fe has been accused of creating a false architectural environment by allowing its design review ordinance to focus more on aesthetics than architectural integrity. In this regard the specific guidelines employed by Santa Fe serve the important purpose of keeping new, quickly executed stucco-on-frame and stucco-on-block construction in visual accord with the city's historic adobe buildings. Architects who work within the limitations imposed by Santa Fe's guidelines comment that the guidelines would not be necessary if the ordinance simply required all new construction to be executed in adobe.

The result, they claim, would be new architecture that automatically complements existing buildings in terms of primary architectural features—height, scale, and mass—because of the limitations inherent in the building material. Furthermore, with no additional architectural restrictions in place, architects say they would be freer to create within the boundaries imposed by the material and, as a result, the regional architectural tradition would evolve more honestly.[29]

If nothing else, through the use of well-defined architectural guidelines, Santa Fe has succeeded in establishing an architectural identity that on the surface appears to represent the continuum of Native American and Spanish Colonial architecture in the region. It is an identity that may prove, given the pressure most American communities are under to build quickly and inexpensively, more sustainable over time, despite the high degree of artifice that is employed in carrying it out, than will the architectural identity Charleston is promoting in its historic district.

By avoiding clearly articulated guidelines, Charleston risks enforcing an obscurely defined conception of what the public considers to be appropriate new construction for the historic district. But, if Charleston prefers to continue to operate its design review process without guidelines, and if it truly intends for its eighteenth- and nineteenth-century buildings to set the tone for all new construction in the city, the city might do better, as has been suggested for Santa Fe, to limit architects to a prescribed list of building materials—for example, locally manufactured and milled bricks and lumber and only those imported materials that were available up to, let us say, the early twentieth century. Perhaps this would anchor new construction more directly to the building traditions of the city's past, while giving Charleston's architects more room to create within a clearly prescribed boundary.

As they currently exist, the standards of neither Charleston nor Santa Fe may ever adequately interpret or honor the *genius loci* that Albert Simons found so essential for the creation of honest architecture. As long as architects are required to adhere to Charleston's unwritten architectural code or Santa Fe's rigid guidelines, the design review boards of both cities may be losing the opportunity to sustain regional architectural styles that are capable of growing beyond what are at best imitative and at worst insulting references to past architectural forms. This is the challenge that faces both the architects designing new buildings in historic communities and the preservationists who, presumably, will seek to protect them one day. This is the daunting obstacle that must be overcome if a city's architectural heritage is to be extended into the new century.

Given the limitations of the process, is design review the most appropriate tool to use to manage architectural change in historic districts? It is easiest to answer yes to this question when the intent is to prevent new construction from dramatically interrupting a well-defined and concentrated inventory of historic buildings. This was the situation in Charleston between 1931 and the 1970s. Then, as Albert Simons believed, the principal objective of design review was not to legislate taste, but rather to prevent "obviously incongruous" new construction from occurring. When the architectural context of an historic district is more diverse, design review becomes a much more difficult mechanism for directing the style of new construction. If the anchor provided by a clearly perceivable architectural context is missing, the process weighs as heavily on good design as it does on the bad. As a result, out of the fear of permitting potential architectural mistakes, we find we must accept the sacrifice of potential architectural epiphanies—innovative architectural statements that advance the record of a community's built environment. Through such compromise we may stand to lose much more than we gain.

If design review is to remain an effective preservation practice it is important that communities closely examine and regularly reassess how it is administered. Charleston serves an important example in this regard, that the sense of security design review provides—the sense that the process genuinely protects historic and architecturally significant resources—is its inherent weakness. The caseload for Charleston's BAR has grown significantly over the years. As a consequence, Charleston's design review board and the preservation organizations that are an essential part of the review process are obligated to spend as much, if not more, time debating the appropriateness of the design of new construction than they do evaluating the significance and integrity of historic buildings in the city that are threatened with demolition or inappropriate alteration.

This is an issue of considerable importance for future generations, especially in a community like Charleston whose public is accustomed to discount the importance of all but high-style eighteenth- and nineteenth-century buildings. As classes of early and mid twentieth-century buildings in the city are threatened with change or destruction, Charleston's design review board members, city planning staff, and preservation professionals would benefit from having additional time to examine and evaluate the architectural and historical significance of the demolition and alteration applications that come before them. Formulating the charters of design review ordinances so that they emphasize preservation rather than aesthetics would go far in ensuring that unwise demolitions and insensitive alterations do not occur. This, I believe, is still the most important issue at stake in terms of Charleston's ongoing preservation, and one that preservationists nationwide should seriously consider if they are practicing design review as a method for controlling change in their historic districts. ◉

(Endnotes)

1 Jason Hardin, "BAR Tastes too Modern for Old City, Critics Argue," *Post and Courier* [Charleston], February 5, 2003.

2 City of Charleston, *Zoning Ordinance* (Charleston, S.C.: City of Charleston, 1931).

3 Alice Huger Smith and D.E.H. Smith, *The Dwelling Houses of Charleston, South Carolina* (New York: Lippencott, 1917; facsimile ed., 1974), 375.

4 Frederick H. McDonald. Letter to John Codman, 6 January 1954. Albert Simons Papers. SC Historical Society, Charleston.

5 Tom Perry, "Design for New Free Library is Approved," *News and Courier* [Charleston], February 5, 1958.

6 "Bill Banning Modern-Style Library Gets First Reading," *News and Courier* [Charleston], February 13, 1958.

7 Gene Risher, "Library Battle Goes Votal but the Decision May Stick, *Charleston Evening Post*, April 1, 1958.

8 "Modern Library Design Reaffirmed by Council," *Charleston Evening Post*, November 19, 1958.

9 There are two official historic districts in Charleston, the Old and Historic Charleston District, which has evolved from the original 1931 delineation, and the Old City District, which was established in 1973. The two districts differ slightly in the degree of control the BAR has over them. The National Register Charleston Historic District does not directly correspond to the historic districts that are defined by the Charleston ordinance.

10 W. H. J. Thomas, "Yacht Club Unveils Plans for Addition," *News and Courier* [Charleston], December 11, 1971.

11 G. Dana Sinkler. Letter to Louis Y. Dawson, III, February 17, 1972. Albert Simons Papers. SC Historical Society, Charleston.

12 Albert Simons. Letter to Hal F. Hentz, F.A.I.A., December 18, 1939. Albert Simons Papers. SC Historical Society Charleston.

13 Albert Simons. [1950?]. Albert Simons Papers. SC Historical Society, Charleston.

14 Robert Russell. "Who Will Guard the Guardians?" *Charleston City Guardian*, Vol 4, No. 2, April 2000.

15 Projects presented to the Board of Architectural Review in Charleston typically pass through three phases of review—conceptual approval, preliminary approval, and final approval.

16 Robert Behre, "Store Design Praised for 'Saks Appeal'," *Post and Courier* [Charleston], September 15, 1994.

17 Ibid.

18 "SARC Awards 2000," *Architecture South Carolina*, 2000, 26–27.

19 David Munday, "Keeping it Simple Earns Epps Award," *Post and Courier* [Charleston], December 4,1994.

20 Transcription of Board of Architectural Review tape recording, December 13, 1995, tapes 2–3. City of Charleston Archives.

21 Author's interview with Robert Epps and John Edwards, April 2001.

22 Preservation Society of Charleston, letter to the Board of Architectural Review re: application 9601-24-6, January 24, 1996. City of Charleston Archives.

23 Board of Architectural Review. Board review statement, January 24, 1996. City of Charleston Archives.

24 Board of Architectural Review. Board review statement, March 13,1996. City of Charleston Archives.

25 Board of Architectural Review. Board review statement, August 28, 1996. City of Charleston Archives.

26 Robert Behre, "A Beauty? A Blight? Jury's Out on Offices," *Post and Courier* [Charleston], February 16, 1998.

27 Robert Behre, "Fleming Stirs Up Debate on Historic Styles," *Post and Courier* [Charleston], April 5, 1999.

28 City of Santa Fe, Santa Fe City Code, Revised Ordinance Supplement: September 9, 1989, 14-17H, Historical District.

29 Interview with John P. Conron, September 10, 2002.

▨ CALIFORNIA'S HISTORIC DISTRICTS

Preservation in a Vacuum

LAUREN WEISS BRICKER, PH.D.
Associate Professor of Architecture
California State Polytechnic University, Pomona

D esign guidelines and review processes that sanction mediocre new construction in historic districts are legacies of the historic preservation movement of the last thirty years. We settle for compromise solutions in the name of careful stewardship of historic resources, and ambivalence about the most effective ways to respond to the physical and historic context of the property.

The message given to architects and their clients by the design review process is that historic and conservation districts are off-limits to creative, contemporary architecture. This paper will examine several of the systemic problems associated with design in historic districts, and pose alternative design processes that may suggest creative solutions. Case studies derived from historic districts in San Francisco, Pasadena, Riverside, and Redlands, California, will be used to illustrate these solutions.

Design Issues

Perhaps the greatest challenge facing architects designing new buildings or additions in historic districts is how to conceptualize the relationship between the district's historic character and the new project. Official guidance for appropriate ways to address this relationship is provided in the Secretary of the Interior's Standards for Rehabilitation (rev. 1990), a document that many California cities have officially adopted as either *the* design guidelines for historic properties or as the precedent for their own local design guidelines and review. While primarily focused on how to treat existing buildings and materials, the standards do recommend that the design of new construction be compatible with the historic character of the district or neighborhood in terms of size, scale, design, material, color, and texture,[1] and that "new design should always be clearly differentiated so that the addition does not appear to be part of the historic resources."[2]

Due to this advice, the design quality of new construction in historic districts has been inconsistent. More often than not, the new building attempts to be compatible by adding decorative details and ornamentation derived from nearby historic buildings, or imagery from buildings of similar styles. In other cases, the new construction uses the same façade material or similar types and patterns of fenestration. In still other cases roof forms and materials are copied in an attempt to make the new construction compatible with the existing.

Two examples of this approach to new design in historic districts are a three-unit condominium building constructed in the Liberty-Hill Historic District of San Francisco (Certificate of Appropriateness approved in 1991; constructed in 1995),[3] and Mentor Park Place, a four-plex residential development in the Bungalow Heaven Historic District of Pasadena (Certificate of Appropriateness approved in 1997).

The condominiums in Liberty-Hill were built on a vacant lot in one of San Francisco's earliest "suburbs"(Figure 1).[4] Developed from the 1860s through the beginning of the twentieth century, the Liberty-Hill neighborhood includes some 300 buildings, with more than half contributing to the Victorian character of the historic district and another seventy-four deemed potentially contributing if inappropriate alterations were removed and the buildings restored to their original integrity. Within this neighborhood of single-family homes, the three-unit condominium building was constructed. It is a two-and-one-half story high, wood-sheathed structure that sits on a high, podium-like garage. The first floor of the condominiums is set back from the street to provide space for a terrace above the garage. A key design motif of the building is a sequence of Palladian windows rising from the terrace through the two-story bay window. The architect uses the double-height window to relate the new construction to its historic neighbors, some of which have multi-story bay windows. The design also borrows the massing found in many Victorian-era houses in San Francisco, simplifying and articulating it in a manner that has more to do with postmodernism of the 1980s and early 1990s than historic

FIGURE 1. *(Left) View of 101 Liberty Street, condominiums, Steven Antonaros, architect (1991-95), on the left; 109 Liberty Street (1872) to the right. Photograph: Alice Carey.*

FIGURE 2. *(Right) View of Mentor Place, Pasadena. "Mentor Park Place." Golden Triangle Design Group, architects (1997); Craftsman bungalow on right (ca. 1910). Photograph: Lauren Weiss Bricker.*

buildings found in the district. Seeming to lack a clear commitment to a design philosophy, the building pales in comparison with its neighbor, 109 Liberty Street, a sumptuous 1872 Italianate characterized by a dramatic contrast of simple, geometric mass with highly sculptural door, window, and cornice details.[5]

Mentor Park Place was built in Pasadena's Bungalow Heaven Historic District (Figure 2). With more than 800 single-family houses constructed between 1900 and the mid-1930s, the Arts and Crafts bungalow is the district's defining building type. Typically modest in scale and built in an era before air conditioning, bungalows remain comfortable throughout the year largely because their low-pitched, overhanging roofs, shade windows, doors, and porches. Although Mentor Park Place employs some design features associated with the Arts and Crafts movement, it does so with little, if any, consideration of the environmental motivation behind them. For example, the low-pitched, double-gable roofs on the four-plex are similar to those found in the district, but lack any significant overhang, thus providing little shade. Similarly, the corner porches, intended to echo the porches on the bungalows, are too small to provide comfortable outdoor living spaces.

Oftentimes architects designing new construction projects in historic districts lack an understanding of the architectural history and building style in the area. Yet such knowledge is vital for the production of creative designs. While there are many different ways an architect could go about obtaining this critical understanding, in California, one of the most straightforward and effective means is to examine district nominations (which may be referred to as case reports) associated with each historic district.

The Liberty-Hill Historic District case report, a typical example of these studies, contains information on the individual buildings in the district as well as sections devoted to the district as a whole. These contain a general description of the architectural styles found in the district, a history of the neighborhood including important events and noteworthy residents, and, significantly, an analysis of the architectural character of each street. The report, however, lacks meaningful discussion of the patterns of overall physical development in the district, as well as critical analysis of why the district looks the way it does. Without this deeper understanding of the character of the district, the architect designing a new building tends to fall back on obvious stylistic features in an attempt to maintain continuity with the past.

The case report for Pasadena's Bungalow Heaven Historic District is similar to the one for the Liberty-Hill Historic District. Although the contributing buildings are carefully researched as is a general history of the district, the report does not provide an understanding of the historically significant patterns so that they may function as a basis for new design, such as the climatic sensitivity in the design of Arts and Crafts dwellings.[6] Such an understanding might have prevented the original design for Mentor Park Place from being conceived as Mediterranean rather than Arts and Crafts, or its redesign, in response to neighborhood objections, from simply using imitative Arts and Crafts details and materials while ignoring the environmental motives behind the style.

The new buildings in both the Liberty-Hill and Bungalow Heaven historic districts suffer from a design approach that lacks an understanding of neighborhood patterns as well as the underlying reasons for the original architectural styles. Rather than responding creatively to Victorian or Arts and Crafts architecture, respectively, the new buildings focus on the particular elements of each style, insensitively borrowing ornamentation, materials, and basic forms without deeper consideration of their contextual meanings.

Review of Historic Districts or Individual Buildings?

In San Francisco, Pasadena, and throughout California, the description of an historic district follows the federal definition found in the National Register of Historic Places:

> An [historic] district possesses a significant concentration, linkage, or continuity of sites, buildings, structures, or objects united historically or aesthetically by plan or physical development ... A district derives its importance from being a unified entity (emphasis added), even

though it is often composed of a wide variety of resources. The identity of a district results from the interrelationship of its resources, which can convey a visual sense of the overall historic environment or be an arrangement of historically or functionally related properties.[7]

The identification of an historic district begins with a survey of individual resources studied in the field and interpreted through written and graphic historic documentation. If a district is identified as historic, its components are divided into categories of contributing and non-contributing buildings. Typically, contributing buildings are those whose form, materials, style, location, and other features are good examples of the historic types found in the district, helping to create a sense of "unified entity." Alternately, non-contributing buildings are those that do not contribute to the unity of the "overall historic environment," either because they have been unsympathetically altered or because they were incompatibly designed. While surveys have traditionally focused on the individual elements that are found in a district (buildings, roads, and the like) with little discussion of the components critical to creating a unified entity, a few recent surveys are beginning to discuss the underlying factors that unite the elements into a coherent whole.

Design guidelines developed for historic districts are likewise typically biased toward the treatment of individual buildings instead of the district as a whole, the result of using the Secretary of the Interior's Standards for Rehabilitation as their basis. The standards primarily provide guidance for the treatment of individual historic buildings, the discussion of "streetscape and landscape features" being of secondary concern.[8] This focus on individual elements and their integrity, rather than the underlying unifying factors, may contribute to the slow erosion of a district's value as new buildings are added that pay only lip service to the district's architectural styles, materials, or ornamentation and details.

More recently the Secretary of the Interior's Standards for the Treatment of Historic Properties with Guidelines for the Treatment of Cultural Landscapes (1996) have provided some guidance for assessing the overall character of historic districts. The guidelines note that districts and cultural landscapes reflect in part a balance of change and continuity: "The dynamic quality of all cultural landscapes is balanced by the continuity of distinctive characteristics retained over time."[9] Change and continuity are also conditions found in most historic districts, as buildings, landscapes, transportation systems, and other resources are altered, added, or removed. Over time, this mix of components from different periods gives districts multiple layers of significance and a richer context for new design.

Understanding that landscapes by their very nature change more rapidly than buildings, the Guidelines for the Treatment of Cultural Landscapes state that "preservation and rehabilitation treatments seek to secure and emphasize continuity while acknowledging change." Design guidelines for historic districts would benefit from a similar understanding of the changeability of its various resources over time. Key to this approach would be an understanding of *why* historically significant features have changed and *how* those changes have affected the overall character of the district as it evolved. Similarly, design guidelines for a district should explain building typologies and other character-defining features found within it in terms of their historic associations, as well as indicate and discuss those characteristics that ought to be applied to new construction.[10] For example, guidelines might address siting considerations for new construction, such as setbacks and relationships between the building and the street, climatic conditions, exterior and interior spatial patterns, and the like. This methodology could include architectural styles as part of the design guidelines but, rather than treating style as the principal mechanism for conveying "compatibility" or "contextualism," style would be one of a number of elements used to design a successful new building or addition to an existing building in an historic district.[11]

The Players and the Process

While the proposed basis for design guidelines may have merit in the abstract, the test will be how well it works in reality. Changes to contributing resources in historic districts in California require the issuance of a Certificate of Appropriateness by the local cultural or historic review commission or board. The certificate sets forth the terms and limits of actions affecting an historic property. Typically the certificate is obtained based on architectural drawings reviewed for their consistency with the design guidelines.

The design for new construction in historic districts should begin with a sensitivity to the character-defining features of the district that contribute to its unity so as to allow the designer to understand those elements that are essential to "fit" the new building into the district. The Heritage Square Historic District (designated 1988, with boundaries expanded 1993) is located in the northwest quadrant of the original 1870 town plot of Riverside, California; it is comprised of residential blocks developed in the late nineteenth and early twentieth centuries (Figure 3). The district's principal historic properties are one- and two-story late Queen Anne cottages and houses, Arts and Crafts bungalows, and two-story Craftsman houses.

As is common in many older neighborhoods, Heritage Square Historic District deteriorated as the city expanded after World War II. The City of Riverside Redevelopment Agency in partnership with the Riverside Housing Development Corporation (RHDC), a local non-profit housing corporation, are charged with revitalizing the residential sections of the Heritage Square Historic District as well as other older and historic neighborhoods in the

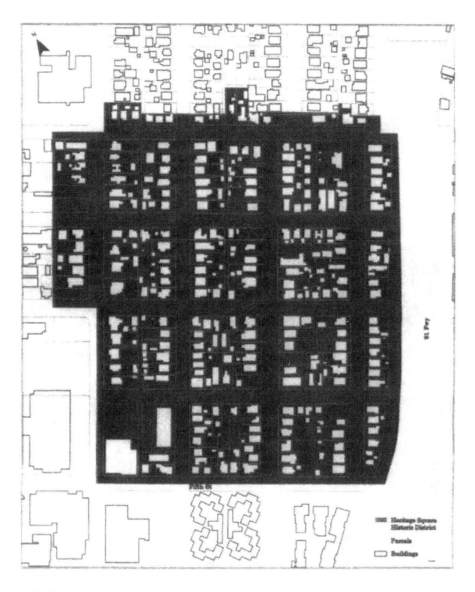

FIGURE 3. *Map of Heritage Square Historic District, Riverside, California (designated 1988, with boundaries expanded in 1998). Map courtesy of City of Riverside.*

FIGURE 4. *Mission Village Infill Housing for Riverside Housing Development Corporation, "The Cottages." Warkentin Architects (3 February 1998). Drawing courtesy of Warkentin Architects.*

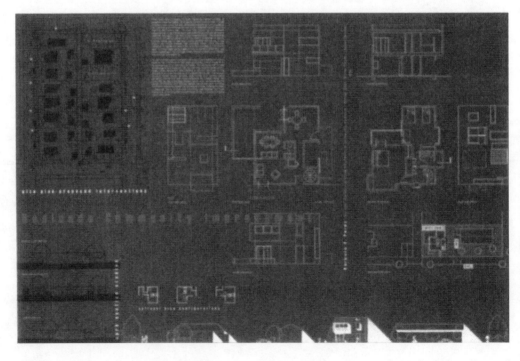

FIGURE 5. *"Redlands Community Improvement – Proposed Interventions." Prototype houses by Barbara Perez and Jorge Garcia (12 March 2002). Drawing courtesy of Barbara Perez.*

city. As one of its citywide initiatives, RHDC created the Mission Village
Home Ownership program to construct new, affordable infill housing on
vacant lots in the Heritage Square district.[12] It hired local architect William
Warkentin to design two prototype houses that could be built in any of
the older neighborhoods in the city, including Heritage Square. While
Warkentin's prototypes, known as "The Cottages," reference the Arts and
Crafts bungalows fairly specifically, his designs provide opportunities for
responding to the variety of architectural styles found in other neighborhoods
and historic districts (Figure 4). Given the wide distribution of potential
building sites, Warkentin took what might be called a geographer's approach
to design.[13] He analyzed parcel maps and conducted a reconnaissance survey
of pertinent neighborhoods to determine the geometric properties of vacant
lots and housing patterns. Through this process Warkentin then established a
minimum standard for the prototype houses. They were designed to fit on a
50-by-120-foot lot, with a 20-to-25-foot front yard set back and 7.5-to-10-
foot side yard setbacks. Garages were sited at the rear of the property, with
access from either the street via a "Hollywood Style" driveway (two parallel
concrete paths with area for a central landscape strip) or from the alley behind
the property. In keeping with the district's historic houses, the prototypes for
new houses were modestly sized at 1,191 and 1,300 square feet. Warkentin
selected an Arts and Crafts vocabulary because it was the most common style
in the neighborhoods where the new houses would be built. However, instead
of simply using decorative elements drawn from the style, he based his design
on its components that responded to climatic and environmental factors. His
prototypes had large shaded porches to provide comfortable outdoor spaces
and were sited to create useable yards.

A special topic studio, "Affordable Housing and Historic Preservation,"
offered at California State Polytechnic University, Pomona for upper-level
undergraduate and graduate students, took a similar approach in the design
of new affordable housing of older and potentially historic neighborhoods.
Kris Miller-Fisher and the author taught the studio in winter 2002. The
studio focused on the area of Redlands, California, known as the Northside.
Its housing stock, consisting primarily of small-scale, detached single-family
houses constructed from 1890 to 1930, was home to many of the area's
citrus workers.

During the first three weeks of the studio the students conducted a
building-by-building architectural survey of 1,800 properties. The survey data
was incorporated into a database designed by the City of Riverside. The class
also analyzed the development of the Northside through a series of Sanborn

Fire Insurance Maps to establish an understanding of how the neighborhood changed over time. The remainder of the academic quarter was devoted to related projects ranging from full documentation, including as-built drawings, of a threatened 1880s house to the development of housing concepts for a typical city block within the survey area, titled "Redlands Community Improvement" (Figure 5). Students identified ways to improve the community, including the rehabilitation of existing dwellings, subdividing lots to create new parcels for construction, fronting on the neighborhood's alleys, and infilling empty lots with new buildings to increase density. The group also sought ways to make the streets more appealing to encourage more outdoor activity and interaction among the residents.

As a starting point the students constructed a large-scale model of a typical neighborhood block showing houses, alleys, streets, and open spaces. This identified the spatial patterns formed by the dwellings and the setback conditions, which in turn governed the suggested locations for new parcels and buildings. One of the designs for infill houses borrowed from the Craftsman tradition, simplifying it to its most elemental form—essentially a gable room sheltering wall planes articulated by a contrast of wood siding and exposed concrete. Other designs were more overtly modernist with careful consideration of parking at the lower level and open interior space. But because of the understanding of the historic patterns of the "unified entity" that was the neighborhood, the different styles worked well together, reinforcing the existing historic architecture while adding a new layer of history and meaning.

Conclusion

Improving the quality of new construction in historic districts requires developing a design process that focuses on conditions that make an historic district a "unified entity" and treats architectural imagery as one, but not the primary, defining elements of the district. Incorporating some of the concepts of continuity and change associated with cultural landscapes helps create a process that allows historic elements to be preserved as the context changes. Fundamental to this process is an analysis and understanding of why a district developed as it did over time. Indicating the character-defining features of an historic neighborhood in a language that can be applied by contemporary designers and their clients is also critical to the development of more sensitive, creative designs within these districts. ❂

(Endnotes)

1 *Department of the Interior, Secretary of the Interior's Standards for Rehabilitation of Historic Buildings* (Washington, D.C.: National Park Service, 1990), 51.

2 *Secretary of the Interior's Standards for Rehabilitation,* 58.

3 San Francisco Planning Department, "Property Information Report on 101 Liberty Street" (San Francisco).

4 San Francisco Planning Department, "Liberty-Hill Historic District Case Report, and Statement of Significance" (San Francisco).

5 109 Liberty Street is discussed and illustrated in *Here Today: San Francisco's Architectural Heritage* (San Francisco: Chronicle Books, 1968), 109; Judith Lynch Waldhorn and Sally B. Woodbridge, *Victoria's Legacy* (San Francisco: Chronicle Books, 1978), 56–57.

6 Pasadena Design and Historic Preservation, Planning Division, "The Bungalow Heaven Conservation Plan: Bungalow Heaven Landmark District (LD-1)," amended October 5, 1993 (Pasadena, 1994).

7 Department of the Interior, *National Register Bulletin 15. How to Apply the National Register Criteria for Evaluation* (Washington, D.C., 1991). The City of San Francisco defines an historic district as "an area containing a number of structures having a special character or special historical, architectural, or aesthetic interest or value, and constituting a distinct section of the city, as an historic district." Article 10, Sec. 1004. *Designation of Landmarks and Historic Districts.* In Pasadena, a "landmark district is an area which has significant historic, cultural, architectural, and aesthetic value as part of the heritage of the city. By city code, a district must consist of ten or more residential properties." *Pasadena Municipal Code,* 2.75.120. And in Riverside, an historic district is a geographically definable area possessing a concentration, linkage, or continuity, constituting more than 50 percent of the total, of historic or scenic properties or thematically related grouping of properties which contribute to each other and are unified aesthetically by plan or physical development which has been designated an historic district by the City Council upon the recommendation of the Cultural Heritage Board pursuant to the provisions of this title. Section 20.25.010, *Historic District Designation Criteria.*

8 *Secretary of the Interior's Standards for Rehabilitation,* 49–52. This emphasis is made especially clear in the section that addresses "Design for Missing Historic Features" in an historic district. The recommended treatment indicates that "designing and constructing a new feature of the building, streetscape, or landscape when the historic feature is completely missing, such as row house steps, a porch, streetlight, or terrace. It may be a restoration based on historical, pictorial, and physical documentation; or be a new sign that is compatible with the historic character of the district or neighborhood," 51. The discussion of historic districts is even more summarily addressed in the *The Secretary of the Interior's Standards for the Treatment of Historic Properties* (1995), a new, modified version of the standards that presents the four primary treatments of historic properties. The only specific mention of an historic district, is the sidebar which provides definitions taken from Department of the Interior, National Register Bulletin 16A, *How to Complete the National Register Registration Form* (Washington, D.C., 1991).

9 Department of the Interior, *Secretary of the Interior's Standards for the Treatment of Historic Properties with Guidelines for the Treatment of Cultural Landscapes* (Washington, D.C., 1996), 6.

10 See Rachel S. Cox, "Design Review in Historic Districts"(Washington, D.C.: National Trust for Historic Preservation, 1994), especially p. 10.

11 The distinction between "compatible" and "contextual" is discussed in Ellen Beasley, "Reviewing New Design in Historic Districts," in Brenda Case Scheer and Wolfgang F. E. Preiser, *Design Review: Challenging Urban Aesthetic Control* (New York: Chapman & Hall, 1994), 20–30.

12 Planning Department, City of Riverside, Case file for CR-O14-978. Riverside Housing Development Corp., "The Cottages." (Riverside).

13 Interview with William Warkentin, October 4, 2001.

ADDRESSING CULTURALLY INFLUENCED DESIGN ISSUES IN DESIGN GUIDELINES

CATHLEEN MALMSTRÖM, AIA and BRIDGET MALEY
Architectural Resources Group

As an introduction, we would like to note that we are an architect and an historian. Our area of expertise is historic preservation, not market analysis, retail design, or the broader issues regarding urban planning such as transportation. It is our hope that this discussion of design guidelines will encourage a continued debate regarding both new design and rehabilitation in historic settings. Design guidelines are only one of the necessary planning tools for implementing good design practices; others include zoning, height limits, and economic incentives. Economic and political climates are also important determinants in historic preservation planning.

As we travel the world, "design-oriented" individuals are among the most appreciative of local character. We thrive on difference; "sameness" disappoints us. The open bazaar surrounding a cathedral or mosque, the farmers' market in the middle of a fifteenth-century piazza, the ad hoc shops under the arcade of a nineteenth-century railroad station—these provide the sights and sounds that give places identity, character, and meaning, ensuring "sameness" does not occur (Figure 1). These are the places, it seems, we love best. Nonetheless, in many cases, these marketplace functions do not "belong" in these locations—at least, the spaces and buildings were not designed to support them. Many of these activities damaged the physical integrity of some rather significant structures. Further, there is frequently evidence of extreme poverty, lack of maintenance, and a complete disregard for the value of the

FIGURES 1 AND 2. *(Left) An Italian market in Orvieto. Photograph: Cathleen Malmstrom. (Right) Exuberant use of signage, the typical existing conditions in downtown Los Angeles: extensive alterations to storefronts, fairly intact upper stories. Photograph: Architectural Resources Group.*

historic architecture. And yet we find these places pleasing; they are colorful, friendly, thriving, and alive.

Nonetheless, whatever merit we grant these individual expressions in other cultures and countries, we do not appreciate them here at home–in American cities, on our commercial streets. Certainly, the weekend outdoor market along a closed Main Street, market buildings designed especially for small displays, outdoor flower markets, or newsstands are the exceptions. Nonetheless, the appropriation of sidewalks and building walls for displays of excessive quantities of goods, wares, and signage is rarely considered an asset to an historic downtown. Traditional methods of conducting business and merchandising techniques, including the exuberant use of color and graphics, have an enormous impact on an historic building or district (Figure 2). In particular, some ethnic traditions, specifically the desire for open-air merchandising, frequently lead to the complete removal of street-level façades of historic storefronts. Although zoning and signage regulations in American cities often strictly prohibit these types of treatment and uses, these practices often go unchecked.

Historic Districts and Design Guidelines

Design guidelines in the United States have traditionally been based on the Secretary of the Interior's Standards for the Treatment of Historic Properties.[1] The standards provide general information for stewards of historic resources to determine appropriate treatments. They are intentionally broad in scope to apply to a wide range of circumstances, and are designed to enhance the understanding of basic preservation principles. The standards are neither technical nor prescriptive, but are intended to promote responsible preservation practices that ensure continued protection of historic resources. There are four basic treatments outlined in the standards: preservation, rehabilitation, restoration, and reconstruction. Another tool that addresses change in historic commercial areas is the National Park Service's *Preservation Brief # 11: Rehabilitating Historic Storefronts.*

Unfortunately, neither of the above-mentioned tools factor in the ethnic influences and evolving community traditions that often inform local design. When these localized design issues are overlaid on the standards, many potential conflicts become apparent. For instance, in downtown Los Angeles, excessive use of signage and merchandising often obscures the incredible historic architectural details found on many of the city's commercial buildings, particularly those storefronts that reflect the current Latino *mercado* tradition. When developing design recommendations for evolving historic neighborhoods, such as in historic areas of Los Angeles, a conservative textbook approach can work, but we believe that juxtaposition of the historic uses and the ongoing history of a place is both possible and desirable. Design guidelines recently developed by San Francisco-based Architectural Resources Group for historic downtown Los Angeles will provide a point of departure for this discussion.

According to the National Park Service's *National Register Bulletin 15*, an historic district "possesses a significant concentration, linkage, or continuity of sites, buildings, structures, or objects united historically or aesthetically by plan or physical development." Generally, these resources must be over fifty years of age in order to be eligible for the National Register or to be included in the period of significance. The Secretary of the Interior's Standard Number 4 states: "Changes to properties that have acquired historic significance in their own right will be retained and preserved." The general assumption with the standards is that such alterations occurred some time ago, most likely within the defined period of significance of the building or historic district.

Adherence to this defined period often results in limited consideration of recent physical modifications by a newer group of building users. Most large commercial districts reflect the American downtown from circa 1900 through the end of World War II. Thus, while alterations that occurred during the 1920s, 1930s, and 1940s may be considered as contributing factors to a district's significance, many postwar alterations, including changes that reflect an evolving community of immigrants, do not fall within the period of significance. As a result, the achievements and design overlays of newcomers are often overlooked.

For example, downtown Los Angeles is comprised of a remarkably intact district of exceptional buildings from the heyday of commercial development in Los Angeles—but only from the second story up! At street level, the district presents an entirely diverse view of urban development in the thriving Latino marketplace of present-day Los Angeles. It is, in a sense, schizophrenic; integration of the conflicting "personalities" into a healthy vital whole is the challenge.

Effects of Changing Urban Demographics

During the last forty years, there has been a dramatic change in the United States' immigration patterns and in the resulting racial diversity of the population. In 1890, 97 percent of foreigners in this country were immigrants from Europe or Canada. By 1960, only a slight shift occurred: 75 percent of the foreign-born population came from Europe, 10 percent from Canada, 9 percent from Latin America, and 5 percent from Asia. The physical evidence of this transformation was significant in only a few places, such as the Latino immigration gateway cities of Los Angeles, New York, and Miami as well as the "Chinatowns" of New York and San Francisco.[2]

However, by 1999, American demographics had radically changed. In that year, only 16 percent of immigrants were from Europe, 3 percent from Canada, and 2 percent from Africa. Twenty-seven percent emigrated from Asia, and over half (51 percent) originated in Latin America. For a complete picture, however, it must be noted that the overall population of the United States continues to be predominantly non-Hispanic white (69 percent).[3] In fact, non-Hispanic whites account for more than 85 percent of the population in sixteen states and more than half of American counties. Thus, many metropolitan areas and historic districts do not presently have to contend with the issues being highlighted here. Nonetheless, with these trends expected to continue, even smaller cities of middle America will eventually find their minority population reaching a significant level. California has over 3.6 million Asians and almost 11 million Latinos; approximately 8 million are

FIGURE 3. *An example of a removed storefront and theater entry now used as display area for merchandise. Photograph: Architectural Resources Group.*

foreign-born. Their combined influence on the culture and the appearance of our cities cannot be ignored.[4] The following five points illustrate this fact.

First, over the years, many historic downtown centers in both small and large cities were abandoned by a variety of occupants: retailers to malls, corporations to newer high-rise commercial and office districts as well as office campuses, and theaters to suburban multiplexes. In many older downtowns, as the original users relocated, businesses catering to growing ethnic populations moved into the historic commercial buildings vacated by earlier users. Particularly in the West and Southwest, where the Latin American immigrant population has grown rapidly, these downtown areas have become increasingly Latino. This demographic change has had important effects—both good and bad—on the character of historic downtowns. Much of the historic building stock remains because there was no perceived viability in "urban renewal." Buildings that might have been lost in the building booms of the latter part of the twentieth century have been retained as growth occurred elsewhere—in the suburbs and in other areas of the city where development was easier due to lower property values and larger available tracts.

Second, as the Latino population has increased, the heavily used markets, which offer a wide range of merchandise from produce to blue jeans, have economically sustained some neighborhoods. Again, the existing storefronts and the larger "swap meets" in some of Los Angeles's historic theaters provide a very generous income for both merchants and their landlords. Although these market-type activities are often jammed into historic buildings with little regard for architectural components and features, these unplanned businesses are quite profitable because of the sheer number of sales generated within or just outside the building (Figure 3).

Third, many buildings are underutilized or vacant at the upper floors, including theaters and other "white elephants." For instance, in historic downtown Los Angeles, income from existing street-level retail establishments can be so high that building owners have no need and little incentive to invest in the substantial rehabilitation required to attract tenants to the upper floors. Indeed, many upper stories in historic downtown Los Angeles are completely vacant.

Fourth, the Latino *mercado* or market tradition of merchandise display often leads to the complete removal of historic storefronts for retail expansion onto the sidewalk. The northern European architectural roots reflected in most American historic commercial buildings do not seem to be compatible with the types of merchandising common to the heritage of Latino immigrant populations. Certainly, ungoverned retail displays are found in northern climes, but most of these are temporary or seasonal and do not have the potential of irreversible impact on commercial structures.

Last, nighttime desolation, roll-down doors, limited storefront glazing, and cultural unfamiliarity lead to a perception that an area is unsafe. On Broadway in downtown Los Angeles, the streets are active during the day from 9 a.m. to 5 p.m., after which time shops are closed, merchants roll down solid metal doors, and pedestrians abandon sidewalks.

The above factors are obvious in some downtowns and subtle in others, yet they are important indications of our changing culture. While it is important to preserve as much of our past as possible, bestowing a higher priority on the preservation of our commercial past than on the culture of the current inhabitants smacks of elitism and can lead to serious political clashes. The designation of historic districts can be perceived differently depending on one's point of view: either as a means to preserve buildings or districts that may be currently threatened or underutilized, or as the imposition of the antiquated values of a few on the new diverse population and an added layer of municipal review (i.e., red tape) in the design process. In his book *History in Urban Places: The Historic Districts of the United States,* David Hamer asks, "Whose history is being preserved?"[5] Is it that of the people living in the districts or that of a city's glory days? And for whom is it being preserved: the tourist seeking a nostalgic trip into the past, or the individuals and businesses creating and supporting a vital community? Hamer contends that historic districts convey "a decline in optimism about the future, a turning away from the linear model of faith in progress to nostalgic invocation of the past."[6] Some cities have employed strict design guidelines to "restore" the historic character to their compromised downtowns, but perhaps at too great an expense to building owners and local merchants, some of whom choose to leave these "regulated" areas. In developing design guidelines, a conservative textbook approach can work, but we believe that juxtaposition of the historic and ongoing history of a place can greatly contribute to the design process.

The Role of Design Guidelines

Jane Jacobs, in *The Death and Life of Great American Cities*, offered numerous observations and arguments as to what makes a city "work," the primary idea being that it is the unplanned mix of uses that creates a thriving urban environment. In developing design guidelines for a downtown district possessing a rich architectural heritage and lively, if not wholly compatible, community uses, we have asked ourselves the following series of questions, with the resulting observations. The questions are applicable to any historic district that is being examined; the observations are both generic and specific to Los Angeles.

What types of uses are appropriate for the historic building stock, both in terms of preserving its physical integrity and sustaining its economy? Most buildings in America's downtowns have a traditional configuration of first-floor retail with commercial or residential space above. This configuration has had great success in the past and is working again today in districts where mixed use is promoted and truly encouraged. Study after study, and now hard evidence, indicates that bringing residential uses into older commercial centers can be a key to their renewal. Innumerable instances of historic office/commercial building conversions to residential use have successfully breathed new life into many historic downtowns. For instance, the City of Los Angeles has recently instigated the Adaptive Use Ordinance that promotes compatible uses of historic office buildings by allowing some leniency on otherwise restrictive building or zoning regulations. This, coupled with the use of California's Historic Building Code, allows for alternative means to reach building safety requirements. The Historic Downtown Los Angeles Design Guidelines (LA Guidelines) encourages creative mixed-use development of downtown buildings. At this stage, the guidelines offer a vision of what is possible. The intent is to provide assistance and even inspiration for those farsighted property owners and investors who, spurred by Los Angelinos' renewed desire to live downtown, are willing to take the risk and be at the forefront of the area's renewal.

How can "design" expand the range of user groups for the district without the loss of its present users who, in addition to giving it character, are also its economic base? Several things can stand in the way of the wider use of downtown districts by community members, number one being the perception that they are unsafe. Guidelines need to address ways to enhance both the security of an area and the appearance of security. For example, open grilles that allow the merchandise to be both protected and viewed in a contained, yet attractive manner can replace the solid metal pull-down panels, used to protect shops during closed hours. Solid metal roll-down doors isolate the pedestrian and create an unfriendly, and perceived unsafe, streetscape.

Successful downtowns do not thrive only during day or night hours, they are alive at all times.

In downtown Los Angeles, resistance to the replacement of pull-down doors is expected. Until a critical mass of evening activity is reached, the perception of an unsafe neighborhood will persist. Again, a critical mass of committed individuals and organizations is the key to success. The first projects are already being implemented, and others are in the planning stages. Most of these early projects are conversions of historic office buildings to housing, with commercial uses continuing at the street level.

Another example is Cleveland's Euclid Avenue, which recently underwent a much-needed revitalization. Components of the plan involved transportation, housing, offices, hotels, theater, and retail; with both new construction and adaptive reuse of historic structures providing the infrastructure to achieve the plan goals of the public/private partnerships.[7] Daylight and nighttime uses abound, bringing people back to downtown Cleveland.

What design parameters will both complement the historic resources and maintain the ethnic diversity that gives the district its vitality? This refers to the fine line between enlightened management and obliteration of the more exuberant modes of retailing. Various approaches were proposed—the best of them requiring dialogue between preservation entities and building owners and merchants. The two most egregious affronts to our significant commercial building stock are rampant merchandising (signage and displays) and the removal of historic fabric to allow alternative modes of retailing. In downtown Los Angeles, signage now overwhelms the historic character of many storefronts. Nonetheless, Broadway, once that city's entertainment and shopping corridor and today a vibrant, Latino-oriented shopping district, can retain this vitality with signage guidelines that use color and light, rather than size or quantity, as their primary means to send a message.

FIGURE 4. *Signage and merchandise in the Grand Central Market. This project benefits from some signage and display oversight. Photograph: Architectural Resources Group.*

The Grand Central Market on Broadway achieved this with reasonable controls on signage and displays (Figure 4).

Most of the recent conversion projects mentioned under the previous question pursued a "gentrifying" approach, without benefit of the new LA Guidelines. The hope is that the LA Guidelines, although not legally binding, will encourage creative compromise through the use of case studies and very specific suggestions, including a clear interpretation of the city's arcane Sign Ordinance.

What public actions can be taken: Creation of a districtwide identity? Streetscape improvements? Signage restrictions? Review of new construction? Every city has distinct circumstances, but certain ideas can apply in one form or another to most historic downtowns. The level of jurisdiction that public agencies hold over private spaces must be determined. Parameters for use of the public way for permanent or temporary merchandising must be established. Often investment in public right-of-way improvements leads to private investment as well. For instance, in Los Angeles a unique through-block connection extends from the Angels Flight funicular, down Bunker Hill, through the Grand Central Market, and across the street to a small, historically themed, open-space element. This collection of spaces provides an important link between the newer, high-rise commercial buildings of Bunker Hill and their respective users to the older area of downtown and its wide variety of Latino-oriented shopping. The LA Guidelines suggest that this existing through-block corridor be considered as a model for other such connectors, allowing a higher level of "restoration" of historic façades along major streets and public spaces, with a greater degree of flexibility in prescribed treatments in the privately owned interstitial spaces. Once a distinction has been made between public and private space, property owners will understand what types of design alterations they can implement to achieve their goals.
The improvements (street furniture, signage, etc.) made to the publicly held components of the network will provide a model for private participation to follow.

How can the design guidelines engage and involve government agencies, property owners, and tenants, address their competing priorities, and help them find common ground and direction? Based on the above, clearly the local government agencies must take a lead in promoting and implementing "design" in the historic district. It is essential that all interested parties come to the table to discuss the localized issues that must be considered in the design guidelines. The involvement of local stakeholders, including members of the represented ethnic groups, is necessary at every stage of their development.

This is often difficult; in historic downtown Los Angeles, the current retail clientele is predominantly Latino, while the merchants and landlords are not. Creative means, like public events, workshops, charettes, et cetera, are essential as they involve all of these stakeholders in the process. On another level, Business Improvement Districts (BIDs) are very effective in encouraging revitalization through historic preservation and design enhancements. This has occurred in New York City with great success. Of the forty-one BIDs active in New York, many BID areas overlap with the boundaries of historic districts. As such, many BIDs become advocates for preservation within their districts.[8] In addition to the New York example, the recent project to create design guidelines for historic downtown Los Angeles was co-sponsored by the three downtown BIDs.[9]

How can the document become a tool for educating both owners and merchants on the value of preservation and on methods of signage and display that both serve their commercial needs and complement the historic character of their property? Design guidelines can become the basis for workshops to educate building owners and merchants about the value of working with the resources at hand. During the 1990s, battle lines were drawn between preservationists and activists for the disabled over the application of the Americans With Disabilities Act (ADA) to historic buildings. Preservationists were regarded as elitists who considered buildings as more important than their occupants, and it took years of effort on both sides to prove that accessibility and preservation can co-exist, without sacrificing design or access. Similar issues apply in regard to historic downtown revitalization and competing cultural groups, and similar compromises are required. The involvement of design professionals familiar with local ethnic traditions is also needed. In Los Angeles, these activities are underway, dialogues are ongoing, and more and more owners and merchants are becoming involved in the process; the new guidelines are serving as a basis for discussion.

Finally, just how large a role can design guidelines play in the revitalization process? The best design guidelines are only one component of a successful downtown revitalization strategy. The economic and political climate will continue to be the most critical determinant of the success or failure of a district to grow and prosper. However, without thoughtful guidelines, addressed to the specific concerns of a unique urban district, and commitment to their implementation, the choices will remain urban decay or gentrification. Visually interesting and easy-to-read guidelines can spark interest in the revitalization process. The LA Guidelines project utilized three case studies to illustrate how the guidelines might be implemented in individual building projects.[10] This chapter of the document allowed property owners to understand that the guidelines would not stifle the creative design process. Further, several recent successful adaptive-use projects in the area take advantage of a number of local and federal incentives during rehabilitation resulting in creative design solutions for reuse.[11]

Downtown Los Angeles: Broadway

With regard to the use of older commercial districts by a generation of new users, we look specifically to Los Angeles's Broadway (between Third and Ninth streets) and its retail storefronts, as a case in point. Broadway illustrates the challenges posed in revitalizing an extremely significant historic commercial core, where maintaining and restoring historic building integrity potentially conflicts with the successful uses introduced by merchants catering to a predominantly Latino consumer market. Some argue that Broadway needs little revitalization at the storefront level—its shops and sidewalks are frequently overflowing with Latino shoppers.[12]

Within the LA Design Guidelines study area there are numerous surviving historic commercial structures because new development, beginning as early as the 1960s, was concentrated in what was a residential neighborhood, Bunker Hill. Today, dozens of downtown blocks and hundreds of Los Angeles's historic buildings (especially at the upper stories) look essentially as they did in the 1920s and 1930s. Broadway contains the largest intact collection of historic movie palaces anywhere in the world, while adjacent Spring Street, commonly known as "The Wall Street of the West," possesses historic financial and commercial structures unmatched elsewhere in the city. The flamboyance and architectural grandeur of the movie palaces on Broadway reflect Los Angeles' early days as an entertainment center.[13] The Broadway of old was a street of constant activity, including running trolleys, shoppers frequenting its many department stores and specialty shops, entertainment buffs attending movie premieres, and locals visiting professional services that occupied the building's upper stories. The Broadway of today also bustles, but only at the storefront level and only during daylight hours.

The vitality of Los Angeles's Broadway has always been dependent on the existence and the success of storefront commercial businesses. In prescribing design guidelines for Broadway, ignoring the postwar, Latino-oriented merchant practices would have been a serious error. However, the current exuberant character of the storefronts, signs, and displays is not a completely positive contribution to the preservation goals for this important National

Register-listed historic district. At the street level, a visual jumble of signage obscures the façade and, in many cases, prevents the pedestrian from any appreciation of the incredible architectural features of the buildings themselves. However, guidelines with the single-minded focus of creating an attractive atmosphere and that do not consider the real circumstances—the success and needs of the existing merchants and clientele—could reverse the commercial successes in the neighborhood. While the LA Guidelines are based on the Secretary of the Interior's Standards for the Treatment of Historic Properties, the recommendations for Broadway, particularly with regard to storefronts, signage, lighting, color, and new construction, take into consideration both the flamboyance of its past and the bold uses of its current character.

Threats to Los Angeles's remarkably intact assembly of early twentieth-century downtown commercial structures are very real. Downtown contains a large number of individual locally designated landmarks. However, the weakness of the existing design review process is that these policies address only individual buildings, not the overall urban fabric. Further, existing signage regulations are rarely enforced by the city. These factors, coupled with deterioration due to years of neglect, have left many historic resources at risk. Development of design guidelines offered an opportunity to foster careful design practices within the historic area.

The LA Guidelines project included a number of important components: promoting the sensitive use and placement of well-designed and crafted (and in the case of Broadway, bold and colorful) signage to complement the unique character of historic commercial Los Angeles; illustrating ways in which historic building rehabilitation projects, as well as proposed infill construction, can be designed to contribute, rather than detract, from the existing character of the area; and respecting the varying histories, cultures, and activities that have shaped the development of downtown Los Angeles when making design recommendations.

With the incremental conversion of many historic commercial and office buildings in downtown Los Angeles to residential use, neighborhood services will be needed. Some new and long-term residents and occupants have concerns about displacement of existing building users. While a level of turnover in merchants will likely occur in the neighborhood, it is hoped that locally based commercial venues will prevail and that the proliferation of "chain stores" will be kept at a minimum. Local merchants will be encouraged to rehabilitate storefronts following the recommendations in the guidelines, ensuring both limited additional modification to historic features and creative lighting and signage to draw a variety of shoppers at all times of the day.

Linda Dishman of the Los Angeles Conservancy, a local non-profit preservation advocacy group, recently addressed residential life in downtown: "The early success of the Grand Central Market project and the recent popularity of [converted lofts] demonstrate there is a ready appetite for living units in a more gritty atmosphere. More people are placing a higher priority on low commute time versus single-family living in outlying suburbs."[14] Following on this thought, Tom Gilmore, a Los Angeles developer, quips that "L.A.'s been a movie set for long enough ... Now it's time for it to become a real city."[15]

Historic Downtown Los Angeles Design Guidelines

To educate the public and ensure that the LA Guidelines was a truly useful document, specific guidance was provided in a number of areas. The guidelines included:

- a matrix to assist building owners and merchants in interpreting the city's arcane Signage Ordinance, which is almost incomprehensible and, thus, unenforceable;

- illustrations of signage and lighting at the proper scale to interest pedestrians, rather than the oversized and excessive vehicular-oriented signage that now exists;

- suggestions for glazed infill systems that respect the rhythm and physical structure of an historic building's street-level opening, allowing a shop to be completely open during the day while providing a secure, but transparent, closure at night;

- suggestions for setting limits on the expansion of retail displays onto public sidewalks through the use of attractive portable display racks;

- a proposal for the creation of interior arcades (along the lines of the Grand Central Market) in several monumental historic through-block spaces; these could be thematically developed (apparel, children's goods, et cetera) to provide incubator spaces for small merchants; and

- case studies that illustrate how the options for storefront design, signage placement, and merchandise display can be incorporated into actual buildings within the study area. These include "before and after" illustrations of many of the guideline recommendations to assist building owners, merchants, and users in understanding the nature of the recommended alterations (Figures 5 and 6).

FIGURES 5 AND 6.
(Above) The typical downtown Los Angeles missing storefront. Sketch with recommendations regarding storefront enclosure, materials, and signage. (Below) Sketch by Kellie Phipps, Architectural Resources Group.

One of the unique aspects of the LA Guidelines was the involvement of the principal stakeholders and decision-makers in the study area. The fact that three Business Improvement Districts (BIDs), facilitated and coordinated by the Los Angeles Conservancy, came together to create the design guidelines is a major demonstration of their ongoing commitment to the area. The existing role of the BIDs to make the area clean, safe, and attractive to the public was enhanced by this additional commitment to ensure that historic buildings are both used and preserved in the downtown.[16] The involvement of key stakeholders facilitated responsive guidelines because each of the BIDs supports a diverse group of property owners. The BID organizations provided a unifying umbrella for community involvement in enhancement projects in each of their districts, facilitating the community outreach process for the guidelines. Concurrent with the guideline project, the BIDs embarked on a way-finding signage program for downtown.[17]

It was the goal of all key participants to produce design guidelines for downtown Los Angeles, a truly diverse urban district, that would encourage effective preservation and adaptive reuse projects, while at the same time considering the vibrant, current character of the place, especially on Broadway. Through a public review process of the draft document, which included meetings with the BIDs, merchants, preservationists, design professionals, and city representatives, the guidelines were completed. Use of the guidelines is voluntary at this point. Nonetheless, the partnership of organizations that prepared the document may consider pursuing codification of the guidelines in the future, if widespread community support is obtained.

Conclusion

Time will judge how effective the LA Guidelines will be, and if it goes far enough in addressing the culturally influenced current configuration of Broadway to ensure that its successes are not impaired. Author Todd Bressi noted, "The hope is that Broadway will retain its Latino-oriented shopping character but emerge as something more—a place where ... employees come for lunch; where Latinos, Anglos, and others come for entertainment and shopping; and where residents, workers, and tourists mingle on the street."[18] The LA Guidelines are intended to provide a tool for the implementation of this wonderful vision. The Los Angeles Conservancy, one of the sponsors of the LA Guidelines, has applied for and received a grant from the federal Small Business Administration to develop a façade improvement program in downtown. It is hoped that with the combined efforts of individual property owners and the Conservancy, a balance can be reached that incorporates both the vivid colors of the Latino marketplace and the incredible architectural details found on many of the area's historic buildings.

The questions related to culturally influenced design issues in design guidelines are evolving ones. As more and more cities begin to address these issues in guidelines, there will be additional creative solutions to potential conflicts. Further, as more commercial areas formulate BIDs there will be new programs to implement, including those that relate to street, façade, and signage improvements within many commercial areas. There are many ways in which new design and historic resources can mingle. It will be the prerogative of each community to balance local historic preservation efforts with the cultural traditions that have evolved locally to ensure that diversity, not "sameness," prevails. ❂

(Endnotes)

1 Kay D. Weeks and Anne E. Grimmer, *The Secretary of the Interior's Standards for the Treatment of Historic Properties with Guidelines for Preserving, Rehabilitating, Restoring, and Reconstructing Historic Buildings* (Washington, DC: National Park Service, Government Printing Office, 1995).

2 Population Reference Bureau. Main Region of Origin in U.S. Shifts to Latin America. http://www.prb.org/AmeristatTemplate.cfm?Section=Foreign-Born&template

3 The US 2000 Census uses "Hispanic" or sometimes, "Hispanic or Latino." In our documentation, we have generally used the term "Latino." In addition, the Census specifies that "There are also two minimum categories for ethnicity: Hispanic or Latino and Not Hispanic or Latino. Hispanics and Latinos may be of any race." Thus, "non-Hispanic white" refers to white persons who are not of Latino ethnicity. http://www.census.gov/population/www/socdemo/race/racefactcb.html *Source: U.S. Census Bureau, Population Division, Special Population Staff*, Maintained By: Laura K. Yax (Population Division) Created: April 12, 2000.

4 Population Reference Bureau. The Geography of Diversity in the U.S. http://www.prb.org/Content/NavigationMenu/Ameristat/Topics/2000Census/The Geography_of Diversity. and Brad Berton. "Colorful Trends," Real Estate Southern California, June 2001, 30–33.

5 David Hamer, *History in Urban Places: The Historic Districts of the United States* (Columbus: Ohio State University Press, 1998).

6 Ibid., 26.

7 Leslie Holst, "New Kids on an Old Block." *Urban Land* 60: 9 (September 2001): 46.

8 New York City Department of Neighborhood Services.

9 Bridget Maley, Cathleen Malmstrom, and Kellie Phipps, "Beyond Safe and Clean: BIDs Help Create Design Guidelines for Historic Downtown Los Angeles," *Urban Land* 61: 2 (February 2002): 71–73, 76.

10 Architectural Resources Group, Historic Downtown Los Angeles Design Guidelines, Draft Document February 2002. Prepared for the Los Angeles Conservancy, Downtown Center BID, Fashion District BID, and Historic Core BID.

11 Frances Anderton, "Swank Plans in Skid Row Los Angeles," *New York Times*, January 25, 2001, B–1, B–14.

12 Curtis C. Roseman and J. Diego Vigil, "From Broadway to 'Latinoway:' The Reoccupation of a Gringo Retail Landscape," *Places* 8 (August 1993): 20–28.

13 David Gebhard and Robert Winter, *Los Angeles: An Architectural Guide* (Salt Lake City: Gibbs Smith, 1994): 216–18. National Register of Historic Places Inventory-Nomination Form for the Broadway Theater and Commercial District (1977 and as amended) and the Spring Street Financial District (1977).

14 Christopher Keough, "Downtown Players See Vital, Burgeoning City Center," *Los Angeles Business Journal*, June 11, 2001, 35–37.

15 Anderton, "Swank Plans in Skid Row Los Angeles," B-14.

16 Maley, Malmstrom, and Phipps, "Beyond Safe and Clean," 71.

17 Hunt Design. *LA Walks Downtown Los Angeles Wayfinding System*. Program Statement: February 9, 2001.

18 Todd W. Bressi, "Broadway's Next Move: From 'Latinoway' to Common Ground," *Places* 8 (August 1993): 29.

Multi-Scale Design Guidelines for the Rural Landscape of Nelson County, Kentucky

NED CRANKSHAW
Associate Professor of Landscape Architecture
University of Kentucky

JULIE RIESENWEBER
Assistant Director
Center for Historic Architecture and Preservation
University of Kentucky

KRISTA SCHNEIDER
Assistant Professor of Landscape Architecture
University of Kentucky

Preservation in rural areas addresses environments large in area and diffuse in focus. In response, rural preservationists have traditionally emphasized agricultural land preservation over design control. Design controls are commonly reserved for towns and cities and emphasize individual buildings. The goal of the Nelson County, Kentucky, Rural Design Guidelines is to preserve agricultural lands and the historic buildings and landscapes associated with them. To preserve patterns of cultural landscape in rural areas, the Nelson County project used landscape analysis, historic landscape surveys, and planning tools to create guidelines whose implementation will achieve historic preservation aims at scales from the planning level to site design. The guidelines address the locations of new development, the processes by which land division takes place, the ways in which additions to communities are designed, and the arrangement of buildings and other elements on individual rural properties.

Introduction

The recent history of development in Nelson County, Kentucky, is a familiar story for those who study or care about rural areas. The county seat, Bardstown, is a small town unusually rich in historic resources and cultural significance to the Commonwealth. It is particularly significant to the history of Catholic settlement in Kentucky, and was the home of the first diocese west of the Alleghenies.[1] Bardstown's historic commercial district thrives with a mix of locally oriented and tourist-dependent businesses. The inner ring of neighborhoods is more than liveable, with houses dating from the federal period onward, small or non-existent front yards, and large backyards and gardens. Bardstown possesses an urban configuration of buildings and streets at a small-town scale.

The countryside of Nelson County is diverse in character. It has a more understated agricultural character than the renowned horse farm area of the Inner Bluegrass region.[2] The productive land in the middle of the county supports large farms that concentrate on tobacco, cattle pasture, hay, and corn. The farms of the hilly eastern part of the county are smaller and are mainly devoted to cattle pasture and small tobacco fields. Much of the western and southwestern sections of Nelson County are rugged knob terrain at the edge of the Muldraugh Hill escarpment. These areas are mostly forested, with pasture on the lower slopes of the knobs and in the stream valleys.

Other settlements punctuate the rural landscape of the county and vary from small shopping and agricultural service centers, to villages centered on a parish church and school, to crossroads hamlets. Nelson County is a center of bourbon whiskey distilling, and some of these hamlets center on a distillery.

The concentration of historic sites in Bardstown and the diverse character of its rural landscapes have long drawn tourists, and a small but significant segment of the county's economy is based on tourism.[3] Equally important, tourism sustains the preservation of historic sites and stimulates entertainment and shopping choices that raise the quality of life for local residents.

Bardstown has long had an active preservation community. A local historic overlay district provides a mechanism for architectural review within the central portion of town. While the community has never ignored the rural landscape's historic qualities and its ability to provide a compatible context for Bardstown, they also have not had to worry about it. The rural lands with their historic houses, barns, and agricultural patterns appeared to be there forever.

But Nelson County's northern border is fifteen miles from the Interstate 265 beltway around the southern edge of Louisville. Accessibility to a major

FIGURE 1. *The agricultural zone in Nelson County allows five-acre lots to be developed two rows deep along existing county roads.*

urban area, combined with housing pressure from within the county, has instigated rapid development of new housing on the county's rural lands. One-acre and smaller lots in subdivisions at the periphery of Bardstown and near some of the county's other communities have supplied a significant amount of the growth in dwelling units, but the vast majority of the land area converted from farms to housing has been in the form of agriculturally zoned five-acre lots. In 1987, about 10,000 acres of Nelson County were in residential use. By 1998, 7,000 acres of residential land had been added to that area.[4]

Current agricultural zoning offers little protection for farmland and the historic resources associated with it. Land divisions of five acres or greater with frontage on an existing road do not require re-zoning or subdivision approval. The agricultural zone even allows double rows of piano-key lots to be developed by permitting driveway rights-of-way to extend between road-front lots. Many of the five-acre lots in Nelson County are surveyed, marked, and advertised, and then sold at auction. It is a remarkably efficient system for converting large areas of farm property into extremely low-density residential use (Figure 1).

Agricultural land area is not the only thing lost by this and other methods of residential development. The spatial and visual system that is a rural landscape is lost as well. The scale, pattern, and texture of roadside vegetation, fence rows, and tree lots are removed along with houses, barns, and other outbuildings. The new construction that results is not uniformly poor in quality, but it rarely considers the form of traditional rural houses or the pattern and scale of rural house yards.

The most common approaches to these problems have been to protect agricultural land in rural areas and to protect *cultural and historic resources, especially buildings*, in towns. This study recognizes that compatible design of individual sites is of little value when the uses of land in the larger rural landscape are drastically changed, and conversely that conserving rural land uses without compatible design patterns will not preserve rural landscapes.

To do both requires that historic preservation processes be integrated into planning processes. The significance of this project is in its effort to integrate historic preservation into the continuum of planning and design scales in a rural county.

Background

In 1999, thirty-six community members came together in an intense two-day Rural Design Guidelines Workshop facilitated by the National Trust for Historic Preservation, and co-sponsored by the Kentucky Heritage Council and local governments in Nelson County. Participants identified the elements of Nelson County's current character, and described preferences for future development. A summary document outlined the results and recommended guiding design principles for urban, suburban, hamlet, and rural areas.[5]

This study built on the interest that coalesced around the National Trust workshop. The Nelson County Rural Design Guidelines project was a collaborative study conducted by faculty and students of the University of Kentucky's Department of Landscape Architecture and the Center for Historic Architecture and Preservation. Funding was provided by the Kentucky Heritage Council and the Joint City-County Planning Commission of Bardstown and Nelson County.

The goal of this study was to develop rural design guidelines that would preserve Nelson County's rural character through compatibility with traditional settlement characteristics. The study worked within the premise that cultural landscape preservation requires attention to all scales of intervention, from the county's comprehensive plan to the design of individual properties. In order to achieve this goal, it became necessary to identify the significant elements that define the county's cultural landscapes and the environmental systems that support them.[6]

Landscape analysis took place in several ways and at several scales, including the county landscape and its subregions, historical and contemporary settlement patterns at both the county and community scale, and rural design characteristics at the site scale. The resulting recommendations propose countywide preservation and conservation areas, areas for new development, and design guidelines for how that new development should occur to preserve traditional settlement patterns.

Several sites were selected on which to develop prototypical design examples that demonstrate the recommendations. These examples illustrated existing landscape resource types, development opportunities and constraints, site analysis methods, design processes, and proposed land use policies.[7] The report contains illustrations of these designs to inform future planning and development projects. This paper focuses on the rural aspect of the project with only contextual discussion of recommendations for towns, hamlets, and suburban areas.

Analysis Process
Sensitivity Modeling

Environmental and agricultural resources: Development practices are degrading the environmental and agricultural resources that have sustained residents of Nelson County for over 200 years. Resource sensitivity to new development should guide future land use decisions. This required analysis of several factors, including the locations of high-quality farmland,[8] streams, wetlands, waterbodies, and floodplains, forest vegetation, steep slopes, and wildlife habitat[9] to determine areas with more significant resources. The greater the occurrence or overlap of these environmental features, the higher the significance and the higher the environmental sensitivity to new development. This resulted in an Environmental Sensitivity Model.

Scenic resources: Cultural values influence visual preferences. To avoid making decisions based solely on the authors' values, a visual survey was given to over sixty residents of Nelson County to determine landscape characteristics they most commonly liked and disliked. Sixty-three photographs represented different landscape types and settlement patterns. The highest-ranked photos generally had the following characteristics: water and riparian corridors, agricultural land in floodplains with forested hilltops in the background, and historic rural landscapes and residential properties. Map analysis of the visual preference survey resulted in a Visual Preference Model.

The Visual Exposure Model derived from GIS viewshed analyses of state roads and U.S. highways. High-exposure areas were visible from primary U.S. and state arterial roads. Moderate exposure areas were visible from state secondary arterial roads. The model treated areas visible from all other county roads as having low exposure. This model does not necessarily target roads that may be considered for scenic corridors or tourism. Recommendations for such designation would be based on looking at those roads that pass through the most highly preferred areas.

The Visual Sensitivity Model combined the Visual Preference Model with the Visual Exposure Model. Those areas that were most visible and had characteristics most preferred were considered the most significant, and therefore most sensitive to new development.

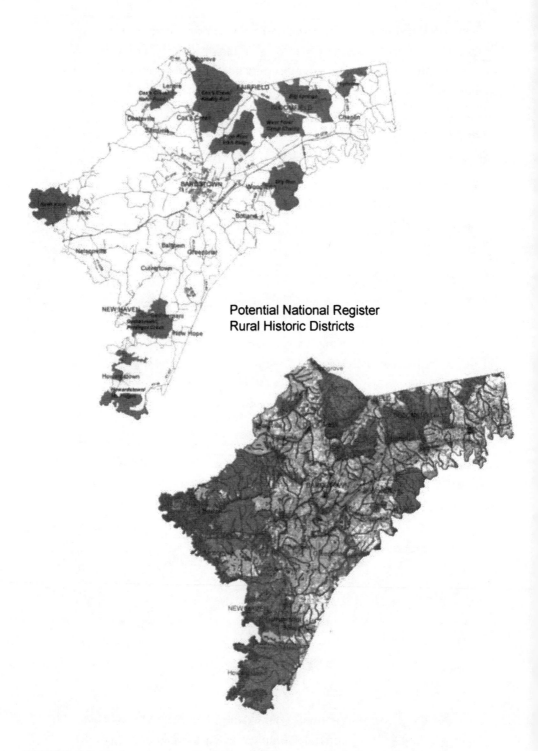

Potential National Register
Rural Historic Districts

FIGURES 2 AND 3. *(Above) Ten potential rural historic districts were identified in Nelson County. They are concentrated in the Outer Bluegrass, in which the largest farms are found, but they represent all landscape regions of the county. (Below) The Composite Sensitivity Model identifies the relative sensitivity of all landscapes in the county to land development.*

Rural historic landscape resources: Because contemporary development trends threaten the integrity of historic rural landscapes, this study identifies those areas that best represent these landscapes so that they may be targeted for preservation. The Rural Historic Landscape Sensitivity Model was built on two information sources. GIS analysis of areas of contiguous agricultural properties and locations of sites on a countywide historic resources survey[10] completed in the late 1970s was used to establish large areas with the greatest potential for historic districts. To actually assess their integrity and significance, and to develop preliminary boundaries, a survey of the Nelson County landscape was undertaken.

Staff of the University of Kentucky's Center for Historic Architecture and Preservation (CHAP) undertook field and documentary research to assess the potential for National Register eligibility of Nelson County's rural historic landscapes. A team drove every state and county road within Nelson County, conducting a reconnaissance survey to ascertain where modern development had obscured traditional land use and architectural patterns and to assess the integrity of more intact rural landscapes. Because the field survey method was reconnaissance, the boundaries described are approximate and intensive field and archival research beyond the scope of this project is necessary for determining final boundaries that could be used for National Register nomination. Research into Nelson County's history was used to develop a sense of the themes and patterns of local development and to outline the types of historic buildings and landscapes expected to represent these.

This work identified ten potential rural historic districts (Figure 2). The ten rural historic landscape areas that were identified have the greatest integrity and are most sensitive to new development. They also provide models for traditional residential development patterns.

Composite resources: Overlay analyses of the environmental, cultural, and visual sensitivity models resulted in the Composite Landscape Sensitivity Model (Figure 3). This model identifies all those essential areas throughout the county that should be protected or conserved in order for Nelson County to maintain its rural historic character, ecological health, and valued scenery.

Site Development Patterns

Communities: Hamlets and towns were examined to determine the essential dimensions of their traditional development pattern. Specific concerns that affect the perception of spatial pattern continuity and the experience of a traditional small community include block lengths, street widths, lot widths, house setbacks, and driveway locations. In the small town of Bloomfield, for

FIGURES 4 AND 5. *(Left) A house on Chaplin-Taylorsville Road illustrates vernacular site design principles that govern the layout of traditional farm residences throughout Nelson County. The yard is approximately one half-acre in size. (Right) A stream, pond, and pasture are part of the continuity of agricultural land along the road. Fences, trees, the stream corridor, and other elements contribute to spatial complexity and create multiple layers of visual division between the house and the road. Overlapping positions of outbuildings, tree lines, and individual trees connect the house site to its background.*

example, blocks are irregular, streets are narrow, lots are deep and relatively narrow, street setbacks are irregular but relatively shallow, back yards are large, and driveways enter off of the street and pass by the house to a garage in the rear yard. The prototypical design examples and design guidelines were influenced by these community patterns.

Rural sites: The potential register districts were well distributed throughout the county and intentionally represented different subregional landscape types. We analyzed a group of house sites that was representative of all of the potential districts to determine site development patterns that could inform site-scale design guidelines.

Analytical description began with the types of settings in which rural residences are found. The next level of description dealt with the landscapes of individual properties in the different setting types. An analysis of these examples then derived the features that are similar in most rural residences and those features that vary significantly. The design guidelines that followed were based on maintaining a similarity with these features so that new construction would be compatible with the existing rural landscape.

Particular setting types tended to be found more frequently in particular landscape subregions of the county, but were in no way exclusive to a sub-region. Features and organizations also did not vary from one region to the next significantly enough to develop different guidelines for different districts. Instead, the guidelines recognize a variety of settings and responses to those settings and incorporate them into one set of site-scale guidelines.

While specific features were used as a basis for the development of design guidelines, four essential concepts were seen to transcend measurements of individual features and to govern the relationship of any house site to the larger rural environment (Figures 4 and 5). Because these concepts describe the ways that rural house sites contribute to the wider rural landscape of Nelson County, they were treated as the guiding principles for design guidelines.

- **Size** of apparent yard: though traditional rural properties have land area that would allow much larger yards, the typical yard is only one-half to two acres in size.

- **Continuity** of foreground: farmland or naturalized areas along streams or slopes often continue between a house site and a road; house sites adjacent to roads often have tree lines that continue road-edge fence rows.

- **Complexity** of arrangement: while simple in detail and point features, traditional house sites often have fences and tree arrangements that create multiple layers of visual division between the road and the house.

- **Connection** to background: tree planting around houses and the vegetated fence rows that connect to yard edges serve to connect yards to wider vegetation patterns.

Current Development Trends and Impact on Historic Landscapes and Other Resources

With an understanding of cultural landscape patterns and environmental considerations, attention was turned to the future of Nelson County if current development trends continued. Trend analysis was based on the county's comprehensive plan, field observation of recent development patterns, and GIS mapping of recent land subdivision.

The Nelson County Comprehensive Plan (adopted in 1996)[11] recommended concentrating 60 percent of future development in and immediately around Bardstown. Incorporated towns, unincorporated villages, and hamlets were recommended to receive ten percent, and the remaining 30 percent was recommended to occur in the rural area. While this plan strives to consolidate public services and infrastructure and limit development in the rural regions by concentrating development around Bardstown, there are some issues that should be reconsidered in light of the significant resources discussed in the previous section.

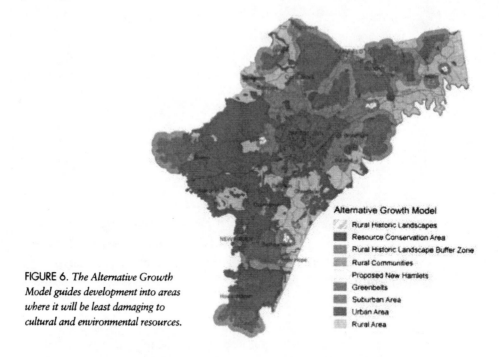

Alternative Growth Model

☐ Rural Historic Landscapes
■ Resource Conservation Area
■ Rural Historic Landscape Buffer Zone
▨ Rural Communities
Proposed New Hamlets
■ Greenbelts
■ Suburban Area
■ Urban Area
▨ Rural Area

FIGURE 6. *The Alternative Growth Model guides development into areas where it will be least damaging to cultural and environmental resources.*

There are several historic communities surrounding Bardstown that will become part of the larger suburban district. Based on the precedent of similar growth models (Lexington, Kentucky's Urban Service Boundary, for example)[12] several negative impacts will likely result. Suburban development will surround the small hamlets and crossroad communities, infringe upon their boundaries and destroy the unique identity that sets them apart from the Bardstown area. Secondly, without preservation policy controls, land use development demands will intensify in the rural communities and long-time residents will be under pressure to either sell their property for redevelopment or move to a new location where their rural lifestyle can be maintained.

Comparing the projected build-out of the comprehensive plan to the Composite Sensitivity Model identified several conflicts. As mentioned earlier, 30 percent of future growth is planned for the rural areas. Without changes to land use legislation, five-acre tracts and small subdivisions will likely continue to be developed along rural roads scattered throughout the county. These rural corridors contain the most highly sensitive visual resources and play a great role in supporting tourism. Projected suburban growth around Bardstown will also infringe upon several sensitive rural areas. The impact of this trend will be the continued fragmentation of farmland, destruction of the integrity of rural historic landscapes, loss of identity for rural towns and hamlets, and the degradation of environmentally sensitive areas.

Recommendations

Nelson County Alternative Growth Model

The Alternative Growth Model is a county-scale vision for Nelson County's future that reinforces traditional settlement patterns and protects significant resources (Figure 6). Using the sensitivity models, the rural preservation plan recommends land-use designations to guide future development in ways that will better preserve and protect the character valued by citizens.

Design Guidelines: Rural District Scale

Resource Conservation Area: The Resource Conservation Area comprises those areas containing the most highly sensitive rural historic landscapes, prime agricultural soils, floodplains, steep slopes, wetlands, endangered species habitat, visual resources, and large mature forest patches protecting the region's biodiversity. Because of the sensitivity of these areas to development impacts, this district is recommended for down-zoning to thirty-acre-minimum lot sizes to reduce density of development and to minimize disturbance of resources on individual sites.

    Rural Historic Landscape Overlay District: The goal of this district is to preserve agricultural lands and the historic buildings and landscapes associated with them in areas with the greatest integrity and significance. In addition to the down-zoning policies that apply to the resource conservation area, the Rural Site Design Guidelines are recommended to be mandatory for any new development in these areas.

    Rural Historic Landscape Buffer Zone: These areas are recommended to provide a half-mile buffer zone around the Rural Historic Landscapes. Without these buffers, the physical and visual integrity of these historic landscapes can easily be degraded by new development incompatible with traditional settlement patterns. This area is recommended for down-zoning to ten-acre minimum-lot sizes and the implementation of rural site design guidelines. Five-acre lots are recommended as an alternative if 60 percent of each lot in a land division is placed in a conservation easement.

    Other rural areas: Land within the rural area but outside of the proposed overlay districts should be down-zoned from five- to ten-acre-minimum lot size. It is recommended that five-acre parcel subdivision be permitted if conservation easements are integrated into 60 percent of all lots. Conservation easements need not be entirely restrictive and should encourage the following land uses: continued farming/grazing, timber production, creation of wildlife habitat and stream protection areas, or other agricultural uses.

Design Guidelines: Community Scale

Rural communities and their expansion areas: Because rural towns, villages, and hamlets are an essential component of Nelson County's historic settlement patterns, new development is encouraged around these communities. During the Rural Design Guidelines Workshop, community members expressed their desire to see future growth accommodated through the expansion of existing rural communities, but expressed concern for the protection of each community's historic qualities. In order for new development to respect the traditional settlement patterns and site design characteristics of the existing communities, Rural Community Design Guidelines were developed based on the physical measurement of community site design patterns (Figure 7). It is recommended that Rural Community Design Guidelines be mandatory for those communities falling within the Rural Landscape Overlay District. New development falling outside these districts should be encouraged to follow the design guidelines through incentives provided in associated zoning and land use policies.

Proposed new hamlets: Several new hamlets have been proposed to accommodate future development (one has already been adopted in the comprehensive plan). These new hamlets are recommended to have a small mixed-use civic and commercial core that facilitates and encourages pedestrian travel. It is also recommended that development in these new communities be regulated by the Rural Community Design Guidelines.

FIGURE 7. *A prototypical development plan in the hamlet of New Hope builds on the existing street and lot pattern, and preserves significant natural features.*

Greenbelts: Greenbelts are an essential component of each town, village, or hamlet (whether new or historic). Traditionally, they were comprised of privately owned farmland. Though privately owned, the public valued them because they provided views and accessibility to the rural landscape.

In contemporary times, a greenbelt could be comprised of lots on the outer periphery of each development parcel that are either owned in common by the community and subject to an open-space conservation easement, or comprised of larger, privately owned estate lots (with a small buildable area), having a conservation easement on a portion of the property.

Greenbelts can be incorporated into the new or expanding rural communities over time as new development is added. By requiring a minimum percentage of open space to be included within any new development tract, developers (in consultation with county officials) would be able to identify opportunities where that open space could serve as a greenbelt. The overall gross density of any new development tract would actually be higher than the existing zoning (to provide incentive), and the lot sizes would be allowed to be smaller.

Urban area: These neighborhoods will provide close proximity to the civic, commercial, and retail centers and recreational amenities located in and around Bardstown, so it is important to establish a strong network of pedestrian, bike, vehicular, and greenspace connections between what is proposed and what already exists. It is recommended that this area also encourage a variety of lot sizes (mostly small lots that maximize density), trail and/or sidewalk systems, storm water detention/groundwater recharge areas, and the incorporation of multi-family housing in the same development.

Suburban area: Small-scale commercial development is encouraged within this district. Proximity to everyday services will reduce travel on county roads, and promote better pedestrian connections to commercial land uses. It is recommended that this area require trail and/or sidewalk systems, and stormwater detention/groundwater recharge areas. Resource Conservation Areas lying within the suburban boundary should also be preserved as open space and incorporated into the design of new neighborhoods as conservation easements on privately owned land or collectively owned parcels maintained by the community or property owner associations.

Design Guidelines: Site Scale

Site scale design guidelines deal with the issues of site development at the larger scale. In the initial workshops, citizens were clearly more concerned with larger scale issues and less concerned with issues of detail. Our analysis

FIGURES 8 AND 9. *(Left) A house on U.S. 62 exemplifies traditional site patterns, with a small yard and a fore-ground of agricultural land and natural features – a stream, pond, and associated vegetation. (Right) A neighboring house on U.S. 62 illustrates the effects of removing natural features, fences, tree lines, and agricultural use of land.*

of the county agreed with their collective thought and could be summarized by this observation: *the types of houses currently being built in the county could fit more compatibly within a traditional rural landscape context if their sites were laid out and managed in a traditional way, than could a house built in a way completely compatible with traditional architectural patterns that was placed on a property laid out in the most common contemporary patterns.* The site-scale guidelines for the rural area addressed house location, yard size and location within the property, garages and other outbuildings, driveways, fences, and landscape plants (Figures 8, 9, 10, and 11).

Project Status and Conclusions

The study is now in the discussion phase that must take place before any provisions can be implemented. Implementation of all the recommendations at one time would be extremely unlikely, though many citizens agree with their intent. Nelson County and Bardstown have been willing to more intensively regulate property for the cause of conservation than have neighboring localities. Some of the provisions of this study could be written into the existing comprehensive plan and zoning ordinance as modifications. Other provisions, such as the creation of new zoning districts or overlay categories will involve more political discussion and more extensive change in land-use regulations.

Any specific recommendations aside, the importance of this study is its example of a process for cultural landscape preservation at multiple scales. Analysis was directed at the very specific qualities of one county, but the issues are universal and the methods are transferable. The legal framework and the political will for implementation will vary widely from place to place and will be partially subject to ongoing debate on the balance between private property rights and public interests in land use and design. ⊛

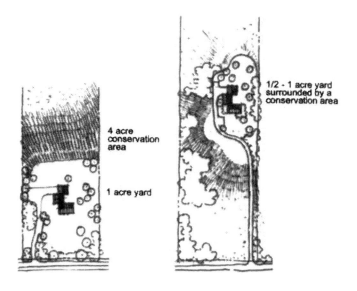

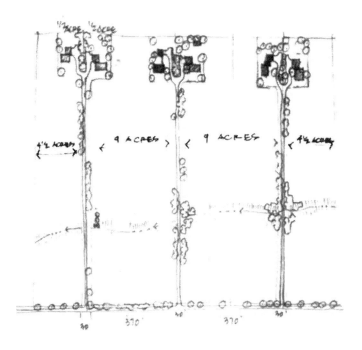

FIGURES 10 AND 11. *(Above) A site plan for a house built near a road illustrates how traditional rural features can be maintained when lots are developed. (Below) A site plan for a group of houses built at the rear of their lots illustrates how conservation easements organized across all the lots can be used to provide space for pasture, tobacco, or other agricultural uses that do not require larger fields, and can preserve the traditional character of road corridors.*

(Endnotes)

1 Abbey of Gethsemani, *Life at Gethsemani* (Trappist, Kentucky, 1958).

2 Christine A. Amos,"The Bluegrass Cultural Landscape: a Regional Historic Preservation Planning Overview," 1988, on file at the Kentucky Heritage Council, Frankfort, Kentucky.

3 Lorraine Garkovich, Ph.D., Nelson County Economic Development Plan (Lexington: University of Kentucky, 1999).

4 1:12,000 Digital Ortho Quarter Quadrangles (DOQQs) were used to develop residential land use data. Distinctions were made between residential development existing by 1987 and development that occurred afterward by comparing the DOQQs with older 7.5 minute series 1:24,000 USGS quadrangles.

5 Nelson County, Kentucky, Rural Design Guidelines Workshop (presented by the National Trust for Historic Preservation, 1999).

6 Historic, agricultural, environmental, and visual resources were mapped in a GIS database using ESRI ArcView software. By identifying the most significant resources and by determining areas of resource concentration or overlap we found landscapes that were most sensitive to new development. Regional environmental analysis and land planning methodologies first developed in Ian McHarg's suitability studies, and GIS modeling described by Carl Steinitz's framework for modeling process, change, impact, and visual preferences, serve as modeling precedents for this study.

7 The principal theories and land use policies promoted in conservation-style subdivisions and developed primarily by Randall Arendt have been applied to specific rural communities within the county. These concepts have been modified to conform to Nelson County's context and with much stronger emphasis on historic patterns.

8 Department of Agriculture, Soil Survey of Nelson County, Kentucky (Washington, D.C: GPO, 1971).

9 Kentucky State Nature Preserves Commission, *Nelson County Natural Heritage Program Database for Endangered, Threatened, or Special Concern Plants and Animals or Exemplary Natural Communities Monitored by the Kentucky State Nature Preserves Commission* (Frankfort, 2000).

10 Historic Resources Inventory Forms for Nelson County, Kentucky, on file at the Kentucky Heritage Council, Frankfort.

11 Pflum, Klausmeier & Gehrum Consultants, Inc., *Nelson County: A Comprehensive Plan for All of Nelson County* (Bardstown: Joint City-County Planning Commission, 1996).

12 Lexington-Fayette Urban County Government, *Our Rural Heritage in the Next Century: Rural Service Area Land Management Plan*, 1999.

PART THREE
*Modernism and Postmodernism
in Preservation Design*

▦ IS LESS MORE?

Twentieth-Century Design Attitudes
and Twenty-First-Century Preservation

PAMELA WHITNEY HAWKES, AIA
Ann Beha Architects

A bstract: Can a good preservationist be a good designer—and vice versa? And how might preservation guidelines strike a balance between preserving physical fabric and leaving space for the imagination, for creating memories for new generations? Design is a critical factor in understanding heritage and planning for its management. Good design involves editing for emphasis, yet preservation argues for leaving as much historic fabric in place as possible. This paper looks at the issue of balancing old and new through the work of two twentieth-century designers, Joze Plecnik (1872–1957) and Carlo Scarpa (1906–1978). It compares the philosophical underpinnings of their work and their time, through writings such as *The Modern Cult of Monuments* (1903) by Austrian Alois Reigel and the 1933 *Athens Charter* of the Congrès International d'Architecture Moderne (CIAM). From the work of these two architects and their eras, the paper suggests how their attitudes might apply to twenty-first-century preservation challenges in the United States.

Modernism and preservation have been at opposite poles throughout the twentieth century. Preservationists decried the large-scale demolition of historic fabric in the decades of urban renewal following World War II and the façadism that continued through the 1970s and 1980s. Some architecture critics currently blame preservation and contextualism for the stagnation of new design. Yet several especially striking preservation projects are found in the work of two architects trained in the formative years of modernism—Joze Plecnik (1872–1957) and Carlo Scarpa (1906–1978). True to modernist principles, their design work shunned direct historical references, but instead used craft and materiality, as well as dramatic removals of historic fabric, to create new forms with remarkable sensitivity to their surroundings.

Both Plecnik and Scarpa trace their artistic roots to late nineteenth-century Vienna which, as capital of the Austro-Hungarian Empire, was a meeting point for the cultures of East and West.[1] The third-largest city in Europe by the end of the nineteenth century, its newly developed Ringstrasse had provided a fresh canvas for a phalanx of monumental structures clad in various Classical and Medieval styles. An unprecedented period of peace and power led to the growth of Vienna's strong middle class, which in turn supported a rich mix of artists and thinkers who advocated breaking with the eclectic tradition, to create art and architecture that related to its own age, not the past—what we now call modernism.

At the heart of the artistic movement was Otto Wagner. In *Modern Architecture* (1896) Wagner declared that "modern forms must correspond to new materials, contemporary needs, if they are to be found suitable for mankind today. They must embody our own development, our democracy, our self-confidence, our idealism. They must take into account the colossal technical and scientific advances of our ages, as well as the practical requirements of society—that is self-evident!"[2] Wagner's theories on new forms and materials were drawn in part from the mid-nineteenth-century writings of German architect Gottfried Semper, who advised that "whenever art loses its true direction, it has to refer back to the arts and crafts, in order to reestablish a harmony between construction and decoration."[3]

Wagner's ideas about the creation of a new style of art and architecture found parallels in the work of Viennese scholar Alois Riegel. Riegel's book, *Problems of Style: Foundations for a History of Ornament*, published in 1893, was both a product of the nineteenth century and a precursor of the twentieth. It reaped the legacy of nineteenth-century archeological excavations in focusing on the importance of applied decoration or ornament as a major form of expression in all media and all cultures. It evoked the spirit of Darwin in looking at production of art as a continuous evolution, without the judgments of "high" or "dark" periods typical of other Victorian art historians.[4] Riegel captured Wagner's attitude in concluding that not only each age, but each culture must have its own art.[5]

Riegel applied many of the basic concepts found in *Problems of Style* to the question of architecture and preservation in his essay, "The Modern Cult of Monuments," written in 1903 as the preface to a proposal for legislation to protect historic monuments within the Austro-Hungarian Empire.[6] He identified several universal values, which corresponded to different kinds of monuments and thus suggested different treatments. The most basic concept was "Commemorative Value," applied to "intentional monuments," memorials or markers to people or events and which "fundamentally require" restoration to keep their communicative power intact.

The second category, "Historical Value," referred to buildings or objects that are representations of "the development of human activity in a certain field." These monuments required connoisseurship to appreciate, and demanded conservation to counteract the process of decay. However, Riegel cautioned that "any speculation and restoration remain subject to human error; therefore the original document ... must be left untouched in order to serve for better and more coherent hypothetical reconstructions."[7] This was a clear critique of the work of nineteenth-century restorers such as the Frenchman Eugène-Emmanuel Viollet-le-Duc.[8]

Riegel's third category was one that he suggested had only emerged in the nineteenth century—"Age-Value," which "trigger(s) in the beholder a sense of the life cycle." Riegel pointed out that ruins had a "mass appeal" that affected even an observer with no knowledge of art or history. They communicated through their "incompleteness, ... lack of wholeness, ... tendency to dissolve form and color," and through their contrast to new or modern structures. For monuments relying on age-value, "preservation should not aim at stasis," Riegel stated, "but ought to permit the monuments to submit to incessant transformation and steady decay, outside of sudden and violent destruction."[9]

Riegel's theoretical ideas found expression through the work of one of Wagner's pupils and assistants, Slovenian architect Joze Plecnik. The son of a carpenter, Plecnik had been educated in both "literary" and "applied" arts,[10] then traveled to Vienna, where he trained and worked with Otto Wagner from 1894 until 1911. Riegel's stand on the value of the "kunstwollen" or "will to art" of individual cultures was of particular interest to Plecnik, a member of one of the empire's oppressed minorities, and inspired him to examine more closely the traditional thought and expression of his native country.[11] In 1912, Plecnik left Vienna for Prague, where he had a teaching appointment at the School of Applied Arts.

Following World War I and the breakup of the Austro-Hungarian Empire, Plecnik was commissioned by Tomáš Masaryk, first president of the Czechoslovak Republic, to restore Hradcany Castle in Prague. The fortification, located on a dramatic promontory overlooking the capital, had been built under medieval Czech leaders and enlarged in the sixteenth century under Emperor Rudolf II. In 1755, Empress Maria Theresa sponsored a significant "modernization" by architect Niccolò Pacassi, architect of Vienna's Schonbrunn Palace, which included application of a uniform, classical pattern of façade treatment throughout the nearly four-acre complex.[12] By the end of World War I, the palace had been neglected, and restoration of this national shrine would symbolize the country's triumph over Austro-Hungarian domination. Masaryk set the philosophical and artistic attitude for the project, stating, "The main aim of the renovation is to make the castle a proper seat for a democratic president. At every level the design should express simplicity, but in a noble and artistic way, symbolizing our national independence and democracy."[13]

Plecnik's work at the castle, carried out from 1921 to 1935, included urban design and landscape treatments to set off monuments as well as dramatic new interiors within historic walls. They were subtle moves, not immediately discernable against the context of the massive construction, but had the aim of dissolving the "barracks-like uniformity" imposed on the courtyards and interiors in earlier times.[14] His views on history, preservation, and the work at Prague Castle are not well documented, but one quote is most telling: "Like a spider, I aim to attach a thread to tradition," he said, "and beginning with that, to weave my own web."[15] The work certainly demonstrates an awareness of Riegel's admonition against speculative reconstructions as well as his suggestion of the power of contrast between old and new.

Riegel had focused on ornament as cultural expression, and Plecnik's interest in materials, craft, and the expressive power of details comes through strongly in his work at the castle. His choice of forms was influenced by a trip made by Masaryk and his family to Pompeii and Paestum in 1921, his own trip with students to Dalmatia and Greece in the spring of 1927, and the heritage of his native Slovenia, at the intersection of Roman, Byzantine, and Germanic cultures.[16] Plecnik's unique, classically derived forms were seen by Masaryk as fitting symbols for a democratic republic, but were also remarkably compatible with their Gothic and baroque context while spare enough to fit twentieth-century ideals.[17] Three projects demonstrate Plecnik's approach.

One of Plecnik's first moves was on the castle walls, at the Paradise Garden and the Ramparts Garden, where he created physical, visual, and symbolic links between the castle and the city below. From there, he turned to the three courtyards that linked the buildings of the palace precinct. The Third Courtyard was the largest and situated at the heart of the castle, with the thirteenth-century St. Vitus Cathedral on the northwest side and palace

FIGURES 1 AND 2. *(Left) Statue of St. George in the Third Courtyard, Prague Castle. Photograph: Pamela W. Hawkes. (Right) Entrance to the president's apartments at Prague Castle, Joze Plecnik. Photograph: Pamela W. Hawkes.*

buildings from various eras forming the other boundaries. Plecnik's concept was to blanket the space with a paving of large granite stone slabs, arranged in squares of nine, and based on existing ornamentation in the Third Courtyard and an adjacent square.[18] Then Plecnik created two focal points: a colossal, new unadorned obelisk of granite, and the bronze medieval statue of St. George on horseback, placed on tall base in a pool (Figure 1). From the courtyard, gates led to other parts of the complex, including a flight of steps leading to the Rampart Gardens.

The entrance to the new president's apartments (constructed 1921–25) was in the southeast corner of the Third Courtyard. Here, Plecnik shifted the axes between the three courtyards, avoiding the original main axis through the Matthias Gate, symbol of Hapsburg domination, and recapturing the coronation route of early Czech kings.[19] A shallow arch on the courtyard side led to an entrance hall covered with a curved vault on Minoan pillars (Figure 2). The Minoan style reflects the early democratic symbolism of the Aegean, though the vaulting also recalls the nearby Vladislav Hall, built in the 1490s.

One of Plecnik's final works was St. Matthias Hall (1928–30), now called the Plecnik Room, placed between the First Courtyard and Second Courtyard and leading to the ornate Spanish Hall. The original interior was demolished because it "lacked homogeneity."[20] In its place, Plecnik created a three-story-high stair hall framed with arcades, the lower two Doric and the upper one "pseudo Ionic." The severity of the columns is contrasted with baroque candelabra that further emphasize the vertical divisions of the

FIGURE 3. *St. Matthias Hall, Prague Castle, by Joze Plecnik. Photograph: Pamela W. Hawkes.*

space. The ceiling was covered with sheets of copper patterned in squares with rivets, reflecting an interest in functionalism that owes much to both Viollet-le-Duc and Wagner (Figure 3).

Masaryk abdicated in 1933 and Plecnik left Prague for his native Llubljana at about the same time. His restoration work at the castle had increasingly been criticized by nationalistic Czechs; [21] his distinctive design work, which had been on the cutting edge in Vienna, was already falling behind the times.[22] A new generation of "modernist" artists and architects proposed not simply to break free of historicism, but "with every serious piece of new work [to create] a new newness which would outpace ... the passage of time."[23] Le Corbusier's *Vers une architecture*, published in 1924, sounded a clarion call to modern architecture, recalling Wagner's words thirty years before.[24]

Le Corbusier's ideas on architecture and urbanism were more fully developed and disseminated through the International Congresses for Modern Architecture, which first met in 1928, just after the founding of the League of Nations. The 1933 meeting in Athens was a watershed, and its proceedings were codified as *The Athens Charter*, published ten years later. The focus of the conference was the state of cities throughout the world, and the *Charter* was seen as "the implement by which the destiny of cities will be set right."[25] A chapter devoted to "The Historic Heritage of Cities" conceded that "the life of a city is a continuous event" and proposed to protect architectural assets—but then set strict conditions for what and how they should be preserved:

> They will be protected if they are the expression of a former culture and if they respond to a universal interest ...

> And if their preservation does not entail the sacrifice of keeping people in unhealthy conditions ...

> And if it is possible to remedy their detrimental presence by means of radical measures, such as detouring vital elements of the traffic system.[26]

In these pronouncements can be seen the seeds of urban renewal and façadism in the second half of the twentieth century.

Plecnik, who continued practicing until his death in 1957, found Le
Corbusier's ideas on design and planning sterile. "Es ist auch eine Idee aber
Keine von Gott kommende," he commented—"It's an idea, but it isn't inspired
by God."[27] However, Le Corbusier's *Vers une architecture* was passionately
embraced by the then twenty-year-old architecture student Carlo Scarpa,
who found the treatise "an invitation to seek new forms in the techniques,
materials, and structural discipline of industrial culture."[28] The Academy of
Fine Arts in Venice was undergoing a transition from classicism to the influence
of Secession, which had been brought to Venice via the Biennale at the end
of World War I.[29] Scarpa was also inspired by American Frank Lloyd Wright,
who visited Venice in 1951, and Plecnik's fellow student, Josef Hoffmann,
who he met in the 1930s.[30] In contrast and competition with Wagner was his
contemporary Adolf Loos, who broke with the Secession in his 1908 book,
Ornament and Crime. He had branded ornament as a waste of labor and
material, but advised that "rich material and good workmanship should not
only be considered as making up for lack of decoration, but as far surpassing it
in sumptuousness."[31]

Both Hoffmann's interest in craft and Loos's passion for materials are at
the core of Scarpa's work and its sympathy with the historic context. Despite
his embrace of modernism, Scarpa said, "I have always had ... an immense
desire to belong to tradition, but without having capitals and columns."[32]
His attitude toward the past comes through most clearly in his work on
the Castelvecchio in Verona. Constructed in the mid-fourteenth century on
Roman walls, the fortifications, like those of Prague Castle, bore witness to
foreign domination of a northern Italian border town. The Castelvecchio
had traditionally consisted of a residence portion with an inner court, and
a military zone enclosed in an outer court. Both guarded a bridge over the
Adige River, which bisected the fortification. In 1797, Napoleon conquered
the Venetian Republic. The tops of the towers and the characteristic medieval
battlements were shorn off to punish the town for insurrection, and a barracks
was built in the outer court. Simple and classical, with stuccoed walls and
regular rectangular openings, the barracks closed off the northern edge of the
court and its historic access to the river.[33]

By 1923, when Verona officials decided to locate the city's art collection
in the Castelvecchio, the building was largely derelict. Museum director
Antonio Avena sponsored a "restoration" of the fort by architect Fernandino
Forlatti in 1924–26. The macchicolated battlements were rebuilt and the front
of the barracks was plastered with a collage of Gothic doorways and window
surrounds salvaged from nineteenth-century buildings around Verona. An

FIGURE 4. *First-floor galleries, Castelvecchio, Verona, by Carlo Scarpa. Photograph: Pamela W. Hawkes.*

entrance was provided in the center of the long façade through a formal garden on axis with the entrance gate and the interiors of both the historic residence and the barracks were decorated like a Renaissance palazzo as a backdrop for the paintings and sculpture.[34]

Scarpa, asked to collaborate on new museum designs beginning in 1957 and continuing through 1973, declared that "Castelvecchio was all deception." He spent considerable energy on the façades of the old barracks, where the fraud was first apparent. "I decided to adopt certain vertical values, to break up the unnatural symmetry," he said. "The Gothic, especially Venetian Gothic, is not very symmetrical."[35] The entrance was shifted from the center to the east end of the façade, which also created a more logical visitor flow (Figure 4). The symmetry was further broken down by applying a one-story bay to the façade, sheathed in stone squares, their rich texture creating a modern equivalent of Byzantine mosaics. This created a niche housing a small treasure chest, its objects lit from above. New window sashes were set behind the principal façade of the former barracks, relating more to the interior than the exterior.

Within the barracks wing, the early twentieth-century details were completely stripped away, creating an enfilade of simply finished rooms where the sculpture and paintings are the main source of color and interest. Ceilings were exposed concrete on the lower level, and covered with floating gray panels that incorporated lighting on the upper level. In the historic residence, the "restoration" elements were also removed, highlighting authentic decorative painting on walls and ceilings. Paintings were hung on walls or portions of them that had lost their decoration, with no concern for symmetry.

Throughout the complex, Scarpa's work was distinguished by an obsession with joints between forms, materials, and surfaces. This was at the crux of his attitude toward history. "See how a building inevitably establishes new identities over time," he said. "Once acknowledged, this basic principle makes it fundamental for the architect to leave conspicuous and characteristic evidence of this own era within the historic fabric, trusting time to fuse it into a comfortable whole."[36] At Castelvecchio and other projects, he did not simply leave to history to fuse the whole, but used "the possibility of discovering joints to reconstitute the whole."[37]

FIGURE 5. *Sculpture of Cangrande della Scala, placed at the second-floor level of the Castelvecchio, Verona, by Carlo Scarpa. Photograph: Pamela W. Hawkes.*

Throughout the galleries, Scarpa broke down the joints between the floors, the walls, and the ceilings.

> The paving [is] one of the key surfaces in defining the geometry of a space. I had to solve the problem of the dihedron between the wall, which is a luminous vertical surface, and the dark, horizontal floor … Thinking of the water flowing round the walls of the castle, I got the idea of creating a version in negative. The floor of every room is individuated, as if they were a series of platforms. By changing the material round their edge for a crowning piece in lighter-colored stone, so as to define the square more clearly, the movement is modulated.[38]

The attention to floor surfaces to unite and set off architecture and art recalls Plecnik's paving of the Third Courtyard in Prague Castle. Just as the medieval statue of St. George provided a focal point for Plecnik's design, Scarpa's placement of the fourteenth-century sculpture of Cangrande della

Scala, a distinguished ruler of Verona, was the ultimate expression of the Venetian architect's dialogue between new and old. Scarpa had sought an appropriate way to suggest the original configuration of the castle, prior to the addition of the barracks. In 1962, the moat along the center wall of the complex was excavated, the last bay of the barracks, with a grand staircase from the Napoleonic era, was demolished. Scarpa positioned the statue at that juncture, raising it in the air below a roof that was peeled back to reveal its contemporary structure and express the break in history (Figure 5). Scarpa described his approach as follows:

> The most challenging item was the location of Cangrande ... It wasn't easy to work that one out. Even set where it is, up in the air, it's related to movement and conditions it, stressing one of the most important historical connections between the different parts of the castle. I decided to turn it slightly, to emphasize its independence from the structure supporting it: it's part of the whole, yet still lives its own separate life.[39]

Scarpa considered preservation "a dialogue between what is there and what might be,"[40] and there may be found a source for innovative design in our own preservation efforts. Some of the challenges of the early twenty-first century are large-scale sites that sheer size, intractable layouts, limited craftsmanship, and years of neglect have placed beyond consideration by most developers. In the case of jails, mental hospitals, industrial and military installations, for example, it may be infeasible to preserve all elements and appropriate to consider more innovative solutions. In doing so, one might look to Joze Plecnik and Carlo Scarpa and to three concepts found in their work—the contrast of old and new, the use of craft details, and the selective removal of historic fabric.

Both architects chose not to restore missing details, but rather to create their own. Their work abstracted the character of the setting to its essence, using it to both inspire the new work and to heighten appreciation of the older elements nearby. Their work became yet another chapter in the history of Prague Castle and the Castelvecchio, a history that will be more clearly understood by future generations because they resisted the temptation to impose their vision of what had been there before.

Both Scarpa and Plecnik exploited the richness of their materials, heightening their color and texture and delighting in craftsmanship, subtle or bold. In this, they broke ranks with modernists like Le Corbusier, who touted the highly engineered, highly uniform roadsters and ocean-liners of the machine age. Their attention to details and the way elements were put together gave their work authenticity and enabled it to fit comfortably in the historic settings, despite the contrasts of form.

Most radically, both Plecnik and Scarpa removed elements of historic fabric to create space for their own insertions. Reigel had pointed out that it was the "incompleteness" and "lack of wholeness" that made ruins and other monuments with "age-value" so appealing. In each case, Plecnik and Scarpa's removals were not wholescale gutting, as we have seen in "façadectomies" or much adaptive reuse, nor were they straightforward additions. The removals were surgical in their precision and in their intent, weaving in "healing" sutures for sites that had become overrun by confusing and speculative restoration efforts. As a result, they were able to strike a balance between preserving physical fabric and leaving space for the imagination, for creating memories for new generations. Thus, to paraphrase ardent modernist Mies van der Rohe, perhaps "less can be more" for modern preservation. ❂

(Endnotes)

1 Alain Arvois and Christina Conrad von Eybersfeld, "Plecnik, Vienna, and the Arcana of Baroque Tradition," in Francois Burkhardt et al., eds., *Joze Plecnik Architect, 1872–1957* (Cambridge: MIT Press, 1989), 16.

2 Peter Vergo, *Art in Vienna, 1895–1918* (London: Phaidon, 1975), 95.

3 Damjan Prevlosek, *Joze Plecnik, 1872–1957: Architecture Perennis* (New Haven: Yale University Press, 1997), 9. Semper's books were *Wissenshaft, Industrie und Kunst* (Science, Industry and Art), published in 1852, and *Der Stil in den Technischen und Tektonischen Kunsten der Praktische Asthetik* (*Style in Industrial and Structural Arts, or Practical Aesthetics*), published in 1860–63.

4 David Castriota, "Annotator's Introduction," in *Alois Riegel, Problems of Style: Foundations for a History of Ornament* (Princeton, N.J.: Princeton University Press, 1992), trans. Evelyn Kain, xxvii.

5 Kurt W. Forster, "Monument/Memory and the Mortality of Architecture," *Oppositions* 25 (Fall 1982): 6.

6 Ibid., 3.

7 Alois Riegel, "The Modern Cult of Monuments: Its Character and Its Origin," trans. Kurt W. Forster and Diane Ghirardo, *Oppositions* 25 (Fall 1982): 14.

8 Eugène-Emmanuel Viollet-le-Duc in *The Foundations of Architecture* (New York: George Braziller, 1990), Kenneth D. Whitehead, trans., proclaimed that "to restore an edifice means ... to reestablish it in a finished state, which may in fact never have actually existed at any given time." See p. 195.

9 Riegel, "The Modern Cult," 32, 42. Riegel mentioned a fourth criteria, "Use-Value," acknowledging that "an old building still in use must be maintained in such a condition that it can accommodate people without endangering life or health." He noted that, just as ruins may be innately appealing, so buildings which are simply neglected are repellant. "Only works for which we have no use can be enjoyed exclusively from the standpoint of age-value," he remarked, "while those that are still useful impede such pure contemplation."

10 Arvois and von Eybersfeld, "Plecnik," 16.

11 Prevlosek, Joze Plecnik, 12. Also Damjan Prevlosek, "The Life and Work of Jose Plecnik" in François Burkhardt, Claude Eveno, and Boris Podrecca, *Joze Plecnik* (Cambridge: MIT Press, 1989), 37.

12 Charles, Prince of Schwarzenberg et al., *The Prague Castle and Its Treasures* (New York: Vendome, 1994), 83.

13 Peter Krecic. *Plecnik: The Complete Works* (New York: Whitney Library of Design, 1993), 55.

14 Charles, *The Prague Castle and Its Treasures*, 84.

15 Prevlosek in Burkhardt et al., 36. Friedrich Achleitner said, "Plecnik did not look to history for a means to distinguish himself from the present; for him, history was the present." "A Slavic Gaudi?" in Burkhardt, 5.

16 Burkhardt et al., 2.

17 Greek forms had likewise been considered the most fitting symbols of democracy in the decades following the American Revolution. Plecnik's choice may have gained further justification from the writings of Gottfried Semper, who had claimed that "only one nation has succeeded in breathing organic life into its architectural creations and its industrial products. Greek temples and monuments were not built, they grew." Prevlosek, *Joze Plecnik, 1872–1957: Architecture Perennis* (New Haven: Yale University Press, 1997), 9.

18 Prevlosek, *Plecnik*, 145.

19 Krecic, *Plecnik*, 65.

20 Prevlosek in Burkhardt et al., 59.

21 Though Plecnik's initial work at the castle was well-received, the paving of the Third Courtyard was not. The Society of Friends of Old Prague organized an inquiry into Plecnik's work and published an article which exclaimed, "We have so many excellent Czech architects who would lovingly and patriotically take charge of the necessary adaptations without harming the monument left to us by our ancestors. We are now allowing a foreign architect, using a foreign style, and with neither love nor sensitivity for our historical monuments, to do what the former hostile government did not do." Vladimir Slapeta, "Jose Plecnik and Prague" in Burkhardt et al., 92.

22 Riegel's discussion of monuments had also noted that "the masses have always enjoyed new things and have always wanted to see the hand of man exert its creative power rather than the destructive forces of nature," which he called "Newness-Value." Riegel, "The Modern Cult," 42.

23 Forster, "Monument/Memory," 8.

24 "The history of architecture unfolds itself slowly across the centuries as a modification of structure and ornament, but in the last fifty years steel and concrete have brought new conquests, which are the index of a greater capacity for construction, and of an architecture in which the old codes have been overturned. If we challenge the past, we shall learn that 'styles' no longer exist for us, that a style belonging to our own period has come about; and there has been a revolution." Le Corbusier, *Towards a New Architecture*, trans. Frederick Etchells (New York: Praeger Publishers, 1974), 250.

25 Le Corbusier, *The Athens Charter* (New York: Grossman Publishers, 1973), 25.

26 Le Corbusier, *The Athens Charter*, 86–87. Emphasis by the author. For those monuments that met these rather daunting criteria, the *Charter* proposed to seize the opportunity to create "verdant areas" by removing the slums around them. While acknowledging that this might "destroy an age-old ambiance," the writers felt that this was "inevitable" and that "the vestiges of the past will be bathed in a new and possibly unexpected ambiance." Interestingly, the first International Congress of Architects and Technicians of Historic Monuments had met in Athens in 1931 and published their own proceedings, also known as *The Athens Charter*. Their focus was more particular, and their recommendations assumed that preservation of historic monuments was an accepted goal. Among the articles was one on "Aesthetic Enhancement of Ancient Monuments," which recommended "the suppression of all forms of publicity, of the erection of unsightly telephone poles, and the exclusion of all noisy factories and even of tall shafts in the neighborhood of artistic and historic monuments," and one on "Restoration of Monuments," that "approved the judicious use of all the resources at the disposal of modern technique and more especially of reinforced concrete." (*The Athens Charter* at http://www.icomos.org/docs/athens_charter).

27 Prevlosek in Burkhardt et al., 66.

28 Nicholas Olsberg, "Introduction" in Olsberg, George Ranalli, Jean-François Bedard, Sergio Polano, Alba de Lieto, and Mildren Friedman, *Carlo Scarpa, Architect: Intervening with History* (Montreal: Canadian Centre for Architecture/Monacelli Press, 1999), 12. See also Maria Antonietta Crippa, *Carlo Scarpa: Theory, Design, Projects* (Cambridge: MIT Press, 1986), 26–33.

29 Sergio Los, *Carlo Scarpa* (Koln: Benedikt Taschen Verlag GmbH, 1994), 8.

30 Olsberg, "Introduction," 12.

31 Kenneth Frampton, *Modern Architecture: A Critical History* (New York: Thames & Hudson, 1985), 93.

32 Olsberg, "Introduction," 13.

33 Richard Murphy, *Carlo Scarpa and Castelvecchio* (Boston: Butterworth Architecture, 1990), 5-6.

34 Murphy, *Carlo Scarpa*, 7.

35 Ranalli, "Renovation and Reorganization of the Museo di Castelvecchio" in Olsberg et al., 70. A slightly different translation is found in Los, p. 74. Olsberg says that Scarpa "despised the false 'certainty' with which nineteenth-century positivists approached restoration and rebuilding," p. 13.

36 Olsberg, "Introduction," 14.

37 Los, 12.

38 Ranalli, "Renovation and Reorganization," 72.

39 Ibid., 70.

40 Olsberg, "Introduction," 14.

Reconsidering the Guidelines for Design of Additions to Historic Buildings

PEYTON HALL, FAIA
Historic Resources Group and University of Southern California

The guidance from the National Park Service for exterior and interior additions to historic buildings emphasizes harmony, invisibility, and adherence to existing spatial patterns while de-emphasizing the importance of additions as expressions of contemporary culture. This paper argues that as buildings and environments change over time, they should simultaneously retain their historic character and evolve richly.

The adaptive use of Grauman's Egyptian Theatre in Hollywood as the new home of the American Cinematheque demonstrates an approach to adding bold contemporary features to an historic structure while respecting its historic character. A key to the design's success is understanding historic character through identifying significant spaces and features and limiting areas where modern interventions occur. Respecting that character while allowing the new features to be of their own time involved separating new structural and functional elements, and new building systems, from the historic building shell. The paper concludes that while the Secretary of the Interior's Standards for Rehabilitation allows for contemporary additions, it does not promote bold additions that express current culture nor ones that create rich new relationships between old and new in historic structures.

The practice of historic preservation in the United States is guided by the values expressed in the Secretary of the Interior's Standards for Rehabilitation interpreted by the State Historic Preservation Offices and the National Park Service. Compliance with the standards is particularly important in financing many rehabilitation projects since they are directly linked to certain federal and state tax benefits for reuse of National Register income-producing buildings.[1] The Standards for Rehabilitation address changes to the appearance, materials, and spaces of listed buildings, including exterior and interior additions and the removal of character-defining features.

The guidance provided by the National Park Service includes the principle that "a modern addition should be readily distinguishable from the older work; however, the new work should be harmonious with the old in scale, proportion, materials, and color. Such additions should be as inconspicuous as possible from the public view."[2] The Park Service's guidance goes on to state, "Interior components worthy of preservation may include the building's plan (sequence of spaces and circulation patterns), the building's spaces (rooms and volumes), individual architectural features, and the various finishes and materials that make up the walls, floors, and ceilings."[3]

While the Park Service does not address interior additions as directly as exterior ones, it does recommend that alterations should "avoid subdividing spaces that are characteristic of a building type or style or that are directly associated with specific persons or patterns of events."[4]

The Standards for Rehabilitation recognize that past alterations to buildings may have gained architectural or historical significance in their own right. If so, they should be respected and treated with the same care as the original building. The same consideration, however, is not currently extended to new additions or alterations to historic buildings. That is, modern additions to historic buildings are not viewed as important in their own right, but rather as subservient to the original architecture or significant changes that have taken place in the past.

This seems to be at odds with not only today's reality, but also even the acceptance of past changes. Buildings and their contexts are not static but continuously evolve, linking together past, present, and future. Thus, since buildings can be thought of as collaborations across time, contemporary interventions should be allowed to express the character of the present as assuredly as the original design expressed its past. This layering of time gives richness to a building, such as a Gothic cathedral where the hundreds of years of construction can be seen as the design and building materials evolved. Collectively, a time-dense context has given us cities such as Rome or Prague

FIGURE 1. *Museo di Castelvecchio. Interior gallery with additions. Photo: © Guido Guidi from project "Carlo Scarpa Architect."*

where one can see a thousand years of architectural history in a single street.

Witold Rybczinski writes that "the best buildings ... are precisely of their time," not timeless.[5] Thus, if the value of old buildings is their reflection of former values, then a future look back at today's work should reflect our best values. Take, for example, Carlo Scarpa's design for the Museo di Castelvecchio in Verona, where he weaves "new work into the ongoing dialogue of an evolving fabric."[6] Scarpa's projects "demonstrate his relentless concern with context in its broadest sense: time past, present, and future; the common sense of a place and the careful reading of its visual character; the methodical traditions of design; and artisanal techniques in building" (Figure 1).[7] Thus, the challenge to stewards of historic buildings and the architects who change them is to retain their existing character while bringing today's qualities to alterations and additions. The alternative is buildings and environments that, over time, will be characterized by mediocre interventions that ultimately devalue the historic resource because they do not reflect our time.

<hr />

The American Cinematheque's adaptive use of Grauman's Egyptian Theatre in Hollywood, California, is an example of an historic building and context that required significant interventions to meet today's functional requirements. It is also an example of a project that preserved original fabric and important spaces, and replicated missing features, while adding clearly contemporary and bold interiors that are not subservient to the original character.

In 1922, Sid Grauman developed the Egyptian Theatre, the first movie palace in Hollywood. Based on vaudeville theaters, it was designed as a complete theatrical environment for patrons, with live music and pageantry as well as the movies shown. Contributing significantly to creating this environment was the architecture of the building (Figures 2 and 3). Meyer & Holler, a noted Los Angeles firm, designed and constructed the building. In 1992, the City of Los Angeles Community Redevelopment Agency acquired the vacant building from a private owner and resold it to the American

FIGURES 2 AND 3. *(Left) Grauman's Egyptian Theatre. Forecourt during 1920s movie premiere. Photograph: Bison Archives. (Right) Grauman's Egyptian Theatre. Original 1920s auditorium proscenium. Photograph: Bison Archives.*

Cinematheque on favorable terms. The building is listed as a local and state historic landmark as well as in the National Register of Historic Places; thus all work to be performed needed to comply with the Secretary of the Interior's Standards for Rehabilitation. Over time, the building had lost most of its original forecourt, portico, foyer, and painted plaster proscenium arch. The 1994 Northridge Earthquake destroyed a substantial portion of the unreinforced infill masonry walls and cracked portions of the reinforced concrete frame.

American Cinematheque, a non-profit organization with the mission of exhibiting good and interesting film, required a facility with the highest standards of acoustics, projection equipment, and comfort, as well as one that recaptured its past association with Sid Grauman and early Hollywood. To undertake the rehabilitation, the organization hired Hodgetts + Fung, an architectural firm known for its contemporary design and its experience in visual and performing arts centers. In addition to the municipal funds, private donations, and other federal programs, funding for the project came from a number of sources, including a grant from the National Endowment for the Arts that recognized the importance of the project to the entire Southern California visual arts community.

The project used bold contemporary interior additions that reflected today to contrast with the retained and restored historic theater. This required that the important historic character of the building be identified and evaluated so that significant spaces and features could be retained. It also required that areas of possible intervention be noted. This led to the concept of physically and visually separating new spaces and systems from the historic building shell. It also resulted in the careful composition of new features to complement the historic building through contrast as well as compatibility.

The identification and evaluation of significant spaces and features was greatly assisted by an existing historic assessment report that documented the significance of the building.[8] It described past alterations and changes, providing a basis for determining which features could be removed without negatively affecting the historic character of spaces as well as those features that should be retained and restored.

Early movie theaters in states with mild climates such as California sometimes featured open-air forecourts that created a transition between the public sidewalk and the building's interior. Probably the best-known extant example of this type of theater is Grauman's Chinese Theatre, built a few years after the Egyptian Theatre was completed. The forecourts also served as open-air lobbies where fans could glimpse stars on the red carpet at premieres.

At the Egyptian, patrons passed through a long, narrow forecourt decorated with ancient Egyptian motifs then under a stoutly proportioned portico to low entry doors. Moviegoers proceeded to a low, darkly lighted foyer that opened onto the rear of the auditorium through heavily draped portals. At the rear of the auditorium they passed under a low, stencil-painted ceiling, down sloping aisles to emerge under a high dramatically lighted ceiling of silvery stars in a night sky. Ahead, the elaborately decorated proscenium arch came into view with its draped silver screen crowned by a gold-leafed scarab.

By 1992, the original builders would not have recognized the building. A series of alterations had drastically changed not only its appearance but also the processional sequence from the street to screen. In the 1940s, a tall marquee wall was constructed at the entrance to the forecourt with a steel-framed canopy connecting it to the front of the building enclosing the open forecourt. Low-walled planters along both sides hid the forecourt sidewalls. The original cast stone columns of the historic covered portico were removed to create an aluminum- and glass-enclosed lobby and concession area. On the interior, the open foyer wall had been filled to create an acoustical barrier between the lobby and auditorium. In the auditorium itself, a projection booth had been added at the rear center. Gypsum plaster absorptive acoustical panels had been added to the surface of original decoratively painted sidewalls to improve the acoustics of the auditorium when "talkies" were introduced. Perhaps the most significant alteration in the auditorium was the demolition of most of the painted plaster proscenium for installation of a wider projection screen. At the same time the original orchestra pit and stage floor were removed, thereby erasing features associated with live stage performances that took place before a film was shown.

In the Egyptian Theatre, the historic forecourt was considered important while its alterations and additions were not. Thus they were removed, restoring the forecourt's original configuration as well as its relationship to the street. In addition, the historic portico was restored, storefronts of the adjacent retail building reconstructed, and the historic neon signs reproduced, helping to bring back the historic relationship between the theater and Hollywood Boulevard.

To accommodate its new use as a screening room, the historic auditorium had to meet stringent technical requirements for both sound and sight. Originally the Egyptian's 1,800-seat auditorium had decorative plaster walls and ceiling that gave it a reverberant acoustical environment. The new program required a more intimate room of only 600 seats placed close to the screen and a surround-sound speaker system with low reverberation. To meet programming and financial constraints, the auditorium also had to accommodate a second, smaller screening room for presentation of video as well as an improved projection booth.

Separating the interior additions from the existing spaces allowed greater flexibility of design while reducing the risk of harming important historic features. It allowed the new construction to have its own scale, proportion, color, and texture as well as made it easily removable should that become necessary in the future. In addition, it allowed new structural systems necessary to meet current seismic safety standards, as well as new heating, air conditioning, plumbing, and electrical systems to be inserted without harming the original character of the building.

The architects treated the historic auditorium space as a richly sculptural backdrop of restored ceilings and walls into which the new systems could be placed. Simple pipe column frames set in new footings under the auditorium floor supported the new spaces (Figure 4). Air supply ducts were attached to the new frame, as were speakers for the new audio systems. Lighting focused on the historic plaster walls were also attached to the frame. Motorized, movable, sound-absorbing panels stacked in the original stage-house space slide into place only after the lights go down.

FIGURES 4 AND 5. *(Left) American Cinematheque. Auditorium with new armature to hold air conditioning ducts, and sound and lighting systems. Photograph: Randall Michaeleson. (Right) American Cinematheque. Lobby with new ramp and combination torchiere and fire sprinklers. Photograph: Randall Michaeleson.*

Another example of separation of new systems from the historic building envelope is in the lobby. Freestanding torchères attached to the floor provide ambient lighting, and also contain fire sprinkler pipes attached to sprinkler heads pointed up to the ceiling. Thus the typical solution of cutting decoratively painted plaster ceilings to install wiring, plumbing, and lighting fixtures is eliminated and important historic fabric remains untouched (Figure 5).

<hr/>

Originally the spaces in the Egyptian Theatre were organized as a processional from the sidewalk through a long, narrow forecourt, under a boldly proportioned portico, through low doors to a foyer with a low ceiling, then into the low-ceiling portion of the auditorium that raised dramatically to the starry-sky-high ceiling. The rehabilitated theater recaptures this sequence even as it divided the original auditorium space into a new lobby with a low ceiling, a small screening room and the large theater space. The new interior lobby was added by extending the foyer into the rear of the auditorium on a flat, light-framed floor supported above the original concrete, sloping floor. The small screening room was added within the expanded lobby. The high-ceiling original auditorium accommodated the new large screening room. Steeper risers, constructed above the original sloping floor on light framing, provide unobstructed sight lines of the screen. A new shallow balcony, with an acoustical separation wall at the rear, positions one-third of the new seats at mid-screen viewing level, thus reducing the distance between the rear seating

FIGURE 6. *American Cinematheque. Auditorium side aisle with new stairs to balcony. Photograph: Hodgetts + Fung.*

rows and the screen. Stairs that lead to the original sidewall exit doors serve the balcony. Armatures were inserted to support HVAC and other building systems while acoustic panels flank the new seating, balcony, and stairs to create the new screening space. The original side aisles were retained to visually and physically separate the interior additions from the original plaster walls (Figure 6).

The walls of the small screening room were stopped below the historic plaster ceiling, keeping the majority of the rear auditorium space visually open to patrons as they enter the building. The decorative ceilings above the walls were untouched and visible from most points in the room. Since the small screening room is suppressed below grade, an emergency exit passes through a subterranean tunnel to the exterior. Thus both new screening spaces are treated as additions floating inside the historic auditorium. In the words of Nicolas Olsberg in his introduction to *Carlo Scarpa Architect*, these spaces are "articulated intervention(s) consisting of a disposition of separate parts which thereby emphasize the historical elements between the parts."[9] That is, the new spaces are consistent with the principles articulated in the Secretary of the Interior's Standards for Rehabilitation, which require new features to be differentiated from the old. Bold articulation of new features not only clarifies the relationship of old to new, but also enriches both by creating contrast between components. In the Egyptian, this was achieved by a number of architectural devices including narrow reveals, offsetting features in plan and elevation, separating them in space, and changing colors.

The design of the Egyptian Theatre's new balcony was developed to minimize the physical and visual impacts on the adjacent auditorium rear wall by articulating the two elements. The balcony is supported on a row of four pipe columns that are independent from the structural system of the historic theater. There is a narrow gap between the rear of the balcony and the rear of the auditorium wall. Patrons who look up from the lobby level see an open slot that is glazed horizontally to provide acoustical separation between the cinema and the lobby. Each of the two stairs to the balcony was separated from the rear wall and the balcony by narrow slots.

Each new addition within the auditorium space has four faces. The rear wall of the balcony expresses the column supports and bends to accommodate the coves of the nearby rear auditorium wall. The freestanding stairs are clad in acoustical panels, becoming dark, textured boxes. The stair interior is an extension of the theater's mysterious theme and entertaining past, using expanded metal lath and accent lighting to create dramatic textures, layered space, and shadows within a confined volume.

The Secretary of the Interior's guidelines also encourage new features to serve multiple functions, since additions that serve more than one purpose typically reduce the amount of intervention required. A multi-functional design can reduce cutting and replacement of original fabric as well as the number of new elements inserted. The Egyptian Theatre's new balcony stair towers in the main screening room are clad with acoustical panels that provide a substantial proportion of the additional absorption needed for the sophisticated electronic sound system. The room has two acoustical environments—one designed for live music and the other for electronic movie soundtracks. Closing or opening sliding side panels as required achieves this dual environment. Using the stair tower walls to support the panels allows the original walls and ceiling to remain uncovered and avoids the need to provide separate elements for the purpose of holding acoustical panels.

The sidewall armatures also serve other functions, such as holding acoustical panels, speakers, ventilation ducts, and lighting fixtures. Two steel frames support all the mechanical and electrical systems required by the spaces. Since the frames are open, the fixtures and systems can be repaired or replaced as needed without disturbing historic walls and ceilings.

Of critical importance to the Secretary of the Interior's Standards and Guidelines is the principle that design of new features have a visual relationship to the historic character of a building. Colin Rowe, in his book *The Mathematics of the Ideal Villa and Other Essays*, provides a definition of character that is consistent with the National Park Service's view. Character, he states, "is seldom, if ever, defined, but it is generally implied that it may be at once the impression of artistic individuality and the expression, either symbolic or functional, of the purpose for which the building was constructed."[10] Rowe suggests, as do the Standards for Rehabilitation, that we define character both by artisanship and by the ways in which buildings express their functions.

This view of character was used by Carlo Scarpa in his Museo, as well as by the architects for the rehabilitation of the Egyptian Theatre. At the

FIGURE 7. *American Cinematheque. Lobby with new sunken screening room. Photograph: Hodgetts + Fung.*

American Cinematheque, its character is related to the historic context. The new sunken screening room has a cap that curves down to its sidewalls (Figure 7). The curved shape was designed to allow a line of sight over the room to the decoratively painted plaster. Nicknamed the "sarcophagus" to evoke ancient Egypt, its monolithic form and scale are read clearly as a modern element. Darkly lit, the new volume complements the drama of the original procession to the auditorium.

The new balcony stair towers are clad with perforated acoustical panels. Ranks of lozenge-shaped openings recall the scale, shape, and pattern of the historic plaster air grilles in the decorative ceiling. Expanded metal panels form a core around a single column at the center of the structure. The interiors of the stairwell have dramatic up-lighting. Thus the stairwell is an artisanal work, rendered in clearly modern materials such as sealed gray concrete, Masonite, and expanded metal. The procession through this space extends the original procession, augmenting the drama of entertainment architecture.

The colors of new elements and spaces reflect their functions as well as their context within historic spaces. For example, the floors and new partitions in the entrance and lobby are red. The side of the new balcony wall facing the lobby is also red. The colors of new features in the auditorium space are shades of blue ranging from dark royal blue to blue-black. The paint for the Masonite acoustical panels makes the inky surfaces slightly iridescent. In contrast, the historic plaster walls are decoratively painted in warm browns with polychromatic glazes to simulate stone. This causes the darkly painted new spaces and features to recede visually, making them appear to float within the historic shell. Patrons see through and beyond the new features to the more brightly lit warm plaster walls.

Conclusion

Vincent Scully characterizes urban architecture in Europe as "representing communication across generations over time."[11] This view of cities and architecture encourages adaptive use of buildings that achieves the best design and construction of each generation of change, creating a rich, temporally dense environment both inside buildings and on the street. The rehabilitation of the Egyptian Theatre represents an attempt to communicate between the architects of the 1920s and those of the 1990s, as well as among generations of impresarios, tourists, and moviegoers. The Egyptian Theatre represents an expanded understanding of the idea of compatibility as generally defined by the Secretary of the Interior's Standards for Rehabilitation as well as a design solution that respects the past by responding boldly, rather than subtly, to historic character. Significantly for the project's financing, the American Cinematheque's project at the Egyptian Theatre is in compliance with the Standards for Rehabilitation. However, in this case, the modern interpretations of the traditions of the entertainment industry, today's technical requirements, and the intention to create interesting new architecture did not allow the typical solution of designing new additions that are architecturally subservient to the historic. Rather, the functional and symbolic demands of the new use required bold new additions that engaged the historic building in a dialogue, one that created rich, new architectural relationships, as well as reconnected the building to its past in new and different ways. ❸

Acknowledgments

The project team for the American Cinematheque consisted of Barbara Zicka Smith, Executive Director of the American Cinematheque; Craig Hodgetts, Ming Fung, and Eric Holmquist of Hodgetts + Fung, Architects; William Wallace, Englekirk & Sabol, Structural Engineers; Ron Lindsay, Turner Construction Special Projects Division; Christy Johnson McAvoy, Principal Architectural Historian, Historic Resources Group; and Peyton Hall, Principal Architect, Historic Resources Group.

(Endnotes)

1 Rehabilitation is defined by the National Park Service as the process of returning a property to a state of utility, through repair or alteration, which makes possible an efficient contemporary use while preserving those portions and features of the property that are significant to its historic, architectural, and cultural values. Kay D. Weeks and Anne E. Grimmer, *The Secretary of the Interior's Standards for the Treatment of Historic Properties* (Washington, D.C.: National Park Service, 1995), 61.

2 Kay D. Weeks, Preservation Brief 14, *New Exterior Additions to Historic Buildings* (Washington, D.C.: National Park Service, undated), 9.

3 H. Ward Jandl, Preservation Brief 18, *Rehabilitating Interiors in Historic Buildings* (Washington, D.C.: National Park Service, undated), 1.

4 Ibid., 5.

5 Witold Rybczinski, "The Lure of the New," *Preservation* 53 (May/June 2001): 69.

6 Nicholas Olsberg, "Introduction," in Nicholas Olsberg et al., eds., *Carlo Scarpa Architect, Intervening with History* (New York: The Monacelli Press, 1999), 9.

7 Ibid., 10.

8 Christy Johnson McAvoy et al., *Historic Assessment Report, Grauman's Hollywood Egyptian Theatre* (City of Los Angeles, Community Redevelopment Agency, 1992).

9 Olsberg, "Introduction," 14.

10 Colin Rowe, "Character and Composition; or Some Vicissitudes of Architectural Vocabulary in the Nineteenth Century," in Colin Rowe, *The Mathematics of the Ideal Villa and Other Essays* (Cambridge, Massachusetts: The MIT Press, 1987), 62.

11 Barbaralee Diamonstein, *Buildings Reborn: New Uses, Old Places* (New York: Harper & Row Publishers, 1979), 15–16.

▣ IRONIC HISTORICISM

Postmodernism and Historic Preservation

ALISON K. HOAGLAND
Associate Professor of History and Historic Preservation
Michigan Technological University

Although postmodernism, the architectural movement away from modernism that achieved popularity in the 1980s and 1990s, is easily criticized for being overbearing and cartoonish, it deserves a new look for what it brought to historic preservation. The two movements have had an oddly symbiotic relationship: historic preservation engendered a new appreciation for the past, which was in turn exploited by postmodernism's use of historical elements, while postmodernism often provided the most apt solutions to the difficult problem of new additions to old buildings, or new construction in historic districts. Postmodernism's affinity for contextualism accorded with historic preservation's need to create a sympathetic environment.[1] The interplay between postmodernism and preservation will be examined through a discussion of their respective characteristics, illustrated by a brief analysis of their utilization in a handful of selected projects in Washington, D.C.

Although both postmodernism and historic preservation can be seen as sharing a reaction to modernism, their origins are more complex. The historic preservation movement began in the nineteenth century with the first conscious preservation of a building for its historical significance. Although a bias for preserving sites associated with famous events and personages lingered until after World War II, preservation's contribution to urbanism, through the interest in historic districts in New Orleans and Charleston in the 1930s, indicated a new trend. Preservation's identification with built environments and ultimately with quality of life called for measures beyond house museums. Widespread destruction of inner cities in the name of urban renewal in the 1960s, as well as the perceived blandness of the modern architecture that replaced these older neighborhoods, further raised alarms about the quality of the built environment. The National Historic Preservation Act of 1966 created a government structure to recognize historic architecture, and additional legislation at both the national and local levels provided protections. Preservation became institutionalized.[2]

Postmodernism dates to the 1930s in fields such as mathematics, where the inability to prove anything with certainty was proven, and in psychology, where reason was shown to be unable to function apart from emotion, the subconscious, and the unconscious. The postmodern movement, which denied isolated rationalism and valued multiple points of view, influenced many fields. In architecture, challenges to the status quo of modernism appeared in the 1960s, but it was with the new social conservatism of the 1970s that the search for continuity and cultural roots, coinciding with disenchantment with modernism, resulted in a coherent postmodern movement.[3]

Heinrich Klotz defined postmodernism broadly to include any architecture that rejected the tenets of modernism. Postmodernists advocated pluralism and eclecticism, art and poetry, improvisation and spontaneity, as well as regionalism and contextualism.[4] That postmodernism turned so quickly to historicism as an expression of these ideals, though, is probably due in part to historic preservation. Preservationists had kept traditional architecture alive during the modernist era, fighting for it in public forums, honing expertise in restorations, and developing a rhetoric of architectural treatment.[5] As architects cast about for a suitable postmodernist expression, the popular acceptability of historic architectural forms and ornament was already proven.

The historicist trend in postmodernism called upon traditional and vernacular forms to make architecture more accessible. Yet, differing with historic preservation, postmodernism depended on more than a continuation of the past; it insisted on a dialogue with the past, a critical look at the past at the same time that it honored the past. Landmarks of American postmodernism include Charles Moore's Piazza d'Italia in New Orleans (1976–79), where the almost perverse use of historical elements, such as all five classical orders, some in stainless steel, introduced a dialogue, as one critic said, "between the Old World and the New, between wit and seriousness, between perfection and fragmentation, between historical exactness and humorous alienation."

Another of the early postmodern icons, Michael Graves's Public Services Building in Portland, Oregon (1980-83), featured excessively stylized pilasters and keystones that perhaps acknowledged the art deco public buildings of the 1930s. Philip Johnson's AT&T Building (1980-83) in New York, with its historicist top, appeared as the work of ultimate betrayal: a life-long modernist actually decorating his buildings. Although the building was greeted with outrage and mockery—James Marston Fitch called it "idiosyncratic," "self-indulgent," "frivolous," and "preposterous"—it represented a fundamental rethinking of the modernist glass-box skyscraper.[6]

Related to historicism was postmodernism's interest in context. Postmodernists frequently borrowed from a building's surroundings, much the same way they borrowed from a place's past. Often, past and context coincide, as in Robert A. M. Stern's shingle-style houses in East Hampton, New York, which reflected their neighboring late nineteenth-century shingle-style buildings. Further, ornament and color, which had been out of favor with modernists, made a reappearance. Unlike the black-and-white palette of modernism, postmodernists employed color in joyous, vibrant ways, such as in Michael Graves's Clos Pegase winery in Calistoga, California (1987). Colors that drew from their context, along with ornament that expressed historical references, appeared on postmodernist buildings.

Another aspect of postmodernism was its use of irony. Although this incurred resentment and misunderstanding, it was also essential to postmodernism's interaction with historic preservation. Postmodern theorist Charles Jencks pointed to a "double-voiced discourse" that accepted and criticized at the same time. Elements were used both as an acknowledgment and as an ironic critique. At Robert Venturi's Guild House (1960-63) in Philadelphia, a home for the elderly, the façade was originally topped with a large, anodized gold antenna, which Venturi saw as a "symbol of the aged, who spend so much time looking at TV." This ironic commentary was not well received by the residents, however, and the antenna was removed soon after construction. Venturi believed that the use of irony guaranteed that historical elements were engaged in a reflexive dialogue, not provided as mere copies.[7]

While postmodernists were developing a new architecture that drew on historicism, context, and irony, preservationists were confronting the complex issue of new additions to historic buildings and districts. Norman Tyler terms the range of options "matching, compatible, or contrasting." One reaction to preservation demands was to duplicate existing fabric, the "matching" option. If imitation is the sincerest form of flattery, following the lead of the existing historic fabric was both respectful and simple. Bland "background" buildings adopted the massing, materials, fenestration, and general appearance of the original building, subtracting or simplifying ornament so as to appear different. These buildings deflected attention from themselves. But the ability of these copyist buildings to deceive the viewer into mistaking them for actual historic buildings concerned preservationists and the government. The Secretary of the Interior's Standards for Rehabilitation constitute the official guidance on this issue. In 1983, Standard 9 ordered, "Contemporary design for alterations and additions to existing properties shall not be discouraged" if compatible. The guidelines elaborated that exterior additions should be "clearly differentiated." In 1990 revisions, the idea of differentiation received more attention and Standard 9 was altered to read, "The new work will be differentiated from the old," but again assumed compatibility.[8]

The contrasting approach, a radically different yet compatible design that clearly differentiated new from old, called for a bolder treatment that might have satisfied architects' egos but ran the danger of overpowering the historic building. With contemporary design, compatibility became more subjective and projects that were hailed in the 1970s as models of contemporary-yet-compatible design might experience a tougher reception today. Purposely different designs find it difficult to survive the design review process.

The third alternative, being compatible without matching or contrasting, particularly suited postmodernism. The historicist bent of postmodernism offered understanding and acknowledgment of context, while postmodernism's duality promised obvious difference. Described as the "hallmark of postmodernism," contextualism was also fundamental to good preservation. When the Secretary of the Interior's Standards urged compatibility with "the historic materials, features, size, scale and proportion, and massing," they were mandating an awareness and understanding of a building's context. Yet contextualism itself has come under attack; *The New York Times* architectural critic Herbert Muschamp argued that contextualism "has led our architecture into the deadest of dead ends," resulting in a loss of a sense of place.[9] He defined contextualism, however, as "the idea that new buildings should fit in with their surroundings rather than add to them" and this is just what postmodern additions are accused of not doing. Some viewers found postmodern additions to be overbearing and distracting, yet postmodernist additions were often able to walk the fine line between dominating and enlivening.

Postmodernism's acceptance as a preservation solution was due to its ability to provide the contrasting-yet-compatible solution. Its predilection for historicism was detached, not a copying. Unlike revivalists and copyists,

postmodernists employed historical vocabulary in a removed way, imbuing
old historical forms with new meaning. The resulting antithetical relationship
provided a tension that also served to differentiate the new addition from
the old, and thus served historic preservation's goal of obvious difference.
Postmodernism thrived on difference; as Charles Jencks explained in information-
theory terms, "where there is no difference, there is no information."[10] This is
also an implicit goal of the Secretary of the Interior's Standards: if the addition
is different, we gather information from it, and recognize it as an addition.

Postmodernism thus had much to offer preservation: an approach to new
construction that self-consciously borrowed from existing fabric. Washington,
D.C., serves as the locale in which to examine postmodernism's interaction
with historic preservation. Generally architecturally conservative, Washington
experienced a great deal of new commercial construction in the 1980s and
1990s. The city has a strong preservation law governing its twenty-five historic
districts. In some, new construction also faces other review boards.[11] As a
result, the city offers many examples of new additions to historic buildings and
new construction in historic districts designed in a postmodern mode.

Architects working in Washington face a couple of unusual circumstances.
One is that Washington's commercial real estate is expensive, due in part to
the city's height limitation, as well as to the unique prestige attached to the
city. As a result, each commercial project is built out to its allowable density,
a hazardous situation for historic buildings. Often, the unsatisfactory solution
is the preservation of only a building's façade as additional square-footage
is constructed behind, beside, or on top of the original footprint. These
rebuildings appear in a variety of architectural styles, including postmodern.
Secondly, Washington's street plan provides architectural settings that few
other metropolitan cities offer. The wide avenues—as much as 160 feet wide—
intersecting with gridded streets produce numerous sites that are highly visible.
They make successful preservation treatments even more evident, but also
highlight architectural missteps.

While not all postmodernism is created equal, overall postmodernism has
added vitality and originality to preservation projects. The following examples
are not meant to be in any way definitive, but to provide a range of solutions
throughout the city that address a variety of design problems. Through them
it is possible to see an evolution, from outrageous and mocking to more sober
and sensitive. Together, they provide a way to evaluate postmodernism's
contribution to historic preservation.

One of the first postmodern buildings in Washington was Martin and
Jones's Madison National Bank (1980) in Georgetown (Figure 1). The building

FIGURES 1 AND 2. *(Left) Madison National Bank, 2833 M Street, NW, Washington, D.C. Martin and Jones, 1980. Located in the Georgetown Historic District, this bank building acknowledges its neighbors while being radically different and even a touch whimsical. (Right) Willard Hotel, 14th Street and Pennsylvania Avenue, NW, Washington, D.C. Henry Hardenbergh, 1900–1901; addition, Hardy Holtzman Pfeiffer and Vlastimil Koubek, 1979–86. The large addition is set back from the façade of the original building in a series of progressive planes.*

is located in Washington's oldest historic district, amid a collection of small, brick eighteenth- and nineteenth-century buildings. The mixed-use project originally contained a bank and five apartments; it is now the Mongolian Embassy. Entirely new construction, it replaced a gas station on a corner of M Street where it joins Pennsylvania Avenue. The multi-light windows, lunettes, and fanlights, and gable roof with dormers and chimneys refer to the Georgian neighborhood, while the Doric half-columns acknowledge the Greek Revival porticoes traditionally featured on banks. The abrupt termination of an architrave supported by one column, columns framing a non-doorway, and a parapet that curves downward instead of up are some of the deliberate irregularities, intended to jolt viewers out of their placidity and see these elements in a new way. And the idiosyncratic assembly of these common architectural elements clearly differentiates this building from its eighteenth-century neighbors.

Two postmodern projects that appeared in the early 1980s used repetition to evoke a sense of playfulness, or perhaps irony. Hardy Holzman Pfeiffer's addition to the Willard Hotel (1979–86, with Vlastimil Koubek) faced the challenge of augmenting the elaborate Beaux Arts hotel designed by Henry Hardenbergh in 1900 for a prominent site on Pennsylvania Avenue (Figure 2). The architects attached the addition far back from the front façade, bringing it forward in advancing planes to form a U-shaped courtyard. The original exuberant mansard roof was repeated on the addition, but with even more dormers and larger bull's-eye windows. To focus additional attention on the overblown roof, the elaborate rusticated stone walls of the original building were reduced to plain brick on the addition. This is not a design solution that would work on a tight urban site. But here, visible across the broad intersection of Pennsylvania Avenue and 14th Street, the addition can be seen in its entirety. The repetition of the advancing planes caused one critic to comment that it looked as though the Willard had puppies. Was this an homage to the original design, or a mockery? Or was it both, incorporating the double-coding that is integral to postmodernism?

Similarly, the Kerns Group repeated the roofline of the Tudor Revival apartment building at 1915 I Street, NW (Frank Russell White, 1917, altered 1981–82, 1988), when it added four stories (Figure 3). Overlooked by comparison to the Willard Hotel project, this smaller mid-block project, which won a Progressive Architecture Honor Award in 1981, retains both charm and playfulness. However, as preservation, it suffers; only the façade of the original building survives. A National Park Service author cited it as an unacceptable solution to the problem of an addition to an historic building.[12] The building was not designated a landmark and the project did not undergo formal review. As design, though, the addition is more successful, drawing attention to the original building's most distinctive feature, its roofline, by imitating it, yet stepping back from the façade to avoid overpowering it.

After some of these surprising, even startling, projects in the early 1980s, postmodernism in Washington settled into a more conservative mode, which was ultimately more sensitive to historic buildings.[13] Wit and playfulness evolved into healthy respect and a more understated neighborliness. Isolated elements were not misused in the way that single columns and exaggerated rooflines had been in the earlier projects. For example, the Bond Building, a Beaux Arts office building at 14th Street and New York Avenue designed by George S. Cooper in 1901, received additions to its roof and sides in 1987 (Figure 4). The project involved preservation of only the façade of the building and filling out the building envelope to the greatest extent possible. Four new stories added above the original roofline are set back, but are clearly visible due to the building's site. For the façade of the new stories, architect Shalom Baranes maintained the rounded corner and used paired columns and gable dormer-like elements playing off of the original façade. The infill buildings attached to the ends of the original façade are more subtle, copying more strictly the neoclassical vocabulary of the original building. The addition is bold enough to demand recognition in its own right, engaging in a postmodernist conversation with the past.

On Capitol Hill, architects face a different set of considerations when designing additions. The neighborhood experienced some development early in the nineteenth century, but mostly takes its character from the

FIGURES 3 AND 4. *(Left) Office building, 1915 I Street, NW, Washington, D.C. Russell White, 1917; additions, Kerns Group, 1982, 1988. The repetition of the significant cornice element produces a clever effect. (Right) Bond Building, 14th Street and New York Avenue, NW, Washington, D.C. George S. Cooper, 1901; addition, Shalom Baranes, 1987. Rather than defer to the original building, the addition wraps the original façade on both sides and top producing a lively dialog.*

two- and three-story brick row houses erected in the decades after the Civil War. Multi-story, rectangular, brick bay windows dominate the façades of these narrow buildings. One of the most masterful architects to cope with this late nineteenth-century neighborhood is Amy Weinstein, who brings a Furnessian aesthetic to her use of materials and color. For a vacant lot at 317 Massachusetts Avenue, NE, she designed an office building that acknowledged the characteristic Capitol Hill row houses (Figure 5). On the three projecting bays, the upper wall became a mere screen that acknowledged the vernacular while proving its irrelevance. Dark glazed bricks accenting the red brick walls and the second-story entrance recessed behind a wide round arch are also features found on nearby row houses. Yet the building's difference is obvious, and postmodernism's tension is preserved.

Nearby at 518 C Street, NE, on a corner site where Massachusetts and Maryland avenues intersect to form Stanton Square, Weinstein played off the idea of a church—not only the church located diagonally opposite, but generic late nineteenth-century churches that commonly occupied corner sites

FIGURES 5 AND 6. *(Above) Office building, 317 Massachusetts Avenue, NE, Washington, D.C. Amy Weinstein, 1986. The bay windows of nearby nineteenth-century townhouses inspired the façade of this new infill building. (Right) Office building, 518 C Street, NE, Washington, D.C. Amy Weinstein, 1991. The façade of this office building in the Capitol Hill Historic District refers to the church located across the street.*

in Washington. In 1991 she designed an office building that has ecclesiastical elements such as a corner tower, bays that repeat like buttresses on the side, and a gabled entrance. The building's colorful patterned brickwork, stubby clustered columns, and slate roof recalled Ruskinian Gothic church architecture (Figure 6). It holds the corner well, while stepping down to relate to the small mid-nineteenth-century house next door. Tensions between its nineteenth-century church aesthetic and twentieth-century office function create a lively dialogue. It represents a level of design that demonstrates how postmodernist additions in historic neighborhoods can be successful by creating solutions that enhance settings and engage historic buildings, while neither deferring to nor disrespecting their neighbors.

Each of the projects discussed in this paper benefited from postmodernism's influence, which offered clever, sometimes witty ways to respect—and sometimes to question—the original building or neighborhood. Through these, and hundreds of similar projects in Washington and elsewhere, the reciprocal relationship between preservation and postmodernism begins to emerge. The constraints of preservation projects offered postmodernist designers a starting point for the historicism on which they drew. Postmodernism influenced preservation too, by providing dynamic, inventive solutions. Offering compatibility without being subservient, postmodern projects energized preservation designs. Through the difference and duality inherent in their use of irony, postmodernist additions distinguished new from old in original and lively ways, enriching their environment while respecting the historic buildings.

Although it is difficult to date the end of postmodernism, it is clear that by the late 1990s it had passed. Recently, architectural critic Robert Campbell called for a postmodern revival, citing "respect for context" as one of the movement's virtues.[14] However, since the events of September 11, the use of irony is not likely to return in the near future. The historicism popularized by postmodernism continues to survive, but without its reflexive quality, the knowing wink, it threatens to become cloying and unchallenging. Whatever direction the architectural scene takes, preservationists should continue to embrace the richness that postmodernism gave to historic districts rather than return to the mediocrity of the least objectionable new building or addition. Postmodernism advanced historic preservation by bringing viable solutions to difficult design problems: new construction that did not ignore or overwhelm historic fabric, but through historical references, offered ironic commentary to distinguish past and future. Postmodernism honored and preserved historic buildings even as it gently mocked them, and to a certain extent preservationists themselves. But we can survive a little criticism, can't we? ●

(Endnotes)
The author gratefully acknowledges the comments and thoughts of David Ames, Richard Wagner, Richard Longstreth, David Maloney, Mark Schara, Julie Reisenweber, and the participants in the Third National Forum on Preservation Practice.

1 Although the critics of postmodernism are numerous, I will cite just one: Stewart Brand, *How Buildings Learn: What Happens After They're Built* (London: Phoenix, 1984), 56. On defining postmodernism, Charles Jencks, *The Language of Post-Modern Architecture*, 6th ed., (New York: Rizzoli, 1991), 149; Magali Sarfatti Larson, *Behind the Postmodern Facade: Architectural Change in Late Twentieth-Century America* (Berkeley: University of California Press, 1993), 154. Philip Langdon defines contextualism as "design that is strongly linked to, and supportive of, its immediate physical surroundings" in "Avant Garde Against Humanity: The Rise and Fall of Anti-Social Architecture," *The American Enterprise Online* (January/February 2002), http://www.taemag.com.

2 Histories of the preservation movement include Charles B. Hosmer, Jr., *Presence of the Past: A History of the Preservation Movement in the United States before Williamsburg* (New York: G. P. Putnam's Sons, 1965); Charles B. Hosmer, Jr., *Preservation Comes of Age: From Williamsburg to the National Trust, 1926–1949* (Charlottesville: University Press of Virginia for the Preservation Press, 1981); William J. Murtagh, *Keeping Time: The History and Theory of Preservation in America* (New York: Sterling Publishing Co., 1993); and Norman Tyler, *Historic Preservation: An Introduction to its History, Principles, and Practice* (New York: W. W. Norton, 2000).

3 Alan Gowans, *Styles and Types of North American Architecture: Social Function and Cultural Expression* (New York: Harper Collins, 1992), 354–55; Mark Gelernter, *A History of American Architecture: Buildings in Their Cultural and Technological Context* (Hanover: University Press of New England, 1999), 294–96.

4 Heinrich Klotz, *The History of Postmodern Architecture*, English translation, (Cambridge: MIT, 1988), 4, 421; Larson, *Behind the Postmodern Facade*, 154; Charles Jencks, *The Post-Modern Reader* (London: Academy Editions, 1992), 6.

5 Gowans, *Styles and Types*, 354. On rhetoric, see the first chapter of Murtagh, *Keeping Time*, which is titled "The Language of Preservation."

6 On Moore, Klotz, *History of Postmodern Architecture*, 130. On Graves, Klotz, *History of Postmodern Architecture*, 327. On Johnson, full quote is "Idiosyncratic. Self-indulgent. Frivolous ... This preposterous design is perhaps a logical denouement for decades of increasingly mannered historicism." Paul Goldberger, *The Skyscraper* (New York: Alfred A. Knopf, 1985), 153.

7 Jencks, *The Post-Modern Reader*, 6; Robert Venturi, *Complexity and Contradiction in Architecture*, 2nd ed., (New York: Museum of Modern Art, 1977), 116; Klotz, *History of Postmodern Architecture*, 153; Larson, *Behind the Postmodern Facade*, 180.

8 Tyler, *Historic Preservation*, 140. Secretary of the Interior's Standards for Rehabilitation available at http://www.cr.nps.gov/local-law/arch_stnds.

9 Herbert Muschamp, "Measuring Buildings Without a Yardstick," *New York Times*, July 22, 2001.

10 Klotz, *History of Postmodern Architecture*, 420–21; Jencks, *Language of Post-Modern Architecture*, 10.

11 The Historic Landmark and Historic District Act of 1978 (D.C. Law 2-144) governs landmarks and historic districts. By the Old Georgetown Act of 1950, the Commission of Fine Arts also reviews alterations in Georgetown. The Commission of Fine Arts and the National Capital Planning Commission review federal projects as well.

12 This project, though, was cited as not adhering to the *Secretary of the Interior's Standards for Rehabilitation*, illustrated in Kay D. Weeks, *Preservation Brief 14: Exterior Additions to Historic Buildings: Preservation Concerns* (Heritage Preservation Services, National Park Service, 1986). Available at http://www2.cr.nps.gov/tps/briefs/brief14.htm.

13 Gelernter, *History of American Architecture* (304), notes that "eventually, like puns, the visual jokes paled" and maintains that the 1980s saw more accurate revivals of traditional styles nationwide.

14 Robert Campbell, "Critique," *Architectural Record* (February 2002): 53.

PART FOUR
Engineering and Preservation Design

■ KEEPING THE VOLUME UP

Infill and Adaptive Reuse of Atlantic City's Auditorium

MICHAEL C. HENRY, PE, AIA
Principal Engineer & Architect
Watson & Henry Associates

This paper considers the design issues and preservation philosophy for the recent (2001) tax credit-eligible rehabilitation of the monumental Auditorium of the Atlantic City Convention Hall, a National Historic Landmark. This paper includes an overview of the design and preservation approaches to the rehabilitation of selected long-span buildings.

Since Roman times, long-span buildings have awed the public and challenged the architects, engineers, and master builders who designed and constructed them. Early long-span structures, such as the Pantheon (118–28 AD) or the *duomo* of Santa Maria del Fiore in Florence (1420–39), typically served as religious structures. Their monumentality and symbolic value contributed to their longevity. In the late nineteenth and early twentieth centuries, a significant number of long-span structures, made possible by advances in engineered trusses and metal fabrication, were constructed as convention and exhibit halls, arenas, train sheds, and aircraft hangars. In the late twentieth century, many of these structures were rehabilitated or adapted for reuse. Examples include: the Reading Terminal in Philadelphia (1893, clear span: 268 feet, clear height: 90 feet); Union Station in St. Louis (1894, clear span: 141 feet, clear height: 140 feet); Gare d'Orsay in Paris (1900, clear span: 131 feet, clear height: 105 feet), and Union Station in Washington, D.C. (1907, clear span: 125 feet, clear height: 96 feet). The Auditorium of the Atlantic City Convention Hall (1929, clear span: 335 feet, clear height: 131 feet), was considered the largest clear-span building in the world.

The engineered roof trusses of these structures, in various geometries, allowed generous column-free spans, satisfying functional and programmatic requirements for uninterrupted floor areas. These long-span structures also provided the opportunity to make strong architectural and technological statements simply with their sheer size; in fact, "bragging rights" seem to have been an important element in the boosterism that accompanied these buildings.

During World War II, long-span engineering was applied to airship hangers such as Airdocks #1 and #2 (1942) at Tustin Marine Corps Air Station in California. Airdock #1 spanned 328 feet (190 feet clear height) with steel trusses while Airdock #2 spanned 298 feet (177 feet clear height). In the late twentieth century, enclosed arenas such as the 1965 Astrodome in Houston, Texas, and the 1976 Kingdome in Seattle, Washington (demolished in 2001), sported long-span, steel lattice-roof frame and ribbed concrete shell dome, respectively. The Astrodome (clear span: 710 feet, clear height: 208 feet) and the Kingdome (clear span: 660 feet, clear height: 250 feet) effectively doubled the span of the then half-century-old Atlantic City Auditorium.

Many nineteenth- and early twentieth-century long-span structures in the United States have been listed on state and/or the National Register because of their technical innovation, architectural significance, or historical and cultural significance. Abroad, historic long-span structures such as the Pantheon in Rome and the Duomo in Florence have gained protection by being listed as World Heritage Sites or on national lists of historic buildings. Unfortunately, many other examples have been abandoned or razed. The challenges in successful rehabilitation and reuse of long-span structures lie not only in the technical aspects of such an endeavor, but also in adapting an appropriate, economically viable new use within a large-volume building while maintaining the monumental spatial character of the architecture.

Preservation Challenge of Long-Span Structures

The rehabilitation, restoration, or preservation of any historic structure involves risks, capital, and skilled labor. Long-span structures, due to their size, structure, and technology, magnify these challenges and risks. The challenges commonly encountered in any preservation project include: accommodating new uses, dealing with archaic interior and exterior materials, making structural upgrades and repairs, meeting contemporary life-safety requirements, and retrofitting electrical, heating, and air conditioning systems. Monumental long-span structures introduce the additional challenge of identifying new revenue-generating uses, maintaining the interior volume of the space while creating smaller subspaces for the new uses, creating a definable sense of scale that relates the larger space to the new elements, and defining an architectural vocabulary to express the relationship between the historic and new work.

The core design challenge for historic long-span structures is the introduction of interior infill construction without diminishing the fabric, scale, or volume of an architecturally homogenous monumental space.

The late twentieth-century rehabilitations of four historic long-span structures (Union Station, St. Louis; Gare d'Orsay, Paris; Union Station, Washington, D.C., and Reading Terminal, Philadelphia) illustrate the varied design approaches to the above challenges.

Union Station, St. Louis, Missouri, built 1894, rehabilitated 1985 [1]

Theodore C. Link won the 1891 design competition for St. Louis's Union Station with his Richardsonian Romanesque design. He joined with Louis Millet to design the headhouse and midway. Engineered by George H. Pegram, the train shed was the largest ever built, covering 11.5 acres. Union Station was designated a National Historic Landmark in 1976 and closed two years later. In 1985, the station reopened as a mixed-use project containing two hotels, retail and food spaces, and entertainment and outdoor recreation areas. While the restoration and adaptive use of the Richardsonian Romanesque headhouse and midway were straightforward, the design for adaptive use of the train shed was more difficult. The train shed consists of a flattened vault roof 140 feet in height with five longitudinal bays providing an overall width of 606 feet. The center bay has a clear span of over 141 feet, with the flanking and outer bays spanning over 139 feet and 90 feet, respectively. Elegant for the lightness of its exposed structure, the train shed is frankly utilitarian in design. The architects for the rehabilitation, Hellmuth, Obata & Kassabaum, retained the steel roof structure and half of the wood roof deck area. The remaining roof area was replaced with glass, increasing the apparent lightness of the structure as well as introducing natural light. Under the shed, a set of "neighborhood" buildings house the new uses, including a 480-room hotel, retail stores, restaurants and food areas, a public plaza and park complete with a lake, and automobile parking. The free-standing infill buildings are purposefully understated, using contemporary materials and style to contrast with the historic roof structure. The height of new construction was minimized to avoid visual intrusion into the historic space.

Gare d'Orsay, Paris, France, built 1900, rehabilitated 1986 [2]

The French architect Victor Laloux was selected to design the Gare d'Orsay in Paris. The train station and hotel were to serve as the Paris terminus for travel to/from southwestern France. Proximity of the station to the Louvre and other historic buildings demanded a sensitive exterior design. Laloux accomplished this by wrapping the French Renaissance Revival-style hotel structure along the cast iron and glass barrel-vaulted train shed. Completed in 1900, the Gare d'Orsay remained a train station until 1969. In 1973 the hotel closed. In 1977 it was determined that the building would be renovated as a museum devoted to the arts of the nineteenth century. The conversion of Gare d'Orsay to Musée d'Orsay was completed in 1986.

The 131-foot-wide, 453-foot-long, and 105-foot-high nave-like train shed was the focal point of the rehabilitation. New museum galleries are organized along a pedestrian "street" at the track level, with most new infill construction set below the line of the original balcony. The balcony parapets and two massive end stair/elevator towers project into the volume of the historic shed. New infill construction is strongly expressed in contemporary design, in direct contrast to the vocabulary and ornament of the original building.

Union Station, Washington, D.C., NHL, built 1907, rehabilitated 1988 [3,4]

Designed by Daniel H. Burnham in the Beaux Arts style interpretation of the Diocletian Baths, Washington D.C.'s Union Station was the world's largest train station when completed in 1907. Measuring 760 feet long by 344 feet wide, it contained two monumental clear-span spaces, the headhouse and the concourse. The station housed a hospital, mortuary, restaurants, police station, swimming pool, bowling alley, and basketball court. In 1969 Union Station was declared a National Historic Landmark. In 1981, the United States Congress passed the Union Station Act, funding the restoration of the headhouse and adaptive reuse of the shed for retail space and Amtrak. The architects were Harry Weese & Associates for the headhouse and Benjamin Thompson & Associates (BTA) for the train concourse. The renovated building, completed in 1988, primarily serves as a train station, while housing more than 100 retail shops and food concessions as well as nine movie theatres.

Weese's treatment of the headhouse was a straightforward restoration with highly sensitive, well-executed introduction of new design elements. Thompson's adaptive reuse of the concourse was more challenging. The shallow vaulted concourse (125 feet wide, 45 feet high and 600 feet long) was originally an open flat-floored space under a coffered and glazed ceiling that concealed the steel structural trusses. BTA's design included restoration of the ceiling, removing the cast iron and glazed partitions in the train waiting areas (leaving only the cast iron entry frames), inserting a mezzanine structure to increase the available retail space, and opening a portion of the concourse's floor to allow views to the new lower-level food court. BTA up-lighted the vaulted ceiling to enhance its visual effect and utilized glazed pavilions for the mezzanine to foster a sense of transparency and reduce visual intrusion into the monumental space.

Reading Terminal, Philadelphia, Pennsylvania, NHL, built 1893, phased rehabilitation 1985 through 1999 [5, 6]

Philadelphia's Reading Terminal is composed of a Venetian Revival headhouse designed by Francis Kimball and a utilitarian train shed set above a street-level urban market. Built in 1893, Reading Terminal was used until 1984. Unlike other train station projects, restoration and adaptive reuse of the train shed and headhouse were undertaken as separate projects. In 1985, the headhouse underwent partial restoration and, in 1999, work was completed for its adaptive use as a convention hotel and public entry to the Pennsylvania Convention Center. In 1993-94, the train shed was adapted as a convention hall, now linked to the Pennsylvania Convention Center. On street-level the building retains its original use as the Reading Terminal Market.

Architects Thompson, Ventulett, Stainback & Associates and the Vitetta Group were responsible for design for adaptive use of the train shed. The train shed uses three-hinged arch metal trusses to span 260 feet with a floor-to-ceiling height of 90 feet. The rehabilitation retains the shed's trusses and wood roof deck. At the headhouse end, the shed retains its original height and width forming a "great hall." At the track end, originally open, a new multi-level infill structure accommodates conference rooms, a ballroom, and service facilities. The new construction is contemporary in style to contrast with the appearance of the historic shed.

The Restoration and Rehabilitation of the Atlantic City Convention Hall's Auditorium

> It is an exaltation of one's idea of space, so that entrance seems not so much a going-in as a going-out, while the supreme beauty of the structure is a splendidly sustained simplicity of the whole, a vast enclosed clearness.
>
> —*The World's Largest Convention Hall, brochure, Atlantic City, New Jersey, 1929*

FIGURES 1 AND 2. *(Left) Aerial View, Atlantic City Convention Center, 1997. Photographer unknown. Photo provided by Martin Photography, Inc. (Right) Rendering, Auditorium interior, circa 1920. Artist Unknown. Postcard by E.C. Kropp Co., 1950.*

Seldom described or referred to without a string of superlatives, even today the Atlantic City Convention Hall tests the power of words to describe the size of the space and its features. The size of the Auditorium impresses current visitors, much as it did early twentieth-century conventioneers (Figures 1 and 2). However, the Auditorium's significance goes beyond its record-setting size. Completed in 1929, it was a state-of-the-art, sophisticated machine for entertainment designed to attract national and international audiences to Atlantic City and its boardwalk, grand hotels, amusements, and sideshows. To accomplish this, the Auditorium not only achieved feats of structural engineering, but also pushed the limits of electric lighting. The Auditorium ceiling, a 220,000-square-foot barrel vault of silver-painted acoustical tiles, became the reflector for dazzling color light shows, anticipating today's laser light entertainment by over sixty years. For centuries, natural light had been used to define monumental interior architecture, but the designers of the Auditorium boldly brought an electric sun inside, creating sunsets and sunrises on the ceiling overhead and consciously eschewing exterior windows and natural light. The innovative lighting also rendered an impressive palette of architectural finishes and colors with themes that stretched from the seashore of Atlantic City to the Mediterranean. The proscenium featured exotic architectural styles, with its neo-Assyrian pylons and capitals set above steaming basins on tripods. Overhead, the barrel vault, ceiling tiles, and loggia recalled the monumental public baths and gymnasia of Rome. Details such as sea monsters, scallop shells, ibis, and sea turtles abounded. Seals of forty-eight states and territories, as well as flags of many nations, ringed the interior. Enormously successful, the Convention Hall attracted conventions, celebrities, ordinary citizens, Presidents of the United States, and the Miss America pageant for decades.

In 1925 Atlantic City commissioned the Boston office of Lockwood-Greene Engineers, Inc., an association of engineers and architects, to design the Atlantic City Convention Hall. Walter W. Cook and George F. Blout were its chief designers. The Convention Hall opened with an elaborate three-day ceremony beginning on May 31, 1929, coinciding with the Golden Jubilee of Light, a national tribute to Thomas Edison marking the fiftieth anniversary of the perfection of the incandescent bulb. Unfortunately, just three years later the Auditorium's elaborate ceiling lighting was abandoned due to the Depression. To lower costs, less expensive pendant floodlights were punched through the ceiling, illuminating the floor but leaving the ceiling in shadow for the next seven decades.

In September 1983 the American Society of Civil Engineers designated the Atlantic City Convention Hall as a National Historic Civil Engineering Landmark. Four years later it was listed on the National Register of Historic Places and as a National Historic Landmark. In 1993 it was added to the New Jersey State Register of Historic Places. But by the late 1990s, the future of the convention hall as a convention and exhibition space was threatened. The Auditorium failed to meet contemporary expectations for seating, sightlines, revenue-generating concessions, barrier-free access, and event rigging, lighting, and restroom facilities. In 1997, the hall's exhibition venue was supplanted by the new Atlantic City Convention Center. As the new center was being developed, the New Jersey Sports and Exposition Authority commissioned a feasibility study for the adaptive use of the historic hall. In 1996, the Authority retained Ewing Cole Cherry Brott, Inc. as the prime architect/engineer for rehabilitation of the Auditorium, and Rosser International as the arena consultant. Watson & Henry Associates were retained by Ewing Cole Cherry Brott as preservation architects and engineers. The rehabilitation of the Atlantic City Convention Hall commenced in 1998, executed in phases until completed in autumn of 2001. The New Jersey Historic Preservation Office reviewed the work, as did the National Park Service, since historic tax credits were used to help finance the rehabilitation.

The Auditorium of the Atlantic City Convention Hall is the primary space in the building that also houses a 5,000-seat ballroom and the world's largest pipe organ. The Auditorium is 452 feet long and 344 feet wide under a clear-span barrel vault ceiling springing from 38 feet above the floor level at the sidewalls and rising to 130 feet at the centerline. The principal interior architectural elements of the Auditorium include the ceiling, the original lighting, loggia, proscenium endwall and stage, musicians' balcony, and the seating balcony. The Auditorium's design reflects its original function as a large, column-free space for exhibitions and conventions. Its structural frame is similar to those of the large, barrel-arched train sheds discussed earlier. The windowless Auditorium, however, conceals its structural framework with interior finishes. Ten three-hinge, arched box trusses support the Auditorium roof and divide the ceiling into nine recessed bays between the north and south endwalls. The arched box trusses, ceiling bays, and endwalls were originally clad with acoustical tiles made of compressed plant fiber. The original tiles were perforated and measured two feet by four feet. Along the edges smaller, unperforated border tiles were installed, set off from larger tiles by flat-profiled wood moldings. At a distance, the ceiling tiles suggested the terra cotta-clad ceiling of a Roman public bath, evoking both monumentality and permanence in the major public assembly space; close-up, the lightweight, face-nailed and field-cut tiles revealed a remarkable absence of careful craft.

The dramatic effect of the Auditorium's volume was maximized by the pioneering application of indirect lighting. In their earliest architectural applications, lightbulbs were exposed, almost decorative features themselves. However, in the Auditorium, the designers concealed the lamps behind prismatic glass windows on each side of the trusses, aiming them at the silver-painted ceiling. An electro-mechanical system controlled lighting intensity and color, the latter through the synchronized control of colored gel filters in front of the floodlamps. The indirect lighting accentuated the ceiling, giving scale to the trusses and expanding the visual sense of the space and volume.

At the base of the ceiling, a balcony concourse runs along three sides of the building, enclosed by a loggia of tripartite arches set between the trusses. The Romanesque-derived column capitals depict mythic land and sea creatures and motifs. The seals of the forty-eight states and territories (at the time of the Auditorium's construction) and the Great Seal of the United States are located in the spandrels between the arches. Above the arches, between and flanking the seals, are flagpole mounts that originally carried the flags of seventy-five nations.

Below the concourse loggia, a shallow, steeply-raked balcony was cantilevered from the sidewalls; the U-shaped balcony continued across the south endwall; the balcony seating was interrupted by a projecting musicians' balcony centered on the south endwall.

The monumental proscenium opening is set in the north endwall. Over 100 feet wide and nearly 80 feet high, it is framed on each side by broad, flat pylons with rusticated joints rising 88 feet. The pylons, Neo-Assyrian in style, are cleaved at the top with opposing eagles and terminate in a flat denticulated cornice. Above the pylons' cornice are 16-foot-high capitals with cornice and

stepped roof. The left capital features the seal of the City of Atlantic City, and
the right the seal of the State of New Jersey. Each seal is backlighted leaded
glass. Scrolled columns are engaged on the interior jamb of the pylons, also in
the Neo-Assyrian style.

The proscenium arch spans 104 feet and is 18 feet high. The arch
includes an entablature that springs from the capitals of the scrolled columns
featuring alternating recessed and diamond basket-weave patterned panels
capped with a denticulated molding. Above the entablature is a frieze of
recessed panels, and above that a cornice composed of a chevron molding
below a lozenge fret molding. Centered on the arch is a leaded, backlighted
glass globe with the letters "WPG" for World's Play Ground. The globe rests
on the entablature and is buttressed with stylized eagles and cornucopiae. A
double band of rays rings its upper hemisphere.

The proscenium pylons are set out from the endwall by recessed lighting
troughs along the outer jamb and along the top and sides of the pylon capitals.
The cornice of the proscenium arch is also set off from the endwall by a
lighting trough, with yet another trough set in the arch in the top edge of
the entablature. Each lighting trough was finished with reflective silver paint
and fitted with a continuous row of floodlights. Tripod-supported basins
with steam outlets and uplights originally were set at the base of each pylon;
these disappeared in the 1930s. A mythological mural featuring Neptune and
mermaids is painted on the 25-foot-high valance under the proscenium arch.
The 1929 skyline of Atlantic City is depicted on the horizon of the scene,
including the Convention Hall and famous hotels such as the Traymore and
the Marlborough-Blenheim. Originally a stepped curtain framed the top and
sides of the mural; later, a modern curtain concealed the mural entirely. The
stage opening is protected by an asbestos fire-safety curtain painted with a
scene depicting a sailing ship, perhaps one of Columbus, framed by vertical
decorative borders featuring the Atlantic City seal. The colors in the fire curtain
are primarily shades of blue, green, and gold. Flanking the proscenium are two
quadripartite, round-arch openings set above shallow, bracketed balconies and
fitted with elaborate tracery grilles featuring coastal flora and birds. The organ
pipe chambers are set behind the grilles.

The original barrel-vault truss enclosures and endwalls were originally
painted with aluminum-colored paint set off with simple, broad, flat wood
moldings and picked out with non-reflective blue, green, and gold paint.
Decorative elements, such as the proscenium surround, the loggia columns
and capitals, and the organ grilles were elaborately painted in highly detailed
and sophisticated treatments, including glazes, gold, silver, and metallic paints.

All together, the Auditorium's finishes and lighting were designed to enclose viewers in a shimmering, glowing, changeable sensation. One contemporary account shows its effectiveness:

> Throughout the convention hall, a tone of quiet dignity, pleasingly merged with the soothing colors of the sea and sky, has been used in all decorative effects, while floods of pure and tinted light present an infinite array of radiant scenes, restful to the eye and temper. The huge trusses and ceiling are of neutral tone, giving full effect to the many color combinations of an extraordinarily elaborate lighting system, while the balcony faces are in two tones of green and gold. The proscenium arch, of truly regal splendor, and marked instantly upon entering the Auditorium, is an outstanding artistic achievement, with perfect blending of verde, cobalt, Nile greens, and gold gleaming richly under indirect and flood lighting. In fact, by utilization of an entirely new and original principle, lighting of the stage and Auditorium has been so designed as to permit not only the usual projection, spotlighting, and special display of feature objects, but an endless number of color effects, including the warmly gorgeous hues of sunset and sunrise, and illumination of the great ceiling in all manner of shimmering shades and tints. In similar perfection, based upon exact science, lighting of the entire building has been so carefully arranged as to provoke instant admiration.[7]

By 1997, however, the Auditorium's ceiling had become severely deteriorated as well as being altered by the introduction of new, unflattering lighting. The original lighting system had been abandoned as a cost-cutting measure early in the Depression. The elaborate decorative-painting scheme had been painted over. The stage curtain and valance were removed. At the south endwall, mechanical rooms and exposed ductwork intruded into the loggia. However, in spite of these problems, nearly all of the original architecturally significant fabric was intact at the start of the project (Figure 3).

The Restoration and Rehabilitation of the Auditorium

Based on a mid-1990s feasibility study, the New Jersey Sports and Exposition Authority concluded that the Auditorium should be rehabilitated for use as a special events arena incorporating a fixed seating bowl with a capacity of 12,000 to 15,000 people. The new arena would host indoor sports, such as ice hockey, boxing, and wrestling, as well as live performances, either on the

FIGURE 3. *Auditorium interior prior to restoration, 1996.*
Photo: Watson & Henry Associates.

end stage or on a center rink stage. Ewing Cole Cherry Brott, Inc., and Rosser International, Inc., arena specialists, evaluated the existing facility and developed the program for the new functions. The evaluation found that the original Auditorium did not meet contemporary functional needs, including adequate seating with appropriate sightlines, compliance with barrier-free access regulations and emergency egress, adequate concession space, restrooms, performer and athletic rooms, and modern rigging, lighting, and sound systems. In order to make the Auditorium competitive with similar the building had to be brought up to modern standards.

While the original flat-floor exhibition use was no longer a determinant, continued use of the Auditorium as a sports/special events arena would be consistent with the criterion of one of the Secretary of the Interior's Standards for the Treatment of Historic Properties. However, updating the building for continued function as an event space would require significant interventions. These interventions would also need to meet the standards.

Concurrent with the facility assessment and programming, Watson & Henry Associates researched the history of the building. They reviewed copies of the original drawings, researched newspaper accounts of the 1929 dedication, located old photographs of the Auditorium, and obtained copies of the original catalogs of the 1929 lighting and electrical equipment. In addition, the preservation architects/engineers conducted an assessment and inventory of the existing fabric to help understand the original appearance of the Auditorium as well as the perception of its architecture by visitors. Watson & Henry Associates also identified the architecturally significant and character-defining aspects of the Auditorium, such as its record-setting dimensions, details, and features, innovative engineering, and creative indirect lighting.

Watson & Henry Associates developed a preservation philosophy for the project to serve as a guide for design decisions, including how to preserve the surviving significant architectural features, which missing architectural features should be recreated, which existing architectural features could be removed, and what new architectural features introduced in the building, such as a

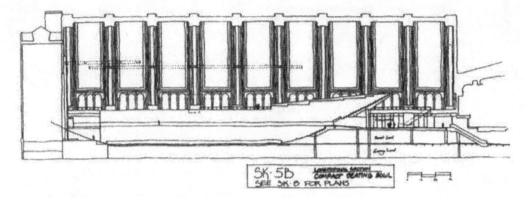

FIGURE 4. *Conceptual section through new Seating Bowl, 1996. Illustration courtesy of Ewing Cole Cherry Brott, PC, Architects.*

seating bowl, should look like. The preservation philosophy primarily drew upon three of the Secretary of the Interior's Standards for the Treatment of Historic Properties. The Standards for Preservation were applied to the proscenium arch and the north and south endwalls, the Standards for Restoration were applied to the ceiling, indirect lighting systems and loggias, while the Standards for Rehabilitation were applied below the balcony concourse loggia. Watson & Henry Associates also developed guidelines for the new freestanding fixed seating bowl in order to maintain the openness of the original space, provide clear views of the proscenium, limit encroachment on the loggias, and minimize the size of rigging, lighting, and sound systems. The guidelines also called for retaining the critical viewpoint from the south endwall, the "musician's balcony."

From a preservation point of view, the seating bowl was the most critical design aspect of the rehabilitation. Seating-bowl geometry is a function of capacity, code requirements, sightlines, barrier-free legislation, structural considerations, and the floor area required by events, such as ice hockey. Several bowl configurations were evaluated for fit in the existing space, for function, and for effect on the historic fabric. Variations included retaining the original balcony, depressing the event floor, and constructing a two-tiered bowl. It became clear that the existing balcony would severely constrain the geometry of a new seating bowl. This led to a design in which the original balcony, not considered to be of primary architectural significance, would be removed, allowing the construction of a functional freestanding seating bowl within the Auditorium. Set as an object within the historic interior, the top of the new bowl connects to the historic building along the side balcony concourse and loggia (Figure 3). A new circulation and concession concourse wraps around the back of the new seating bowl, and opens to the Auditorium above (Figure 4). At the new concourse level, the seating bowl incorporates a

FIGURES 5 AND 6. *(Left) Atlantic City Convention Hall, Auditorium interior after restoration. Photo: Tom Crane and Jeffrey Totaro, 2001. (Right) Atlantic City Convention Hall, Auditorium interior and new seating bowl after restoration. Photo: Tom Crane and Jeffrey Totaro, 2001.*

musicians' balcony, replicating a key viewpoint of the original balcony. The new bowl and concourse are in contemporary materials, but subordinate to the original fabric. Color palettes for new work were derived from, but do not match, the historic Auditorium colors. Samples of the balcony seats were salvaged, restored, and reinstalled in circulation areas (Figures 5 and 6).

The original combustible ceiling tiles, contaminated with asbestos, could not be retained; they were removed and replicated in custom fabricated sheet metal for the ceiling bays and in glass-fiber reinforced gypsum for the truss enclosures. The original ceiling tiles were spray-painted with aluminum reflective paint. Test application of the same paint on the replacement tiles resulted in excessive glare from the lighting system. Therefore, the ceiling was painted with a less-reflective paint that better achieved the original effect. The new lighting system recreates the effect of the 1929 original indirect lighting of the ceiling. The new system includes computer-controlled fixtures at the base of each ceiling bay and backlighted windows in the truss enclosures. Signage design draws from the original iconographic vocabulary of the Auditorium's decorative elements of real and mythical sea animals. In the new graphics, these symbols are abstracted to be more organic and less symmetrical forms than the originals. Finally, the historic decorative paint scheme was restored and the stained glass, state seals mural, and painted fire curtain were conserved. The project received a National Preservation Award from the National Trust for Historic Preservation in 2003.

Acknowledgments

The in-depth investigation into the history of the Atlantic City Convention Hall by Penelope S. Watson, AIA, Principal at Watson & Henry Associates

(W&HA), provided the basis for development of the preservation philosophy of the project; this philosophy was validated when the National Park Service certified the application for the Rehabilitation Tax Credit. Leila Y. Hamroun, Senior Graduate Architect at W&HA, was project manager for the restoration component of the Atlantic City Convention Hall, notably the restoration/ conservation of the decorative finishes by Evergreene Painting Studios. Abby Perlstein, Architectural Intern, performed much of the background research for large clear-span structures for the preparation of this paper. ⊛

(Endnotes)

1 "The Nation's Largest Single Act of Rehabilitation," *Architecture Magazine*, April 1989, 83–87.

2 "Missed connections," *Architectural Record*, March 1987, 128–39.

3 "The Rebirth of a Magnificent Monument," *Architecture Magazine*, November, 1988, 68–75.

4 "Spirit of St.Louis," *Progressive Architecture*, November,1985, 83–93.

5 "Putting a Historic Train Shed Back on Track," *Civil Engineering*, July 1994, 22–23.

6 "Philadelphia Train Shed Reopens," *Progressive Architecture*, May 1994, 35.

7 Inaugural Issue, *Auditorium Magazine*, June, 1929, 62.

▣ BEFORE THE ARCH

Some Early Architects and Engineers on the St. Louis Riverfront

CHARLES E. PETERSON, FAIA, FAPT, FSAH

U rban historians and preservationists visiting St. Louis today might be surprised to learn how the federal Historic Sites and Buildings Act of 1935 was used to justify a spectacular urban clearance on the Mississippi riverfront to build the Jefferson National Expansion Memorial with the great stainless steel arch designed by Eero Saarinen. Little has appeared in print to reveal the whole story of the memorial. It is a long story, full of contradictions and surprises. It was this writer's good fortune to be immersed in the St. Louis project from its inception in 1936 to 1947. Few people around today remember the controversy. It relates closely to what was to happen in Philadelphia in the late 1940s and early 1950s during the creation of the Independence National Historical Park.

Looking back, the outstanding figures in this St. Louis project were the civic leader Luther Ely Smith (1873–1951) (Figure 1) and the brilliant architect who designed the great steel arch, Eero Saarinen (1910–1961). Begun as a recordation and salvage project of one of the most extensive collections of historic cast iron façades in the country, the end result was an almost total defeat for the cause of historic preservation. However, on the positive side, Saarinen's arch is not only one of the most recognized monuments in the country; it is listed in the National Register of Historic Places.[1]

Early Promotions of JNEM

FIGURE 1. *Luther Ely Smith (1873-1951). St. Louis civic leader and promoter of the Jefferson National Expansion Memorial. His enduring efforts over the years to develop the riverfront finally produced the great Saarinen arch and its present setting. Courtesy of Missouri Historical Society.*

Founded under the colonial government of Spain in 1764, the frontier town of St. Louis became the capital of French Upper Louisiana when France acquired the interior of North America from Spain. After the Louisiana Purchase by the United States in 1804, St. Louis became the principal springboard for western exploration and settlement; its levee on the Mississippi River was soon crowded with steamboats. By 1870, St. Louis had become the third-largest city in the country. Four years later it was linked directly to the East by rail when the great Eads Bridge was completed. With the shift in transportation methods, the old riverfront that had been the economic hub of the city began to die. Although various schemes to revive the area were put forth, nothing happened for the next sixty years.

In 1933, during the depths of the Great Depression, times were hard in St. Louis as elsewhere. Bernard Dickmann, the newly elected Democratic mayor, had wrested city hall from the Republicans as well as delivered a lot of votes for Franklin D. Roosevelt. In the same year, Luther Ely Smith, an attorney and a Republican, emerged as chairman of a civic committee intending to build a great memorial celebrating the "Winning of the West" as well as resuscitate the city's waterfront.[2]

Under the Hoover administration, Smith had been appointed to the federal commission that oversaw the design and construction of the George Rogers Clark Memorial at Vincennes, Indiana (Figure 2). The story goes that as he was crossing the Eads Bridge into St. Louis after a meeting of the Clark Memorial Commission, the idea for the Jefferson National Expansion Memorial came to him.[3] Smith sketched out a plan for Mayor Dickmann that envisioned a memorial along the Mississippi riverfront occupying an area of some sixty blocks from the Eads Bridge south to Popular Street. Together they proposed to demolish all of the buildings in what was almost universally considered a blighted area to create a site for the new memorial.

FIGURE 2. *Early proposed architectural development by Louis LaBeaume of LaBeaume and Klein, Architects. Courtesy of National Park Service, Jefferson National Expansion Memorial (JNEM) Archives, St. Louis.*

Luther Ely Smith was energetic and resourceful, a skilled tactician with phenomenal tenacity. In January 1934, Dickmann and Smith presented plans to supporters in St. Louis for a riverfront museum complex that would memorialize trappers and traders who had made St Louis the gateway to the West. Support grew quickly. By April 1934, he and Dickmann had brought together civic and business leaders to form the Jefferson National Expansion Memorial Association. Enthusiastic about the idea, President Franklin D. Roosevelt said that he was "greatly interested in the suggestion for the Jefferson National Expansion Memorial for the St. Louis Riverfront."[4] Legislation to establish the federal Jefferson National Expansion Memorial Commission was introduced in Congress in January, passed in March, and signed into law by the President on June 14, 1934. In a congratulatory telegram dated December 18, 1934, to the Jefferson National Expansion Memorial Commission, President Roosevelt wrote:

> All good wishes for the success of your commission's efforts to recall and perpetuate the ideals the faith and courage of the pioneers who discovered and developed the great West.
> — *Franklin D. Roosevelt*

Louis LaBeaume, a noted St. Louis architect, was engaged by the association to develop the initial scheme for the memorial (Figure 2). Classically trained at Washington and Columbia universities, LaBeaume had toured Europe and worked in various offices in Boston before returning to St. Louis to work on the 1904 Louisiana Purchase Exposition.

The cost of acquiring and developing the riverfront site was estimated at $30 million. In September 1935, the City of St. Louis dutifully voted a bond issue for $7.5 million for land acquisition. Later that same year, Congress appropriated the balance. Things seemed to be moving along until Roosevelt's Attorney General refused to endorse the legality of the project because of the proposed federal funding source. Fortunately, on August 21, 1935, President Roosevelt had signed the Historic Sites and Buildings Act into law. With some quick maneuvering, the appropriation for the Jefferson National Expansion Memorial was recast to allow it to be paid for through the Historic Sites Act. With federal participation secured, the National Park Service was designated to administer the project.

The Park Service Arrives

John L. Nagle, who had been chief engineer of the Arlington Memorial Bridge project in Washington, D.C., was assigned to head the St. Louis project. A sturdy professional of competence and experience, Nagle was assigned to develop this urban project of unprecedented size and complexity, something that had never been attempted by the young bureau best known for natural parks in the West.

Arriving in 1936, Nagle immediately leased office space in the Buder Building, near to the riverfront. The author was appointed project planner, and engaged landscape architect Daniel C. Fahey of the National Capital Parks Region as his assistant. Together Fahey and the author drove from Washington to St. Louis over the great National Road (U.S. Route 40) in June of 1936. They opened their offices using packing boxes as furniture until desks, chairs, and drafting room equipment could arrive. This humble office became the first permanent presence of the National Park Service in St. Louis.

As soon as enough staff had reported, Superintendent Nagle charged the team to conduct a detailed study of the memorial site (Figure 4), examining and recording every building, street, and sidewalk prior to the area being cleared. "I want you men to know more about the site than any other living persons," said Nagle. This was a staggering task; the area consisted of forty city blocks containing over 500 structures.

Under the terms of the Historic Sites and Buildings Act of 1935, the Secretary of the Interior, through the National Park Service, was charged with surveying and researching historic and archeological sites and buildings and documenting them with drawings and photographs. In addition to this work, the team was also charged with developing a plan for the memorial on the site that would be soon cleared.

It was anticipated that as soon as the recordation and research was completed, design and construction work on the memorial would proceed quickly. This assumption meant that the St. Louis office had a number of engineers on staff, including Julian C. Spotts, who succeeded Nagle as superintendent, James Rasbach, Walter Kerlin, and Howard Gruber. Their chief activity lay in carefully closing down the streets and utilities in the memorial area and oversight of the several demolition contracts.[5] However, things did not go as planned. There was opposition to the project, which resulted in it being legally challenged seventeen times in all, dragging completion out some thirty years after inception.[6]

Architectural Staff and Site Studies

While the fate of the memorial was being litigated, the author and his staff were kept busy documenting the historic buildings. Among them was Captain Clarence E. Howard, formerly with Olmsted's office; John Albury Bryan, AIA; G. Vietor Davis; Henry Rice, Jr.; Frank Leslie; and secretary Adele Postmiller.[7] In addition to recording the historic buildings, Howard created alternative schemes for the memorial. In 1939, the architectural office was temporarily expanded when it became the central unit of the Historic American Buildings Survey.[8]

Investigating the original colonial town site was an interesting historical exercise. An intensive study was made of most of the town site, most of which would be cleared for the Jefferson National Expansion Memorial. To place the colonial town in context, we also studied the original plow lands covering some twenty-five square miles, including the older French village of Cahokia east of the Mississippi River. Frank Leslie plotted the results of the study on a map. As part of the study, all the known early maps, including some found in foreign archives, were collected and laid over modern plats. The "emplacements," or building lots of both French and Spanish lands, were compiled to give an accurate picture of a colonial town.[9]

Although the notarial documents were relatively detailed, very few of the colonial buildings had survived to the age of photography and no artists' view, if there ever were any, had survived. To visualize the architectural character of the early French buildings, it was necessary to examine those that had survived in Ste. Genevieve, Missouri, Cahokia and Kaskaskia, Illinois, and the lead mining settlements in the Ozarks. Examples in Louisiana and along the St. Lawrence were also studied, as were the French North American archives in Paris.

Although the earliest buildings had long since disappeared, the original street pattern was extant. In addition, there were many interesting structures, some dating to the rebuilding after a great fire in 1849. The formal 1804 transfer of Upper Louisiana from France to Louisiana was considered a critical point of historical interest. The author spent considerable time examining the physical and documentary evidence from this period.[10]

St. Louis had been sited on a limestone plateau above a convenient landing for riverboats. The original stockaded town was laid out in a more or less regular gridiron in accordance with well-established Spanish colonial policy. In 1762, St. Louis along with much of Spanish North America was transferred to France. Soon the area attracted French Canadian fur traders. Following their legal traditions, they left a remarkably detailed documentary record of their private affairs, including information about their buildings.

One of the earliest existing buildings, the Old Courthouse (1839–59), was not originally included in the memorial area.[11] While the Old Courthouse was not within the authorized boundaries, its architectural importance was always evident to Park Service architects, as well as to LaBeaume, who incorporated it into his scheme. The Park Service architects quietly began our study of the courthouse without specific approval. We wanted to help ignite public interest in the building so it would be included in the memorial area. Eventually that happened; the courthouse was restored for Park Service use. The first public museum displays were opened there and it has continued to be the administrative headquarters of the memorial.

Designed by William Rumbold, who also served as consultant for the dome of the U.S. Capitol, the Old Courthouse was admired by many St. Louisans. It seems remarkable now that Mayor Dickmann had to virtually force its preservation by the federal government.[12] The first part of the Old Courthouse to be restored was the south wing, built in the 1840s. By scraping many layers of paint, it was revealed that the public passages featured grained golden oak trim. The oval courtrooms were restored and adapted for meeting spaces and the old offices upgraded for modern uses. Immediately prior to World War II, the great dome and gabled wings were re-covered with sheet copper. In ignorance, we removed the dome's wrought-iron construction, which we now know to have been a pioneer experiment, later used on the dome of the U.S. Capitol, which should have been saved. But today we can be thankful that the fine old structure was saved at all.

Another prominent historic building in the memorial area that was saved from destruction was the Old Cathedral (1834). Fortunately, the building had been measured and drawn up by an Historic American Buildings Survey group under St. Louis architect Eugene Pleitsch before the Park Service arrived, and a detailed report prepared by John Bryan.

Museums Proposed by the Park Service

The huge monumental structures proposed in the LaBeaume Plan were intended to house an omnibus collection of historical material relating to the "Winning of the West." When the Park Service became involved in the project, the omnibus collection evolved into two specialized museums. One, named the Museum of the Fur Trade, celebrated St. Louis's role as a major fur trading area during the Spanish and French periods, as well as the early American period. The second was to be the Museum of American Architecture.[13]

The Museum of the Fur Trade was proposed and promoted by Dr. Carl P. Russell of the National Park Service.[14] Based in Washington, D.C., Russell was an authority on Indian relations with a special interest in trade goods, trappers' supplies, and firearms. A substantial staff, including Ralph Lewis,[15] worked under museum division's head Ned J. Burns to produce numerous artists' drawings and several dioramas to be used in the proposed museum. They illustrated the early years of contact and trade with Native Americans.

The author was responsible for proposing the Museum of American Architecture, which was described in the November 1936 issue of *The Octagon: A Journal of the American Institute of Architects*. I thought it was appropriate for the Jefferson National Expansion Memorial since:

> Thomas Jefferson was an enthusiastic student of architecture, and through his part in securing the original designs for the United States Capitol and the White House and by his revival of the Roman style in the Virginia State capitol and his own residence "Monticello" and others, probably exercised a greater influence on American architecture than any other single man.[16]

In justifying the museum as part of the Jefferson National Expansion Memorial that was to tell the story of the westward development of the country, I stated, "What more graphic expression of political and social history can be found than in the builder's art? The nature of the American people and the chronology of their movements are permanently recorded in their structures."[17]

Intended for both the scholar and general public, the Museum of American Architecture was to include exhibits consisting of entire buildings, parts of buildings, examples of construction methods and ornament, architectural drawings, as well as photographs of buildings and craftsmen working materials. To begin the collection, I thought it possible to save structural and ornamental fragments from the buildings being demolished for the Jefferson National Expansion Memorial, especially the cast iron façades.

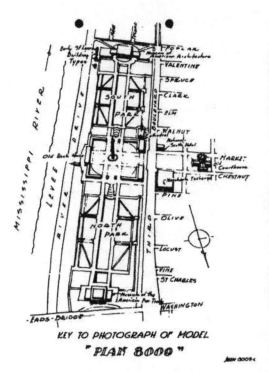

FIGURES 3 AND 4. *(Left) Plan 8009 (October 1937). Key to model of Plan 8009. Courtesy of National Park Service, JNEM Archives, St. Louis. (Right) Plan 8009 (October 1937). Photograph of model. Courtesy of National Park Service, JNEM Archives, St. Louis.*

"Plan 8009"

Superintendent Nagle asked the architects to develop a plan for the memorial along the riverfront that would include the two museum buildings, the Old Courthouse, the Old Cathedral, and the Old Rock House (1818), originally used as a fur traders' warehouse and one of the few buildings to survive the fire of 1849. In addition, Nagle asked us to include a formal approach from the river.[18] Among the plans we prepared was one called "Plan 8009" which was presented to the Jefferson National Expansion Memorial Commission in October 1937. We prepared a site plan (Figure 3) and a model for the presentation (Figure 4), as well as a written description entitled, "A Description and Explanation of Plan 8009 for Jefferson National Expansion Memorial," written by the author.[19]

The boundaries of the plan closely followed those of the French colonial village of St. Louis. Our major design assumption was that the memorial should fill the entire area from Popular Street to the Eads Bridge that was more or less formal in character. Plan 8009 consisted of a major north-south axis parallel to the Mississippi River and a minor axis linking the river to the

Old Courthouse. The memorial was divided into three sections, the South Park fronting the Museum of American Architecture and North Park fronting the Museum of the Fur Trade. Uniting the scheme at the axial crossing was a Central Plaza, containing a tall slender tower or shaft as the focal point. Taking advantage of some of the then new lighting techniques, a central tower was designed with a crowning element of molded glass that was to be internally and externally illuminated. To provide an architectural frame for the plaza, a colonnaded porch surrounded it, facing inward. A parking garage was to be located underneath the plaza.

The two museums terminated the major axis. In addition, the designers retained the Old Courthouse, Old Cathedral, the Rock House, and National-Scotts Hotel, the most significant historic buildings on the site, as part of the scheme. Unfortunately, only the Old Courthouse and cathedral survive today. The original pattern of streets was to be recalled in the pattern of pedestrian walkways. Although only a sketch, Plan 8009 influenced the program for the architectural competition held after World War II.

Over 500 existing buildings were surveyed during the early years of the project. Most were scheduled for demolition. Of these, a number had interesting features that staff architects felt should be saved for the proposed architectural museum. The superintendent agreed. Thus, when clearing of the site started in October 1939, the demolition contracts specified what should be saved and delivered to the Park Service for storage. These varied from small decorative elements to four complete cast iron façades, considered excellent examples of the structures erected immediately after the 1849 fire. At our invitation they were examined on the site by Professor Sigfried Giedion and favorably reported by him in his celebrated volume *Space, Time and Architecture*.[20]

A modern one-story fireproof warehouse in the area called the Denchar Building (after its last owner) was selected for storage. It had a concrete-slab floor and a delivery truck entrance. In this was stored a vast collection of carefully labeled artifacts intended for study and display in the Museum of American Architecture. The repository worked well until sometime during World War II when a bulldozer was used to quickly clear part of the storage area, damaging a part of the collection. The remaining artifacts remained in the Denchar Building until 1956 when the Jefferson National Expansion Memorial Commission decided it had little or no value. The collection was then offered to museums by the Park Service. To its surprise, there was a lively interest. The Smithsonian in Washington got first choice. Dr. Anthony N. B. Garvan and the author went out to St. Louis and selected enough specimens to fill a large truck.[21] With the dispersal of the collection, hope for a major architectural museum in St. Louis ended.

Public Relations

Upon his arrival in St. Louis in 1936, the author immediately began to acquaint the city's citizens with the National Park Service's mission to preserve historic sites and buildings, especially as it pertained to the Jefferson National Expansion Memorial.[22] In addition to preserving buildings *in situ*, or recording them prior to demolition, our purpose was to show how American buildings reflected the society that built them. Another objective was to make sure that the Mississippi Valley would be well represented in the proposed Museum of American Architecture. The St. Louis press and its citizens responded with interest.

Upon arriving, one of the first things done was the publication of the proposal for a Museum of American Architecture in an article in the November 1936 issue of *Octagon*. To make the public aware of research on the project area, an exhibit entitled "The Old St. Louis Waterfront" was held at the St. Louis Public Library in April 1938. In the exhibit's catalog we articulated the main objective of our work for the past two years: "to attempt a thorough understanding of those physical remains in the thirty-seven blocks of riverfront buildings which will be razed, in order that important historical objects not be discarded through lack of information."[23]

Much of the author's own work during the eleven years he spent working on the Jefferson National Expansion Memorial he compiled into *Colonial St. Louis: Building a Creole Capital*. He also pursued other historical activities to promote the memorial, including founding and serving as secretary of the William Clark Society, which saved an historic fur trader's house known as the Campbell House, as well as founding and serving as president of the St. Louis Historical Documents Foundation, which published several books. The author also served on the board of the Missouri Historical Society and was secretary of the St. Louis chapter of the American Institute of Architects when World War II broke out. He also originated the idea of celebrating the 250th anniversary of the founding of Cahokia (1699–1949).[24] In 2001 a compilation of reports and other materials produced by the Jefferson National Expansion Memorial listed over 250 items on a great number of topics, written by dozens of people and ranging in length from one or two pages to hundreds of pages.[25]

The Coming of World War II

Luther Ely Smith had always dreamed of a great international design competition for the Jefferson National Expansion Memorial. Its realization had to wait until after World War II. In 1947, George Howe, FAIA, an eminent Philadelphia architect, was engaged to create the architectural program for

FIGURE 5. *Eero Saarinen's prize-winning arch with naturalistic landscaping over museum that leaks. Undated postcard view published by CharmCraft, St. Louis.*

the competition. Howe managed to satisfy all the various parties involved, a difficult task considering the number of ideas that had been advanced over the past fourteen years.

Over 170 entries were received from across the country. They were reviewed in a two-stage process by seven eminent American architects: S. Herbert Hare, Fiske Kimball, Louis LaBeaume, Charles Nagel, Jr., Richard J. Neutra, Roland Wank, and William K. Wurster. The design of Eero Saarinen was finally selected as winner in 1948. It would take another seventeen years before Saarinen's great arch was finished, four years after his death (Figure 5).

Although the competition was carried out by the commission, it did not directly involve members of the architectural team that had labored so long and hard at the site. Many had been reassigned during World War II and in

FIGURE 6. *The Old Rock House: Manuel Lisa's fur trade warehouse was built in 1818 on a rock ledge. Courtesy of National Park Service, JNEM Archives, St. Louis.*

the years immediately after. The author, for example, was posted in 1947 to begin preliminary studies for the proposed Independence Hall National Park in Philadelphia, two years later moving to Richmond, Virginia, to become regional architect. On one occasion, after Saarinen had been selected, the author toured the site with the new architect. While there, they discussed the idea of retaining the Old Rock House, recently restored by the Park Service (Figure 6).

Saarinen liked the idea of keeping the old stone building because he felt it helped give scale to his soaring arch. Unfortunately, the carefully restored landmark was later removed and no longer exists. ❂

Appendix A

Publications and Exhibits by Charles E. Peterson Related to the Jefferson National Expansion Memorial

"Museum of Modern Architecture: A Proposed Institution of Research and . Public Education," *Octagon: A Journal of the American Institute of Architects* (November 1936).

"A Description and Explanation of Plan 8009 for the Jefferson National Expansion Memorial," National Park Service Memorandum (October 1937).

The Old St. Louis Waterfront: 1938: An Exhibition of Architectural Studies of the Jefferson National Expansion Memorial. St. Louis Public Library, April 11–30, 1938.

Catalog for *The Old St. Louis Waterfront: 1938: an Exhibition of Architectural Studies of the Jefferson National Expansion Memorial.* St. Louis Public Library, April 11–30, 1938. Reprinted for the Domestic Field Tour of the Society of Architectural Historians, May 19–26, 1991.

"Early Ste. Genevieve and Its Architecture," *Missouri Historical Review* 30, no. 2 (January 1941): 207–32.

"French Landmarks Along the Mississippi," *Antiques* 53, no. 4 (April 1948): 286–88.

"A List of Published Writings of Special Interest in the Study of Historic Architecture of the Mississippi Valley," Jefferson National Expansion Memorial (1940).

"The Museum of American Architecture: A Progress Report," *Journal of the Society of Architectural Historians* 1, no. 3-4 (July–October 1941).

"Notes on Old Cahokia," *French American Review* 1, no. 3 (July-September 1948).

"Notes on Old Cahokia" (expanded version), *Journal of the Illinois State Historical Society* (1949).

"Manuel Lisa's Warehouse," *Missouri Historical Society Bulletin* (1948).

Colonial St. Louis (Tucson: The Patrice Press, 2001). Compilation of studies done for Jefferson National Expansion Memorial by Charles Peterson, which appeared in installments of the *Missouri Historical Society Bulletin*, April and July 1947.

"Colonial St. Louis," *Missouri Historical Society Bulletin* Part 1 (April 1947): 94–111; Part 2 (July 1947): 133–49; Part 3 (October 1947): 11–30.

(Endnotes)

1 Two published accounts of the blight of the cast iron warehouses that are useful are: Charles B. Hosmer, Jr., *Preservation Comes of Age*, (Charlottesville: University of Virginia Press, 1982): Vol. I, 626-49; Vol II, 725-33) and Sharon A. Brown, *Administrative History: Jefferson National Expansion Memorial National Historic Site* (June 1984).

2 Previously, Smith had been chairman of St. Louis's General Committee on Civic Needs for four years.

3 Hosmer, 626; Brown, 4.

4 Brown, 4.

5 In this slack period Nagle's talents were to be exploited by other National Park areas. Those included the delicate handling of sculptor Gutzon Borglum at the great Mount Rushmore carving in the Black Hills of South Dakota. Borglum's bills for reimbursement at times appeared to be padded and he was backed by his influential friend, Senator Peter Norbeck. Other problems were the deterioration of the great monument at the Perry's Victory reservation in Lake Erie and the collapse of seawalls at El Morro in San Juan, Puerto Rico. As World War II approached, Nagle finally disappeared on some secret military assignment and did not return to the St. Louis project.

6 The leader in this was recognized as the Mangelsdorf Seed Company, which was championed by Congressman Lambertson of Kansas. Although legal obstacles were eventually cleared one by one, the delays held up physical progress and little more than clearance of the site had been completed by the time of the attack on Pearl Harbor.

7 My most interesting assistant was G. Vietor Davis, son of a local banker who had sat on the original memorial committee. Davis was a lively youngster with degrees from Princeton and Washington universities. He had a genuine feeling for architectural/historical values and had the necessary discipline to run our great project investigation in the land titles in the St. Louis Recorded Archives. That ambitious operation occupied ten busy people for two years, funded by the Works Progress Administration.

Henry E. Rice was a skilled landscape draftsman recruited in the East. He had a disciplined mind and could be relied upon to plot the land title records accurately on our historical base map, which covered the town as it stood in the year 1804—the year of the Transfer.

Frank Leslie was a local architectural draftsman who neatly and conscientiously measured and drew many inked sheets of Historic American Buildings Survey drawings—especially of the St. Louis Courthouse. These were used later as the basis of restoration plans and finally were deposited in the Library of Congress. District Officer Eugene Pleitsch, AIA, of the Historic American Buildings Survey had already produced seventeen sheets of courthouse records, but far more were needed as the basis for detailed restoration plans.

Adele Postmiller, a locally recruited and very competent secretary, took a great deal of interest in our research program and, in the end, produced a very good paper on the Russian log cabin as introduced in Alaska. It would have been part of the western story proposed for the Museum of American Architecture.

Herbert Moscowitz was the team leader, assisted by Colonel Werner Genot. That project produced two sets of 8"x10" transcription cards in the number of some 10,000. One set was deposited at the Missouri Historical Society. The meat of each document was transcribed in English, with the French and Spanish equivalents alongside. The cards were carefully indexed for proper names, some of which had been recorded in as many as twenty different spellings.

That record was eventually the basis for my essay, "Colonial St. Louis: Building a Creole Capital," first published by the Missouri Historical Society in 1949 with a second, generously illustrated edition by the Patrice Press of Tucson in 1993.

8 The survey had been established at Washington in 1933 and was an immediate success. But one just criticism was that the buildings studied had to be in or near cities where the employed architects could reach them. This time around transportation was provided in the form of a station wagon and travel expense money. Many small towns and rural areas could then be reached and recorded.

In the first eleven months, our work was carried through the states bordering the Mississippi River from Missouri and Illinois southward. By October it was possible to open an exhibition in the Fine Arts Room of the St. Louis Public Library titled "Ante Bellum Houses of the Mississippi Valley." Forty-six houses were represented in the fine salon photographic prints, and sixteen by measured drawings.

The catalog carried sixteen pages, mimeographed. Two hundred fifty copies were distributed. The contents were eventually incorporated into Frank J. Roos, *Bibliography of Early American Architecture* (Urbana: University of Illinois Press, 1968). This was a revised edition with a preface by his widow Beatrice Adams Roos.)

It was supervised by F. Ray Leimkuehler, AIA, considered to be one of the finest draftsmen in St. Louis, and staffed by junior architects as follows: William A. Bernoudy, John A. Campbell, Adolph H. Felder, Ferdinand H. Manger, Jr., Joseph P. Marlow, Norman G. Moore, and Herman A. Weiter. Lester E. Jones, photographer, was obtained through a U.S. Civil Service list of eligibles. Ida B. Guild served as secretary.

9 This study was incorporated (with credit) by Dora P. Crouch in *Spanish City Planning in North America* (Cambridge: MIT Press, 1982).

10 The historians F. L. Billon, J. T. Scharf, and Louis Houck had done excellent groundwork well in advance of our work.

11 It is more than possible that Luther Ely Smith's apparent antipathy to old buildings–which became apparent as time went along—was the explanation.

12 A special report was requested from the Missouri Historical Society, who published it under the title "The Old Courthouse," by Stella Drum and Charles van Ravenswaay. It appeared in *Glimpses of the Past 7*, nos. 1-6 (January-June 1940): 3–41. A modern work, highly illustrated, is Donald F. Dosch, *The Old Courthouse: Americans Build a Forum on the Frontier*, Jefferson National Expansion Memorial Association, St. Louis (1979).

13 "A Museum of American Architecture (A Proposed Institution of Research and Public Education)" by the undersigned was published in *The Octagon, A Journal of the American Institute of Architects* in November 1936. The proposal was updated in "A Progress Report" in the *Journal of the Society of Architectural Historians* 1, nos. 3-4 (July-October 1941).

14 Russell's first studies of the Western fur trade began about 1930 for museum use in Yellowstone National Park and were first published in 1967 by Knopf under the title *Firearms, Traps & Tools of the Mountain Men*. Its enduring importance was attested by ten subsequent printings by the University of New Mexico Press by 1998.

15 Ralph Howe Lewis, a distinguished museum specialist, spent five years on the Jefferson National Expansion Memorial staff. He became Chief of the Park Service Museum Branch and authored many professional publications, including *Museum Curatorship in the National Park Service, 1904–1982*, published in 1993. He died at Harpers Ferry in November 2000, at the age of 91.

16 Charles E. Peterson, "A Museum of American Architecture (A Proposed Institution of Research and Public Education)," *The Octagon: A Journal of the American Institute of Architects* (November 1936).

17 Ibid.

18 See Brown, *Administrative History.*

19 Charles E. Peterson, *Report No. 22: A Description and Explanation of "Plan 8009" for the Jefferson National Expansion Memorial.* St. Louis (October 1937).

20 Sigfried Giedion, Space, *Time and Architecture,* (Cambridge: Harvard University Press, 1941).

21 Since then the idea has begun to catch on. The Museum of American Building in the Old Pension Building in Washington is an example. A small museum of fragments is also available for architectural study and is accessible to architects and students at the Independence National Historical Park in Philadelphia.

22 In response to an oral history question on October 22, 1994, about what he did to try save buildings in the JNEM, Peterson responded, "Give slide lectures on the architecture of the area, I gave many talks . . . I talked to the Second Annual Strawberry Festival of Kirkwoos Missouri, the Belleville Women's Circle, the Downtown Stockbrokers, I talked to the — all over the place." Oral history interview by Charles E. Peterson, Architectural Historian. Jefferson National Expansion Memorial, Interviewed by Bob Moore, Historian JEFF.

23 Charles E. Peterson, catalog for *The Old St. Louis Waterfront: 1938: An Exhibition of Architectural Studies of the Jefferson National Expansion Memorial,* St. Louis Public Library, April 11–30, 1938, reprinted for the Domestic Field Tour of the Society of Architectural Historians, May 19–26, 1991, p. 3.

24 Joseph Desloge of St. Louis was a chief supporter of the celebration, which included importing a whole trainload of Indians from out west. "Notes on Old Cahokia," *French American Review* 1, no. 3 (July–September 1948). "Notes on Old Cahokia" (expanded version), *Journal of the Illinois State Historical Society* (1949).

25 Janet S. Ayres and Jennifer Rawlings, *Finding Aid to the Jefferson National Expansion Memorial Research Reports,* National Park Service (St. Louis, Missouri: March 2001): 1.

▨ TEMPLES OF FLIGHT

Preservation by Design at Ronald Reagan Washington
National and Washington Dulles International Airports

H. HENRY WARD
Coordinator, Archaeology & Historic Preservation
Parsons Beinckerhoff/Parsons Management Consultants

T he title of Richard Longstreth's keynote address, "I Can't See It; I Don't Understand It; and It Doesn't Look Old to Me,"[1] to the 1995 "Preserving the Recent Past" conference captures the basic challenge in dealing with the historic resources of the recent past. Preservationists working with twentieth-century properties often feel a special need to explain the relevance of their work. To most of our fellow citizens historic preservation is about restoring glorious monuments of past ages; unfortunately, efforts to preserve the monuments of our own age can be more difficult to justify.

To some, the preservation of a modern airport seems unusual and perhaps even odd. Not only is the familiar refrain of "How can that be historic? I remember when it was built," voiced, but even if historic, an active airport must continue to evolve to meet changing technical requirements, security demands, economic conditions, and public expectations. Without special care, inevitable conflicts will arise between the goals of preservation and imperatives to keep pace with rapidly changing conditions, often leaving preservation on the short end of the stick.

The preservation challenges of the recent past are embodied in the redevelopment of National (now Reagan Washington National) and Washington Dulles International airports that serve the nation's capital. The historic significance and unique architectural character of each presented a variety of historic preservation challenges. At Washington National the primary challenge was the rehabilitation of the 1941 Art Moderne Terminal A as part of a comprehensive modernization program that included a new thirty-five-gate Terminal B/C by Cesar Pelli. The primary challenge at Dulles was completing Eero Saarinen's original design, which will provide for the new capacity and facilities required by rapid growth. This paper will discuss the successful preservation strategies implemented at both active airports.

In 1987, operation of the airports was transferred from the Federal Aviation Administration (FAA) to the Metropolitan Washington Airports Authority. The Authority was created to undertake major redevelopment and expansion at both facilities. As part of the transfer, the Authority accepted responsibility for the airports' historic preservation planning. During the first phase of the redevelopment process, the focus was on background research, facility surveys, long-range planning, and program development. This phase also included developing preservation strategies for both airports. During this first phase, the Authority identified twenty-eight resources potentially eligible for the National Register of Historic Places, ranging from prehistoric Native American campsites at Dulles, to the remains of a colonial mansion at National, to the singular modern design of the Dulles Main Terminal.

In the second phase, the Pelli design for a new terminal at National was completed, as was the restoration of a number of significant historic spaces in the original terminal. At Dulles, the historic Main Terminal building was doubled in length, fulfilling Saarinen's original design. The airport redevelopment projects at both airports are now entering a third phase, as each continues to grow and evolve to meet new changing technology, economic pressures, and political realities.

National and Dulles Airports as Historic Resources

Most people recognize that commercial air travel has profoundly affected twentieth-century history and culture. People readily accept that old aircraft are historic and deserve preservation; however, making the case that airports should be preserved is more difficult. Unlike historic aircraft that are no longer in use, and thus can be preserved as museum pieces, older operational airports must meet modern air travel requirements. As a result, the preservation of a working airport represents unique challenges, particularly in preserving significant elements while the facility continues to expand and change.

National Airport was constructed less than forty years after the Wright brothers flew at Kitty Hawk. Twenty years later, the explosive growth of air travel, fueled by the introduction of commercial jets, forced the airport to expand rapidly. Located on a tightly circumscribed site between the Potomac River and the Mount Vernon Memorial Highway, the airport's growth was hampered by limited available land. The restricted site, along with the lack of a master plan, resulted in haphazard additions as well as non-sympathetic changes to the original terminal building.

Eventually, space limitations of the historic but outdated existing terminal and the overburdened ground transportation and parking networks resulted in the Capital Development Program, which included the construction of Pelli's new Terminal A, new access roads, and garages. Unfortunately, the new construction required the removal of some historic structures. However, the airport's most historically significant structure, the 1941 Terminal A, along with other important resources such as the ruins of Abington Plantation House, were preserved and restored.

Unlike National, Dulles Airport was designed at the beginning of the jet age. Understanding the growing popularity of air travel, Saarinen's master plan originally envisioned a main terminal twice the size of the one the Federal Aviation Administration eventually constructed in 1958–62. As farsighted as he was however, he did not anticipate that the number of passengers would eventually overwhelm the unique mobile lounges used to take passengers directly from the terminal to the planes, helping to reduce the ever-increasing long walks from terminals to Jetways. By the 1980s, however, dramatic increases in passengers led to the construction of temporary midfield concourses, and the mobile lounges were relegated to oversized shuttle buses.

Historic Preservation Planning at National and Dulles Airports

During early phases of the program planning at National, preservation-planning goals were carefully integrated into the airports' overall redevelopment plans. A comprehensive airport survey identified all historically significant resources, and specific historic spaces and architectural elements were documented. When project requirements would affect an historic resource, care was taken to program new uses for the historic spaces that were compatible to their original architectural character and would allow for a high-level restoration of original historic features.

In part, the success of the preservation efforts was due to the natural interest that many of the architects, engineers, and Authority staff had for aviation history. These affinities led many involved to embrace historic preservation as an integral part of the redevelopment plans. During the early

phases of the project, the Authority and its preservation consultants learned
how to successfully negotiate the preservation regulatory process. They
formed a talented "preservation team" with the federal and state preservation
agencies, finding mutually acceptable solutions to problems that arose. Another
critical factor in the success of the preservation program was the airports
themselves. Both Reagan National and Dulles are imbued with tangible, almost
iconic, historic and architectural character, which helped to bring about their
own preservation.

At the core of this successful partnership was a shared understanding that
the preservation program would only be successful if the team could achieve its
preservation objectives while allowing the airports to be upgraded functionally.
This is not to say that the redevelopment plans did not entail differences of
opinion. There was an ongoing balancing act played out through the Section
106 process, which provided the framework to identify, discuss, and resolve
conflicts between modern requirements and historic preservation goals. The
preservation team worked together to demonstrate that restoration of historic
features could be achieved while meeting the functional, cost, and schedule
requirements of the redevelopment program. This already complex process was
further complicated by the myriad standards and regulations that had to be
met, including the Secretary of the Interior's Standards, the Airport Authority's
design standards, FAA security requirements, local and national building
codes, Americans with Disabilities Act Accessibility Standards, Environmental
Protection Agency Hazardous Materials Regulations, and energy conservation
standards to name but a few. In the end the process was successful because the
team was able to reach appropriate and pragmatic compromises that allowed
both the design and preservation requirements to be achieved.

Washington National Airport

Faced with a tightly circumscribed site and an inadequate historic Terminal A
space, the redevelopment plan for National Airport included the construction
of a major new thirty-five-gate North Terminal and the wholesale revamping
of access roads and parking areas. Although the new terminal was located
to leave the historic 1941 Terminal essentially intact, there were direct
and indirect impacts that needed to be addressed. After careful study and
consultation, plans were developed and approved to avoid or mitigate these
adverse effects.

Early in the design process it was decided that the new terminal should
be stylistically distinct from the architectural style of the airports' original

FIGURE 1. *Landside view of main terminal, ca. 1941.*
Courtesy of Metropolitan Washington Airports Authority.

Art Moderne design. In the words of Cesar Pelli, the architect for the new North Terminal, "The design for the terminal is sympathetic to the historic 1941 South Terminal. As in the existing South Terminal, we placed the functional elements toward the landside and created large expanses of glass to see the federal monuments beyond. Both the new terminal and the historic South Terminal buildings have their own character, appropriate to their time and the nature of air travel in each period."[2] The physical connection between the two terminals was provided by a connecting structure of sufficient length to allow for an appropriate visual separation and a gradual architectural transition from the smooth concrete surface of the old building to the more elaborate exposed metal structure and window walls of the new facility.

The 1941 design of Terminal A was not without controversy. Initially the consulting architects preferred the then new International Style for the building since they felt it embodied the futuristic spirit of aviation. This style, however, contrasted sharply with the neoclassical architecture on Washington's federal buildings preferred by the government. Matters were further complicated by an additional request, possibly from Franklin Delano Roosevelt himself, that the terminal reflect the rich colonial heritage of the historic Virginia surroundings.

The design team, lead by Howard Lovewell Cheney, developed an Art Moderne design that integrated architectural references to the colonial and neoclassical styles as well as attempted to capture the spirit of the future (Figure 1). The basic structure of the boxy, horizontal building with its large glazed curtain walls, cantilevered floors, and curved walls was clearly modernist in character. However, the symmetrical, stepped massing, and simplified portico seemed to reflect the composition of earlier styles.[3] As the construction of the airport was to occur as the nation was beginning to prepare for the coming war, the building was designed using economical materials in innovative ways. The exterior walls were cast-in-place concrete finished with a thin wash for a smooth, stone-like finish. On the interior, a mixture of exposed concrete, hollow terra cotta tile wall systems, and restrained ornamental details in patterned terrazzo, molded aluminum, and etched glass was used.[4]

In the early 1940s, air travel was relatively novel. As a result, one of the more significant architectural elements of the design was the focus on providing areas for visitors to watch the planes take off and land. The window wall design for the terminal's main interior spaces and expansive exterior observation decks were intended to provide visitors with unobstructed views of the airfield and with sweeping views of the Washington, D.C. skyline across the Potomac River.

In the 1950s and 1960s, as air travel became more popular, the expressive form of the elegant Main Terminal became obscured with piecemeal additions. At the same time, access roads were widened and parking lots constructed to alleviate some of the landside congestion, and the Washington Metrorail system was extended to the airport. While this helped to reduce the number of vehicles, the elevated station visually detracted from the landside of the terminal.

Rehabilitating Terminal A

As part of the development of the new Terminal B/C to the north, the Airports Authority was able to accomplish the restoration of specific portions of the 1941 Terminal, including the original dining room, Franklin Delano Roosevelt's President's Suite, and the old post office. The original dining room at National Airport featured a curved wraparound window wall providing unparalleled views over the airfield to the national monuments across the Potomac River (Figure 2). The space was graced with an elaborately inlaid blue terrazzo floor, a decorative molded plaster ceiling, and an elegant curved wood panel interior wall. To enter the space, one mounted a grand staircase and passed through a glass and aluminum window wall with doors framed by graceful Art Moderne designs in molded relief.

Over the next five decades, the dining room had undergone a series of "improvements" that gradually obscured most of the room's original charm. Although some important architectural elements were lost, preliminary non-destructive investigations discovered that many of the original components, including the original terrazzo floor and plaster ceiling, still existed in reparable condition. Original plans and historic photographs provided the information for the reconstruction of the missing elements, including a series of graceful lighting fixtures and the art panels decorating the entrance window wall.

One of the most difficult elements of the project was the restoration of the distinctive terrazzo floor. Portions of the original floor underneath earlier food preparation appliances had been severely stained. In addition, it was discovered that large areas of the original floor had received earlier poor-

FIGURES 2 AND 3. *(Above) National Airport dining room, ca. 1941. Courtesy of Metropolitan Washington Airport Authorities. (Below) National Airport dining room President's Club, 1998. Photograph: Eric Taylor for Metropolitan Washington Airports Authority.*

quality patches. The original terrazzo also exhibited such a wide variation in color and aggregate distribution that it was extremely difficult to provide the restoration contractor with a useful terrazzo specification or to approve submitted samples of patch material. A submitted sample might be a perfect match in one location, but completely unacceptable for an area ten feet away. This resulted in an ongoing dilemma for the design and construction teams as they struggled to achieve acceptable results, without the exorbitant expense and time required to prepare the terrazzo mixture on a patch-by-patch basis.

While the final aesthetic quality of the restored floor were somewhat disappointing, the process taught the team useful lessons about the critical differences in construction versus restoration specifications, as well as the importance of a full evaluation of a restoration project prior to determining a final design solution. The repair of the floor also resulted in discussions about the relative merits of rehabilitation versus replacement of historic fabric. Since the patching of the original floor made it almost impossible to restore it to a "good as new" appearance, a complete understanding of the existing conditions prior to the decision to repair the floor might have led to the choice to replace rather than repair. Although this action would not have retained as much historic fabric, as recommended by the Secretary of the Interior's Standards for Rehabilitation, it would have given the floor a much more uniform and aesthetically pleasing appearance.

Once the original dining room was restored, it was divided into two spaces, one housing the terminal's exhibit hall and the other, larger northern portion of the Continental Airlines Presidents' Club, serving VIP passengers using the new airline gates located in the north end of the 1941 Terminal (Figure 3). The remaining south portion of the room was developed into an accessible history museum and public lecture facility with interpretive exhibits on the airport's history, as well as the archaeological investigation and preservation of the airport's colonial Abingdon Plantation Site.

While the division of a major historic space is often problematic, careful design and close consultation with preservation agencies produced a consensus that was an acceptable compromise between the intent of the Secretary of the Interior's Standards for Rehabilitation and the requirements of the architectural program. The room was divided using a "temporary" wall designed to be removable without significant damage to the ceiling or floor. It was also designed with band of clear glass panels along the ceiling allowing the continuity of the original space to be appreciated. The new wall also provided additional space for large-scale interpretive graphic panels that otherwise could not have been included. The new wall also allowed for the inclusion of banks of electrical outlets and telecom jacks that would allow the exhibit space a third potential use as a media center.

Restored to its 1941 condition, the Presidents' Club once again delights visitors with its decor of pale blue terrazzo floors, decorative plaster ceiling, curving wood panel walls, and expansive window walls. Respecting this unique space, Continental Airlines deviated from its standard interior design, selecting furnishings to complement the historic space. The club's patrons now enjoy the same gracious surroundings and remarkable views of the airfield, Potomac River, and national monuments that drew diners and sightseers in years past.

With the opening of the new Terminal B/C, the airport operations office's need for additional space required that it be moved from its current cramped location in space that had originally served as the presidential suite. The apron-level facility was designed to provide President Franklin Delano Roosevelt with an accessible, private waiting room and reception area at the airport. The suite was built on the ground level adjacent to the airfield, allowing the wheelchair-bound FDR to enter and leave the terminal out of public view. With the relocation of the operations' technical facilities, the space could be restored and adaptively reused as an elegant conference room.

Like the rest of the historic terminal, the suite's original design used relatively inexpensive materials. The dark terrazzo floor with a dramatic metal inlay of the Army Air Corps insignia was found to be largely intact. However, like the floor in the original dining room, it did require both small patching and the replacement of a few more damaged floor panels. One of the space's most unusual features was the use of then new wood-veneer plastic laminate produced by Formica. Small mars in the historic walnut-veneer panels were patched and missing panels were replaced with natural walnut panels, bleached, stained, and touched up with faux graining to resemble original plastic laminate.

Upgrading the Presidential Suite's original heating systems to current standards, while preserving the original fabric and character of the rooms was one of the more complicated aspects of the airport's restoration. The system consisted of simple heating coils housed in radiator enclosures below the windows, which were too small to hold new fan coil units. In addition, the ceilings in the suite were too low to allow new ducts to be run above the replaced acoustical ceiling. This problem was solved by connecting the Presidential Suite to the central air handling system through a series of registers located high in the plastic laminate walls behind grilles painted to match the panels.

Many of the Presidential Suite's original windows were found intact, encased behind later walls. Although in excellent condition, the single-pane, steel-framed windows were clearly inadequate to meet current thermal and acoustical code requirements. Because the interior window framing was too shallow to be retrofitted with multi-pane insulated glass, the design team first thought the original windows would have to be replaced. However, by attaching insulating glass to the exterior of the original frames, the historic windows could be retained as well as upgraded to meet current codes. To complete the room, new "deco-style" wall sconces and ceiling fixtures were installed in their original positions. Finally, appropriately styled conference room furnishings were selected.

When the post office at National Airport was first opened in 1941, it was a state-of-the-art facility to handle the flood of airmail flown in and out of the nation's capital. The public lobby was graced with an elaborate inlaid terrazzo floor and decorative molded aluminum wall grilles. When the post office was relocated in the late 1940s, the original lobby was reconfigured for baggage handling. Eventually most of the original room was demolished and replaced by a series of small offices and closets.

In the redevelopment plan for Terminal A, the Authority had decided to reconfigure the existing space and adaptively reuse it to house the office issuing airport passes and identification badges. Following a now familiar pattern, the first step was to carefully remove all of the non-original features. During this controlled demolition, the well-preserved floor and one corner of the original lobby wall were uncovered. Because of the close match between the new pass/ID facility function and the historic post office lobby, the decision was made to reconstruct the historic space. Sections of the original floor that were damaged were replaced and existing original wall panels and grilles cleaned. Compatible new materials were used to reconstruct missing walls, doors, counters, and teller windows. This new construction did not exactly duplicate the original; rather, it was designed to allow the viewer to distinguish between original and new construction. Unlike some of the other restoration projects, the transformation of the original post office into the new pass/ID office was achieved with relatively few problems. A last-minute change in requirements, the installation of remotely operated ID photo equipment, was accommodated by removing a non-historic door and building a photo booth out of an unused portion of the original post office cashier's office.

The completed restoration work has seen the removal of abandoned holding rooms and jet ways that obscured Terminal A's elegant airside façade. Future phases of the National Airport Rehabilitation and Expansion Project will include the demolition of other non-historic extensions to Terminal A, the construction of a new nine-gate South Concourse and the completion of the historic rehabilitation of the 1940s terminal. Although the design of the new concourse will be integrated with the 1941 structure, it is not intended to be a literal extension of the earlier building. As with the North Terminal, the South Concourse design will share a number of basic architectural elements and materials with the historic terminal, but will be of a distinctly modern appearance. Restoration specialists are currently repairing and restoring the terminal's original cast-concrete exterior facades that have deteriorated significantly over the last sixty-two years. This effort includes replacing corroded steel reinforcing members, as well as specialized concrete patching and filling. In addition, the exterior of the building will receive a sophisticated electrolytic treatment intended to reverse the "carbonization" of the original concrete and restore its ability to protect the embedded reinforcing steel from further corrosion.

When the construction of the new concourse is completed, the original 1941 Terminal will undergo continued restoration. The main waiting room will be restored to its original function as a passenger ticketing and lounge area. As with the projects completed to this point, special care will be taken to repair and restore original fabric, while missing original features will be reconstructed based on original plans and period photographs. When complete, Terminal A will be returned to its former glory and will live on to serve future generations of the traveling public, fulfilling its original function as a domestic airline terminal which successfully marries modern efficiency with historic graciousness.

Dulles International Airport

While the preservation and expansion of Dulles Airport may seem simple on the surface—doubling the size of the terminal based on Saarinen's original design—it was actually quite complex. Replicating the building's signature columns and massive centenary roof structure presented myriad engineering challenges. Incorporating new security requirements unforeseen in the late 1950s, presented design challenges in both the existing and new sections of the building. This required the addition of significant new space to the expanded terminal complex. Incorporating these new facilities without dramatically altering the building's unique, striking architectural character and appearance was a central challenge faced by the airport's architects and preservation consultants. Finally and perhaps most significantly, the designers and preservationists were faced with the question of what to do with the functionally inadequate, but historically significant mobile lounges used to move passengers directly from the terminal to the planes.

The Dulles redevelopment also challenged the design team and preservation agencies to re-think some of the basic tenets of historic preservation practice. Current preservation practice and guidelines, embodied in the Secretary of the Interior's Standards for Rehabilitation, emphasize the protection and maintenance of original historic fabric as well as new construction that is visually distinct from the original. Both of these tenets were challenged in the expansion and preservation of Dulles.

Dulles was the country's first commercial airport designed specifically for the jet age. Its architect, Eero Saarinen, took a completely new approach to how an airport should function. Saarinen's innovative design rejected the traditional approach of having passengers walk unprotected from the terminal to planes, as well as the emerging "finger" design where passengers walked down long corridors to jet ways connected to the aircraft. He designed large "mobile lounges" to move passengers from the terminal directly to the planes. This not only protected passengers between the terminal and planes, but also gave Saarinen the freedom to design the terminal as a soaring monumental gateway to the nation's capital, rather than as a utilitarian transportation facility (Figure 4).

The construction of the original structural columns was a complex process involving intricate fiberglass and wooden forms and over fourteen tons of reinforcing steel in each column. Unlike most columns that are vertical, Saarinen sloped his outward, creating the need for massive foundations as well as bracing for the formwork until the concrete cured. In addition, the engineers had to take into account the deflection caused by 2,000 tons of pre-cast concrete panels suspended from hanging steel cables off the roof system.[5] The dramatic curved centenary roof created an expansive free-span gallery space uninterrupted except for a massive sculptural central roof drain. To maintain this openness, low kiosks were used to house ticketing counters, restrooms, and commercial concession spaces. Lacking permanent structural

FIGURE 4. *Landside view, Dulles International Airport, ca. 1960. Courtesy of Metropolitan Washington Airports Authority.*

connections, these service modules could act like "furniture," and be moved, expanded, or reconfigured in response to changing operational requirements.

The airy terminal was placed on a two-story concrete plinth that incorporated separate levels for departures and arrivals. Departing passengers arrived on the upper level and moved through the soaring ticketing concourse to the mobile lounges docked on the airside of the building. Until the 1970s this was done with limited formal provisions for passenger security. The mobile lounges would take passengers directly to their planes parked on the field beyond. Deplaning passengers were transported by the lounges back to the upper level of the terminal where they took an escalator to the lower floor, passed through baggage claim, and exited at the lower level (Figure 5).

Saarinen decided to locate the control tower to the south of the midpoint of the Main Terminal overlooking the runways and airplane taxiways. The bold geometric tower was connected to the terminal by a low, horizontal, concrete and glass structure, which served to emphasize the tower as a striking vertical counterpoint to the horizontal mass of the terminal.

All other structures and facilities at Dulles were designed to be visually subordinate to the Main Terminal and tower. The original parking area was located in a recessed bowl immediately in front of the terminal. This allowed it to be convenient, but not intrude visually on the terminal. The approach road was carefully designed to provide a progression of views as one approached the terminal. Visitors first glimpsed the tower almost a quarter of a mile away, and were then given two additional partial views, finally culminating in a final grand, sweeping view of the entire terminal.[6] Even the landscape plan was a carefully integrated element of the overall architectural scheme, with a progression from less structured, natural plantings on the airport perimeter, to increasingly formalized groves of trees and shrubs in the vicinity of the terminal.[7]

Major service buildings were constructed along two flanking service avenues to the east and west of the terminal. These ancillary buildings were simple, rectangular, flat-roofed structures, limited to one story and clad in uniform, vertically ribbed metal siding (painted a standard "Dulles gray"). Structures outside of the immediate terminal area were allowed to be higher but still maintained the same rectangular design, flat roofs, and gray exteriors.

Not content to simply design the airport and abandon it to the inevitable pressure of future growth, the Saarinen design team compiled developed a Master Plan to direct future development. In the architect's words, "There was a crucial problem of discipline, long-term and imaginative zoning. Of special importance was the problem of some kind of continued control in the terminal and its surroundings."[8] The airport original Master Plan included a graphic

FIGURE 5. *Cutaway diagram, Dulles International Airport, ca. 1960. Courtesy of Metropolitan Washington Airports Authority.*

representation showing the faint white outline of the anticipated expanded terminal (Figure 5).

Almost from the moment it was completed, Dulles was recognized as Saarinen's greatest architectural achievement. Although he did not live to see it completed, the architect had said, "I think this airport is the best thing I have done. I think it's going to be really good. Maybe it will even explain what I believe about architecture."[9] The American Institute of Architects posthumously awarded Saarinen its Gold Medal Award in 1962. The AIA also included Dulles Airport on its 1976 list of fifty of the most significant American structures built since the Revolution. It is also notable that in 1978, Dulles was one of a few buildings placed in the National Register of Historic Places well before it reached the fifty-year milestone usually considered the minimum age for eligibility. In 1989, the airport terminal and its surrounding buildings and landscape still retained a high level of architectural integrity. This led to the designation of the Dulles Airport - National Register Historic District, including the Main Terminal and tower, the twelve original service buildings, the original mobile lounges fleet, the Parking Bowl, access roads, and original landscape features.

Rehabilitation and Expansion at Dulles

The initial planned capacity of Dulles was 8 million passengers per year. By 1989, the number of annual passengers exceeded 14 million.[10] (In 2000, the number of passengers approached 20 million.) The airport faced the twin challenges of expanding the terminal and other facilities to meet the current and future demand, while preserving the unique architectural character of the terminal and its surroundings. Fortunately, part of Saarinen's genius was his foresight in recognizing the potential need for expansion. His plans clearly showed his intent to double the length of the Main Terminal by extending both ends. In fact, the plinth, access roads, and base were constructed to accommodate the 1,240-foot length originally envisioned by Saarinen.

This deceptively simple plan to "expand the terminal" left myriad complicated engineering, design, construction, and historic preservation challenges. One of the basic tenets of historic preservation, formalized in the

Secretary of the Interior's Standards for Rehabilitation, is to protect, maintain, and rehabilitate a building's original fabric. Another is to design additions that are compatible but do not exactly duplicate the design of the original structure. How to deal with an original design, only partially executed, is not discussed in the standards. Thus, completing Saarinen's design was uncharted territory. Not only would it violate the principal of compatibility, but not duplication, but expanding the terminal would also mean removing significant amounts of historic fabric, including original end walls, vehicle ramps, and vertical circulation systems. In addition, modern security requirements, along with the limited capacity of the mobile lounges (now overwhelmed by the sheer volume of passengers) meant that the original experience of moving from ticketing to the planes would be seriously altered.

As the expansion plans were being developed, a detailed inventory of all original building features was undertaken. The goal was to save as many original features as possible, hopefully without compromising aesthetic or operational requirements. Some decisions were difficult; for example, the damaged and discolored original polished concrete floor was left in place. Not only did this preserve a massive amount of original fabric, the resulting contrast between the new and old floors helped to clarify the division between the original and new structures. Despite all the challenges, the final result was an essentially seamless expansion of the Main Terminal to its original intended length.

The preservation challenges at Dulles extended well beyond expanding the Main Terminal. The increasing number of flights, along with the rapidly changing nature of air travel, resulted in the need for new facilities unanticipated in Saarinen's time. The most pressing requirement was the need for more aircraft gates, which would be met by replacing existing temporary gates (at the base of the tower and in the midfield) with new permanent facilities. Unfortunately, Saarinen's original Master Plan offered no specific guidance for the design of these new concourse facilities. Basing the new facility design on the original Main Terminal or service buildings would lead to either a new "mini-terminal" or a "really big, gray metal box"; both were rejected as inappropriate additions to Saarinen's campus.

The solution was to construct the new T-Gates and Midfield Concourse that "recombined elements of the architectural vocabulary" of the original Saarinen facilities to create a new amalgamation that would be compatible with, but not mistaken for, the original new construction. These new concourses were designed as low horizontal structures that harkened back to the original service buildings. The new building rests on solid concrete bases and included expansive areas of windows that relate to the Main Terminal.

Another major problem at Dulles was the parking lot capacity. When the airport first opened, all parking was located in a recessed bowl in front of the Main Terminal. As parking demand increased, this lot became a premium-parking facility, while a series of remote surface lots were constructed in the north of the airport. While it would have been possible to satisfy anticipated future demand by continuing to construct more and more distant lots, it would not resolve passenger demand for more near-terminal parking. Given the conflicting demands, some structured parking solution was required.

In this case, the decision was made to locate parking garages to the north and west of the existing historic parking lot. The lower levels of the garages were recessed below grade, reducing the perceived height of the structures. In addition, the site treatment included landscape buffers of broadleaf trees, consistent with the original Dan Killey landscape plan. The garages are faced with plain, pre-cast concrete panels colored and textured to match the plinth of the Main Terminal.

Since the expanded terminal has been completed, Dulles continues to face increasing numbers of airlines, flights, and passengers. In order to meet this growth, in 1998 the Airports Authority launched a new Dulles Development program (often referred to as the "d2"). Fortunately, the majority of this new development will occur outside of the historic central core, thus limiting direct impacts to the architectural character and contributing properties. The first of three permanent tiers of Midfield Concourses is near completion, and the continued development of these facilities will allow the airport to continue to meet the future demands for more aircraft gates. The concourse design, which was carefully developed in consultation with the preservation agencies, will be followed in the two future concourses. As the new concourses are developed, Saarinen's original mobile lounges will eventually be replaced with an underground Automated People Mover system. At the same time, a new central security mezzanine will be developed in new sub-grade spaces built under the terminal expansions and the reconstructed South Finger between the terminal and tower.

The design for these new underground facilities raises interesting new questions about how to integrate these new spaces into Saarinen's carefully orchestrated passenger experience of moving from the access highway through the Main Terminal and out to their plane. As these new underground facilities are separated both vertically and horizontally from the Main Terminal, the design team and agency representatives reached consensus that the new spaces should have a distinct architectural character, while remaining compatible with the general design of the original airport.

Conclusions

Over the past decade, the Metropolitan Washington Airports Authority and it consultants have carried out ambitious redevelopment programs at both airports. By carefully integrating preservation into the development process, both historic preservation goals and airport development requirements have been achieved. These efforts will continue through the next decade as the next phases of the development at each airport proceeds.

Along with its strikingly modern new Cesar Pelli terminal, National Airport's jewel of a 1941 Terminal has been preserved and is already being restored to the elegance that made it a landmark in early airport design. Despite its explosive growth, Dulles Airport continues to hold true to the remarkable architectural vision of its creator, Eero Saarinen. The expansion of the sculptural masterpiece of a Main Terminal has been completed in accordance with his original plans, while the rest of the redevelopment program carefully maintains and preserves the unique architectural character of this remarkable modern historic resource. Although many future challenges remain, these two very different "Temples of Flight" enter the new century with two very important shared attributes—rich histories and bright futures. ✪

(Endnotes)

1 Richard Longstreth, "I Can't See It; I Don't Understand It; and It Doesn't Look Old to Me," in *Preserving the Recent Past* (Washington: Historic Preservation Education Foundation, 1995), 15–20.

2 Oscar Riera Ojeda, ed., *Single Building Series: National Airport Terminal-Cesar Pelli* (Gloucester, Mass.: Rockport Publishers, 2000), 22.

3 James M. Goode, "Flying High: The Origin and Design of National Airport," *Washington History*, 1:2 (1989): 16.

4 Robinson & Associates, *Historical and Architectural Documentation of the Main Terminal at Washington National Airport.* Prepared for the Metropolitan Washington Airports Authority, 1992, 1–8.

5 Engineering Science, *Historic and Archaeological Survey Report: Washington Dulles International Airport.* Prepared for the Metropolitan Washington Airport Authorities, 1989.

6 Roger Sheppard, *Structures of Our Time: 31 Buildings That Changed Modern Life* (New York: McGraw-Hill, 2002), 112.

7 Ammann Whitney et al., *Dulles International Airport: Master Plan Report.* Prepared for the Federal Aviation Administration, 1966.

8 Aline Saarinen, ed., *Eero Saarinen On His Own Work* (New Haven: Yale, 1962), 104.

9 Ibid., 101.

10 Vitteta Group/Studio Four, *Main Terminal Expansion: Washington Dulles International Airport: Concept Design.* Prepared for the Metropolitan Washington Airport Authorities, 1990, 1–3.

▦ INDEX

Page numbers in italics refer to illustration pages

Made in United States
Orlando, FL
16 January 2024